WORKING IN TALL BUILDINGS
VOL. I

The Cookie Line

Working in Tall Buildings

VOL. I

Buildings

A Wry Look Back
at My Life and Career

DON WILT

LUMINARE PRESS

WWW.LUMINAREPRESS.COM

Printed in the United States of America

Cover Design by Claire Flint Last

Luminare Press
442 Charnelton St.
Eugene, OR 97401
www.luminarepress.com

LCCN: 2020917373
ISBN: 978-1-64388-450-9

To Priscilla Claire Beistel (Grumschwartz) Wilt
My Muse

Table of Contents

Preface

Dear Reader,

I couldn't help thinking of some funnier ways to begin this telling of my life story. One was, "This is my book. How do you like it so far?" But Garry Shandling already took that one for his TV show.

Another was, "When is my editor going to quit giving me these crap subjects to write about?" But that would have been a riff off Steve Martin, I think it was, who opened his first performance at Carnegie Hall with the words, *"When is my agent going to get me out of these shit holes?"*

So I'll just play it straight and say a few different imaginary readers have occupied my mind while I was writing this autobiography. Lord knows I've had plenty of time to imagine them as this endeavor began in the spring of 2018 and here I am wrapping it up in the midst of the Great Coronavirus Pandemic of 2020. (My wife thought I was having an affair because I kept going out for more "copy paper.")

I'll say this: the pandemic has been a godsend; weeks and weeks with nothing to do but write.

Can you tell I'm kidding? If you can't, that could be a show stopper. I'm just sayin', if you aren't going to get the jokes, maybe you shouldn't come to the show.

What's probably most imaginary is that there will be any readers at all; not outside my own family anyway, if in it. Still, I've chosen to write for a general readership if only to challenge myself.

As Marshall McLuhan was saying back when I was in journalism school, the medium is the message. If I, using this brain, can finish a book, any kind of book, imagine what that unbelievably gifted bunch of grandkids of mine might do. Like the kids in Lake Woebegon, they're all above average.

Maybe they can take it to the next level, write a good book. Maybe a scholarly one, as opposed to this mash-up of thoughts and memories pertaining in large measure to my career in organizational communications. (Besides, they say the great writers were fueled by bourbon. I was fueled by Pepsi; you get what you pay for.) And anyway, let's face, it: to write a really successful book you have to have a popular topic and I was never that popular.

I'll just admit at the outset that some of what's in here isn't going to interest everyone. The family parts, for example, might strike some as belonging in that category they use on *America's Funniest Home Videos* to separate incoming entries. I'm told their largest category is one called "O.F.F."—Only Funny to the Family. So yes, there's some of that in here.

On the other hand, it's asking a lot, even of the family, to read those parts about my career in organizational communications in spite of how hard I've worked to make them at least appear interesting.

Sometimes, trying to address these different imagined audiences required me to write in a different voice, and sometimes to even wear different clothes while I was writing..

Still, this is primarily for my kids, their kids, and so on down the line. I hope they find it a useful, if only partial, history of the Wilt family in the West. It's not a genealogy— only what I remember of my part of the family diaspora, starting only a couple of generations back from my own.

You'll read in here that the author Ken Kesey told me once he was not going to fall into something he called *"That Old American Trick."* He was talking about something a little different, but I'll repurpose the idea here. I have not fallen into that old American trick of feeling that a person has to spill their guts just because they're putting pen to paper. If you want to hear that kind of thing, come by the house sometime.

In the meantime, if it makes you feel any better, think of this less as a true memoir and more of an exercise in reputation management on my part. You know: "The older I get the better I used to be."

And while I'm at it, I'll also mention that some of the names in here have been changed to protect the innocent.

As for the working years, when you leave one of the big companies from a position like mine you sign something called a disparagement agreement. It says you won't belittle, mock, ridicule, sneer, criticize, vilify, denigrate, deride or make fingers-down-the-throat gestures about anybody you ever worked with there whether they be living, dead, MIA or in a coma. (Well, that's not the exact language, but you get the idea.)

I know these policies might drain my story of some of its juice, but I weighed a number of opportunities to dish before concluding that what might look like a highly entertaining story to me could look like a libel suit to someone else.

And that's a darned shame, because at the end of the day, big organizations are societies unto themselves, with the same variety of offbeat personalities, dysfunctional behavior, conflicts and injustices that you see anywhere—sometimes writ large. I say this because in my time people in positions of power enjoyed immense latitude. They could get away with all kinds of conduct that wouldn't be tolerated today.

Sometimes the organization would be a highly successful business enterprise with attractive jobs even though it was clearly dysfunctional at some level. At one of the more venerated companies I worked for, I remember one of my co-workers saying in exasperation one day, *"Having this job is like being in love with a beautiful woman who also happens to be crazy."*

Pris and I learned on our trip to South America a few years ago that the Inca ruler was so deified that the ground was considered too unclean for him to touch. When he needed to spit, he did so into the hand of a courtier who then wiped it away with a special cloth that was burned along with anything else the ruler had touched in a ceremonial bonfire once each year.

(I could see the resemblance with some of the more self-important individuals I served under. I learned to carry a little spittle kit with me whenever I sat down with one of them to go over a speech or something. But the annual company bonfire would make it all worthwhile.)

In my time corporations resembled fiefdoms, I suppose, where if you were considered valuable enough to the "court" it might look the other way concerning certain obvious personality disorders. Possibly this was because someone was too valuable to the organization—in revenues, for example. I once knew of someone who was responsible for $50 billion in sales in a single year. That's not a typo. That's billions with a "B." They would have been reluctant to let a person like this go over to the competition just because everyone he worked around thought the reason he wore a comb-over was to hide his horns.

Then there were some that didn't make any sense to begin with—just poor hiring decisions. They never lasted very long. Here I'll mention the highly placed manager who spent a good deal of his time behind closed doors playing with sets of toy soldiers he'd erected in different places around his spacious office.

One elaborate scene represented a famous Civil War battle. It was made up of maybe 80 little soldiers, horses, artillery pieces and so on. He knew a lot about that one. If you were ever in a situation in his office where you needed to change the subject, you could just ask him a question about that battle. He would do all the talking from there.

One person told me that he was in this guy's office once when he got to talking about a different battle scene—this one from World War I and set up on his coffee table—where he could identify each little combatant by name. He said the one in the lieutenant's uniform was Hitler when he was in the Bavarian Army.

I don't know whether he did or not, but the guy who told me this scoffed and said, *"Can you believe he thinks Hitler made lieutenant? He didn't even make full corporal."*

That comment itself was a little odd, I thought. I'm just saying that you'd be surprised regarding some of the things we spent our time talking about instead of working because of the odd personalities involved. (With the additional dimension, of course, that some of these people held your career in their hands and you had to kind of play along with them—like visiting a resident at a memory care center.)

One particularly powerful individual in a company I worked for—we'll call him "Hugh Hundaker" here --was on his way down when I was assigned to support him. He still enjoyed the aura of absolute power accorded top individuals in these organizations, though. My boss told me, *"Hugh might not be as important as he once was, but you are to treat him as if he is."*

I came into a breakfast meeting one morning about 10 minutes early. The conference table was set up with a dozen or so place settings on paper placemats illustrated with examples of how easy it was to convert English measurements to metric. This was all the rage at the time and even the president of the U.S. had called for a national campaign to convert to the easier and more widely used global metric system.

Only a few minutes before the big man was due to arrive, his top assistant came into the room like a bomb-sniffing dog. He took a quick look around and said, *"You gotta get rid of these placemats; Hugh hates metrics."* A quick scramble ensued to trash the offensive mats and replace them with some bamboo ones rustled up in the kitchen.

A few days later I was having coffee with one of the old-timers in the office. He asked me how my work with Hugh Hundaker was going. I told him about the metrics placemat incident. He said, *"Ted Simpson used to have your job. He wrote a poem about working with Hugh."* It went like this:

I was sitting in a meeting
Just as quiet as I could be
When in came Hugh Hundaker
And hung his coat on me

One of my colleagues came back to the department one day with his mouth hanging open. He'd just been instructed by one of these "Mr. Bigs" to change the spelling of a word in something he'd drafted for the guy, making it incorrect. But when the writer pointed this out, the guy told him that because he, Mr. Big, had attended a U.S.

military academy, not merely a state institution like the lowly writer, they would "just assume" that his version was correct. (The lowly state institution, by the way, was UCLA, so it wasn't like the writer had gotten his diploma off the internet or something.)

It didn't help that people in the organization were often only too willing to elevate top people to above-human status. I remember once talking to a young woman who said that at first she was intimidated to be doing secretarial work for George Weyerhaeuser.

"Then one day," she told me, *"I realized he puts his pants on two legs at a time just like everybody else."*

<u>Two</u> legs at a time! I could never get the image out of mind after that of George Weyerhaeuser in his undies standing on the top bunk in the morning preparing to jump into a pair of pants being held open below by his wife, who is looking away.

Anyway, I'm not going to dwell on some of these aberrations of corporate life. I'm quite happy enjoying the rewards of a corporate career in America in the late 20th Century and feel no need to salve old wounds by skewering some of the less lovable creatures I encountered there. Just know that they were part of the scene and had to be dealt with.

I've tried to do enough work-arounds in writing about that sort of thing here to give an authentic flavor of what organizational life involved without maligning anyone. As to anything in here that someone <u>might</u> find libelous, I'll just throw up the same defense I saw a tabloid newspaper use one time in a libel suit. It said, *"Hey, we never said this stuff was true!"*

The adult reader might also find my account of things pedantic at times—what the initials RFK stood for; what "Catch 22" means; or how the Vietnam War draft lottery worked. Doesn't everyone know this stuff already? I'm pretty sure many younger people will not, so I've spelled them out.

In these respects, this is a little bit of a history book, at least for the parts of it I brushed up against. It's also part family history, part communications textbook, part travelogue, part love letter to my family, part paean to ports I have loved, and part just an excuse to string some favorite jokes and stories together.

Feel free to jump ahead.

As for why someone of such average proportions would feel the need to leave a memoir at all, here is why: not knowing more about the generations before ours is something that bugs a lot of people my age. In our family the last generation is now entirely gone; it's too late to ask any of them about anything unless you know a good necromancer.

Seriously, if you know a good necromancer, I could use one. I've only the vaguest notion of the generations before mine except that they were Northern Europeans— English, Irish, Scotch—who settled on the East Coast of the U.S. with the first Europeans then moved west over the next couple of centuries. We're said to go back to William Bradford on my Grandmother Wilt's side of the family. He came over on the *Mayflower* and was the first governor of the Plymouth Colony.

The first major stopping point for our line I ever heard anything about was southeastern Wisconsin around the town of Steuben, a two-hour drive west from Madison. Steuben is where my grandfather, Albert Alford Wilt (b. 1880, d. 1938), was raised on a farm before he headed west to Oregon around the turn of the century. This is where I pick up the story.

I wish I could tell you more. For example, what was life like for my dad and his family on the Willamette Valley homestead before electrification came along in the 1930s? I know just two things: One is that they and the neighbors had to string their own power line over a mile from the state highway; the other is that when it came to lighting the rooms (a process that unfolded over several years due to the Depression), they did the barn first, and then the kitchen because that's where the work got done.

And not just this one thing, but the whole Great Depression experience. Whatever happened to them in this time, it sure produced some intelligent, industrious, resourceful, funny, and sometimes hedonistic people, I'll say that.

We may never know certain other details, such as how Albert got to the West Coast to start the Oregon chapter of the Wilt clan to begin with. He arrived too early to have come by car. That leaves only the train, unless he rode a horse or hoofed it. It's this level of detail about my own life that I wanted to put down somewhere so my kids won't be left wondering about them when they're my age.

I'll also admit to thinking that I thought I might have something to say about the field of organizational communications, which is why I've gone to some lengths to describe what people in the field did and how it was practiced in my time. The world has been so radically altered by the advent of social media, and now the pandemic, that I have no idea whether any of our methodology is still in use today. I know the bedrock principles of communication never change, I can tell you that.

In any event, maybe one of my progeny will follow me into journalism or a related field and find this account helpful. (Or avoid it like the plague.) Either way, mission accomplished!

Otherwise, I'm not sure the story needed to be written, for I have been amazing only in the way that all human beings are amazing. And any adversity I've had to overcome in my life so far, knock wood, has been of the garden variety—never got trapped by a big rock and had to gnaw my own arm off or anything like that.

Neither have I played a part in any kind of monumental or historic undertaking, unless you count the current pandemic; knew none of the famous or accomplished individuals I crossed paths with well; didn't go to war or work on the Alaska pipeline. Never really mastered anything; the old saying that someone knows just enough about a subject to be dangerous would probably apply to me.

And yet I write a book about it.

Here's what I think happened: I had an epiphany around age 11. I was reading one of the *Bobbsey Twins* adventures, a birthday gift from my grandmother, Alma Wilt. Near the bottom of the page I was on, something tragic happened in the story; I think a dog was killed. I teared up.

When I turned the page, the writer so adroitly moved along with the story that within a paragraph or two I found myself laughing out loud. I remember thinking, *"Wow. Words are powerful. You can really affect people with them, make them laugh, make them cry."* (I had to wonder: might it possibly make them give you money, too?)

I'm not sure you could say it was the moment I knew I wanted to be a writer, but it sure put a thought in my head. And when a thought comes into <u>my</u> head, it almost always goes out through my mouth. I must have started talking it up as a quasi-career path way back when and actually did begin to play around with words.

Just recently I heard someone describe one author's ability to *"make the words come off the page and explode in the reader's mind."* Wouldn't that be wonderful? Alas, the reader would probably have to have a fuel depot in their mind for any of the words in here to cause an ignition like that. Having never tried my hand at long-form writing before, I really didn't know what would come out.

I did write a slender book on communications early in my career, which I'll talk about later. But I only got as far as the <u>title</u> for another one about my experience serving as jury foreman for a trial involving a man who had exposed himself in an adult movie theatre in Long Beach, California, once. It was, "The Jury was Hung and so was the Defendant."

I had hoped this one would be better than it turned out to be, but I suppose that was like a cat hoping its tail would get longer. Once a Flack, now a Hack.

I was about 15 the first time I heard someone say, *"You should write a book."* I heard it again many times in the intervening years. (Do you think maybe they were saying I should <u>read</u> a book? That would have made more sense.)

In any event, I obviously took the suggestion to heart because I started hanging on to just about anything I thought could be used for decoration in a work like this. It turned into a voluminous archive of everything from press clippings—some written <u>by</u> me, some <u>about</u> me—to personal correspondence going back 50 years or more. A lot of it is stuff useful for no other purpose than to generate a laugh, which sometimes was all my job called for.

(Did you know, for example, that Lou Gehrig died of Lou Gehrig's disease? What are the chances of <u>that</u>?)

I'd make use of all kinds of this "borrowed" material— like the inane last sentence above, lifted from one of the *Dumb and Dumber* movies I think.

Otherwise I guess I saved it for, like, right now. You'll have to tell me if it was worth hanging onto.

Either way, the pleasure has been all mine.

—Don Wilt
Camp Sherman, Oregon
April 15th, 2020, my 72nd birthday

Introduction

My dad used to tell people that I liked to hear myself talk. He encouraged me to watch for more opportunities <u>not</u> to. Instead, I ignored his advice and made a career of it.

Mine is a story of someone who discovered what you could call his "career track" somewhere around first grade and stayed on it until the end of his working life.

Some would say I pulled a rabbit out of a hat, making the leap from deep in the woods of Oregon to some of the biggest companies in the world, and from there into one of the best jobs there at that. It might very well have been the best job in my field at the time.

But I've heard say that you can't pull a rabbit <u>out</u> of a hat unless you put one <u>in</u> there first, so this is also the story of how my rabbit got into the hat and what the trick was to pulling it out.

I asked a friend's 12-year-old daughter once what she wanted to be when she grew up. She said, *"I'm not certain, but I'm pretty sure I want to work in a tall building."*

It made me laugh at the time, but I'm not so sure my own thinking was too much more evolved at an age quite a lot older than that. I wanted to work in corporate communications because it sounded like the big leagues.

Before the big leagues, though, came the "B" leagues. This is where my story begins.

To set the context, I spent my formative years in an Oregon sawmill town small enough that we played eight-man football in high school. Baseball teams sometimes had to borrow or lend a player so that both sides would have nine men. No doubt about it, this was the bush leagues. My high school class of 26 graduates was the largest in the town's history—by far; my older brother Denny's class had nine, my sister Cheryl's seven.

There wasn't a lot of information coming in or going out of a place like that in the 50s and early 60s, either. We were like the Romanians under Ceausescu.

Without making too much of it, I'll just say I don't know if there's such a thing as "Small Town Complex" (like "Small Man" complex), but it wouldn't surprise me.

Unless someone with more worldly experience took you under their wing, you didn't get much in the way of development in a place like this. In that sense you could remain disadvantaged for a long time.

I'd cite the lack of experience with a large organization of any kind as one example. Another would be the absence of any kind of instruction in debate, organization or critical thinking. (Also, brown-nosing—didn't know a thing about it.)

You could say I just wasn't very well-rounded.

It was years before I could show up at an important occasion and know I wasn't under- or over-dressed. (And this was just last week!)

Small-townism can cause a lot of self-doubt in a person. How could I be expected to keep up with the kind of people I'd meet at a big university, on the newspapers, and later in the big cities and companies?

Yet by the time I came to the end of my career, I was sittin' pretty at a ginormous aerospace company in Southern California—*Fortune Magazine* called it "The World's Most Admired Aerospace Company." And I had the best job there.

I can't <u>not</u> mention that the job came with an access badge that read "Inner-Perimeter Executive Parking." I'm vain enough to have kept it as a little souvenir of my "glory days." (Isn't that like on Maslow's Hierarchy of Human Needs or something, the need to be in the "inner-perimeter?")

I'm <u>not</u> so vain as to think this made me anything special. They called the generation before mine the "Greatest Generation." I call ours the "Luckiest." All the conditions for a person to prosper were in place in our time: good public educations, cheap university tuitions, and jobs for all.

Something that makes my life story a little bit improbable, though, is the coincidence—or luck, maybe—that the giant, 100-year-old industrial organization I'd just gone to work for would decide it needed a complete communications examination and redo right when I'd just taken an interest in the new field of organizational communications and managed to string together a few meager credentials related to it.

One could also surmise that my small-town upbringing would work against me once in the halls of commerce, but actually it was quite the opposite; sometimes I outrivaled others in my profession not in <u>spite</u> of my backwater upbringing but <u>because</u> of it.

That doesn't mean it was always easy, though, and I'll give you one reason why:

One of the Collared Professions

Besides helping to pioneer new ways of doing things in my field, I was also a pioneer on the Wilt family tree—the first of our breed to make my living working for "The Man" my entire career, as opposed to owning my own business or practicing one of the more self-regulating professions like land surveying, trucking or skateboarding.

I've heard this called, "Wearing another man's collar." In our family, that had not been seen as a good thing. My younger brother, Darcy, even told me once, *"If I had your job I'd kill myself."*

To tell the truth, it didn't always thrill me either. Take the time one of my first supervisors told me over coffee one morning that he'd been instructed to give me *"more leash"* because my work had impressed, but then quickly added that he still reserved the right to *"jerk the leash"* any time he felt like it.

That's when Darcy would have killed himself—<u>or</u> the supervisor. I know I felt like it at the time.

But if the corporate life required a certain amount of subjugation, it also provided a financial safety net that I found appealing. Namely, it made it possible for me to feed my family and give them a good life, which was always Job One with me.

It also came with almost unlimited opportunity—not just for advancement and bigger pay, but for recognition, self-fulfillment, adventure and fun—of which I took full advantage. Even that is part of the story.

Spoiler Alert

Just another note or two as you embark on this tour of my life and times. First, you'll notice that I wasn't able to resist the habit of name-dropping. It's <u>so</u> much fun, and some of the ones I crossed paths with were about as big as they get—Bobby Kennedy, Neil Armstrong and Henry Fonda—just to drop a few right here. (You may have noticed I managed to drop Ken Kesey's before I was even out of the preface.)

I'd always considered such persons to be important parts of "My Story."

That was, until the day I had lunch with one of the more elevated individuals I know. He said, *"I'm not like a lot of people; big names don't impress me."*

I challenged him at first. I said, *"You mean to tell me that you would not be interested in reading about the time that Henry Fonda picked me up in a 1953 Chevrolet four-door sedan borrowed from the set of the movie 'Sometimes a Great Notion' and we rode along for quite a while talking about the author, Ken Kesey?"*

He pounced. A little smirk came over his face and he said, *"Yeah, and then what happened?"*

Obviously, the answer was *"nothing very important,"* which is probably what you could say about most of what I've chronicled here.

So, spoiler alert: nothing happens. I mean, I may have joked around with the head of NASA one time (we were talking about staying fit and I told him about a new exercise for people who don't like to work out; they're called "Diddly-Squats.") He laughed, but he didn't then make me an astronaut.

If Only for the Laughs

Sometimes I marvel that someone with my modest abilities found himself in so many desirable positions professionally. My old J-School and newspaper chum Jim Sellers told me once that it was because my ambition exceeded my intelligence. He was probably on to something there.

In any event, for a life in which not very much of importance happened, I sure had a good time putting it down on paper.

If nothing else, parts of it should be good for a laugh, which has always been one of the best reasons I could think of for doing something.

And to think I got paid for it.

Between the Interceptions

Finally, I hope my progeny find inspiration in these pages, that it's a part of the family story that makes them feel good about who they are and where they come from.

If that comes off as *braggadocio*, it's not to say that there aren't some families out there that have it all over ours, but not that many.

It's also not to say that I wouldn't like a Mulligan on some of my own missteps along the way. As my old friend Luther Metke told me once, *"Of course we make mistakes; we only get to do this once."* I plead being human, a phrase borrowed from a good personal bio I just read.

During the NCAA's 150th year celebration of college football, I heard a Hall-of-Fame quarterback say he was watching ESPN with his teenage son once when they put his statistics up on the screen. His son said, *"Man, how'd you ever get into the Hall of Fame with that many interceptions?"*

The QB/Dad says, *"I told him I did it between the interceptions!"*

That's how I did it too. Let the story begin.

CHAPTER 1

Small Fish in a Small Pond

Our Town

When I was in first grade in 1954, a pretty accurate (if "boosterized") description of my hometown of Marcola, Oregon, appeared in the *Eugene Register-Guard*. It was in the form of a letter to the editor from my childhood pal Mike Gambill's mother, Ardith, and ran under the headline *"No Ghost at All."*

> *To the Editor:*
> *Last Tuesday night the people of Marcola gathered around their television sets as usual. This night, however, we couldn't help feeling a bit self-satisfied. At last, the Mohawk Valley was going to get some recognition. What happened?*
> *Many of your readers probably saw the program—most of them, understandably enough, were left with the impression that in a few years they could drive to Marcola, poke around the decaying ruins and then boast that they'd been to a real ghost town.*

We can't blame the producers of the show too much. There have been so many misconceptions built up that very few people outside our community have any accurate impression of us at all.

Not long ago, a new acquaintance said with a raised eye brow," Oh, you live in the bad-lands, huh?" Things like this happen often—too often! It's about time someone set the facts straight.

The majority of people who live in Marcola are honest, hard-working citizens—average people like in any other community. Why rumor has given us the dubious honor of being a sort of last outpost, I cannot imagine.

Now there is another fallacy—the ghost town theory. Do you know that a great majority of our men drive to jobs in Springfield and Eugene and Sweet Home—and did even before Fischer's mill was closed? Do you know that Fischer's employed many non-local men, transporting them from Springfield every day?

Do you want to know why so many of us live in Marcola and will continue to do so, Fischer's or no Fischer's? In the first place, the Mohawk Valley is as beautiful as any of the more publicized valleys in the area. The land is rich and productive. It is a healthful and safe place to raise our children. We have a fine consolidated school district that provides an economical hot lunch program, music instruction and a gymnasium that any school would be proud to have.

There are churches too, despite the fact that the camera overlooked those in favor of a boarded-up store and an empty house—both out of use before Fischer's closed.

Don Wilt

Our organizations here are extremely active. There is an Odd Fellow Lodge, a Veterans of Foreign Wars and its auxiliary, The Royal Neighbors, The Mothers Club and the grange to name a few. These organizations have now united in an effort to obtain instruments for the school band.

Does this sound like the death rattle of a dying community? I don't think so.

There is one disadvantage to living in Marcola and I don't think anyone would deny it. That is the antiquated trail of humps and bumps that passes for a road from here to Springfield. Give the Mohawk Valley its long-promised highway and you would open up a region that could well develop into one of the most prosperous and rewarding in this vicinity.

Why not give us a chance? Marcola has been overlooked too long."

We begin here because I thought Mrs. Gambill painted a pretty vivid picture of the place where I grew up. It was, as she portrayed, a timber town of about 400 people that had just closed its last sawmill—the Fischer's Lumber Company, where most of the breadwinners in town had worked, including my own father. Despite her protestations, the town did have a *"Last Picture Show"* vibe to it.

You'd be surprised how isolated a place just 20 miles from a small city could be in those days. No Internet, of course, or Smartphones to connect us to the larger world. I mean, we didn't speak *Boont* or anything like that, but you could probably tell we were from *someplace* by looking at our haircuts; (Tom Walters was the only barber and he leaned toward a certain style that featured fairly large "whitewalls.")

There were still board sidewalks running along both sides of the main street for about three blocks and the remaining buildings all had false fronts like you see in the Westerns. Easily half of the stores that once lined the main street were boarded up or torn down by the time I was in fourth grade. This included the former Hopkins Café, Curly Hanson's service station, a former auto repair shop big enough for logging trucks and most of the buildings at the old mill.

That left us with only a handful of services—Wayne's Market, Art Moran's Richfield service station, and three taverns (same as the number of churches). For everything else you had to "go to town."

Yet it was also a community with a lot of civic pride. When our basketball teams were doing well people would pack into the high school gymnasium—a little box like the one in *"Hoosiers"*—and cheer and stamp so loud on the wooden bleachers that you could feel the vibration on the covered bridge over the river a couple-hundred yards away.

The schools were well-run by long-time superintendent Barry Mauney. He looked like he could have just stepped out of a Dickens novel with his wire rim glasses and black suit-vest, but he was on top of things. We can probably credit him with having the vision to see that two brand-new additional classrooms at Marcola Elementary were ready for us when my class—the largest in the town's history—showed up for first grade in 1954.

Both our schools—a grade school that went to 8th grade and the four-year high school—were classic beauties built in the 1920s with polished wood hallways, high ceilings and the double-hung classroom windows that you used a big pole with a hook to open when the weather got warm.

The high school was not called Marcola High, but Mohawk, as we were located in the Mohawk Valley and served what once had been several separate small towns—Wendling, Mabel and Donna—all mill towns gone by the bye. The valley was named for the Mohawk River Valley in New York.

Both of the school buildings were later burned to the ground by arsonists, the high school around 1997, and along with it the class photos of me and all four of my siblings that lined the main hallway. It was small enough that they could still do that for every individual in the school's 40-year history.

I took my son, Cooper, to see the old high school one summer when he was about 10. We slipped through an open door and found my class picture. There my colorized self was with my name "calligriphied" beneath my photo in the class of 1966. It said "Donald <u>Wild</u>." Off by one letter.

Coop must have been thinking, "Well, <u>he</u> must not have made much of an impression here." I was more inclined to think, "Man, the guy who did this got it right the first three times a Wilt came through here; he'd had plenty of practice. This must have been around the time his drinking took off."

We had excellent teachers in both schools, some of whom actually taught every one of the five Wilt kids, starting with my older brother, Denny, six years ahead of me, and ending with my little brother, Darcy, four years younger—a period of more than 20 years.

Our Place on the Social Scale

While I consider myself to be a self-invented man, I don't pretend to be a self-made one. My brother and I both knew a guy who inherited a lot of money, along with the company that produced it. He was obnoxious and Denny always said, *"He was born on third base and thinks he hit a homerun."*

With that as context, you might say that we were born on first base. Our parents provided us with a comfortable and safe place to live, no food insecurities, high expectations in school, and admirable role modeling. But once we were no longer in danger of getting run over crossing the road or falling into an abandoned well, we lived highly independent and self-directed lives. No allowances, no family councils. Certainly no "guidance counselor" in high school. Who ever heard of that?

Sometimes when I'm watching sports on television with friends I'll say, *"I would have gone to Stanford, but I ended up going to Oregon."*

Invariably someone will bite and say, *"Oh really, why?"*

I tell them, *"Nobody told me about it."* They didn't tell me about Gonzaga either, or even Linfield for that matter, which is more the size of college I probably should have been looking at.

Tax Day Birthdays All-Around

The town was highly-populated with GI's back from WWII. You know they call them the *"Greatest Generation."* They really were. Very capable, resourceful, dependable people— men and women alike—running a pretty good little town and, in large part, serving as commendable role models for our generation. I always liked to say that ours may not <u>be</u> the greatest generation, but we rubbed up against it.

This is the town I came home to after being born at Sacred Heart Hospital in Eugene on Tax Day—April 15th, 1948. I was born at almost exactly the same moment that my first childhood friend, Kathie, was being delivered in the adjoining hospital room to my mother's best friend, Louise Kintzley. If that wasn't crazy enough, my sister, Susan, had been born on the same date in the same hospital exactly one year before us. (People called this "Irish twins" at the time but you probably wouldn't use the term today.)

In order for this remarkable coincidence to occur I had to come into the world a couple of months early, arriving as a premature infant that the hospital was not sure was big enough to make it. My mom used to talk about being able to put her wedding ring over my hand and wrist.

She always credited our family physician, Dr. George Guldager, with pulling me through. I later met and became friends with an outstanding neonatologist named Charley Hoffmeister who routinely saved infants born weighing in the <u>grams</u>, so my situation would have been no big deal today. But in 1948 I guess it could have gone either way. (Sorry about that.)

Louise and Mom had known each other since their late teens and my dad spent a lot of time with Louise's husband, Dick. We were close enough that we referred to them in our household as *Uncle* Dick and *Aunt* Louise. Kathie celebrated all our birthdays with us so we had some great birthday parties. It was always hamburgers at our house, a tradition that continued clear up to the end of our college years.

Mom would always come up with an idea like a cake made up of railroad cars with each of our names on one of the cars. There would also be a fourth cake for Darcy who couldn't get his act together and ended up being born two days "late"—April 17th.

Out Peeling Chittum

At first we lived in a small, two-bedroom house on Murdoch Lane. My folks later sold that house to the Kintzleys when we moved to another house in Marcola where I grew up.

A while back Kathie came across receipts her father had saved for the payments they made to my folks on the Murdoch Lane property.

The total price was $3,300. It appeared to be a pretty friendly arrangement in which Dick paid whatever he apparently was able to pay each month. His payments hovered around $70 but sometimes dipped as low as $50 or went as high as $135. You can see he was logging or working in the woods because the payments were smallest in the winter when they were snowed out. In December of 1951 there was no payment at all.

If I know Uncle Dick the sums on the checks suggest he was making "double payments" whenever he could. This would have been his style, so the skipped payment would have been no big deal and it's consistent with a scribbled note from a friend of theirs I found in the same batch of papers.

It mentioned that times were so hard that, *"Everyone's out peeling chittum to make ends meet."* Chittum was bark stripped from the wild Cascara tree, prized for its medicinal purposes. You peeled it off the trees, dried it out, then turned it in for cash at Wayne's Market for around 17 cents a pound. A burlap bag full of dried chittum might put seven or eight badly-needed bucks in your pocket.

I did my share of it. Even came face-to-face with a seven-foot long cougar doing it one time. Thank God they're even more skittish than humans. First the big lion looked surprised and then he looked gone.

From Extreme Stability into a World of Change

Somehow both "Uncle" Dick and my dad managed to pay for their houses through these lean times, making it possible for both Kathie and I to spend all our childhood years in Marcola until we left for college in 1966.

Kathie's early life had a little more variety in it than mine did. For one, her family had a television early-on. I went to her house sometimes after school in first grade where we watched the test pattern of an Indian chief on the screen for a while because that was all that was on in the afternoon.

We didn't have television at our house until 1959 when I was in 5th grade. My cousins up the road in Corvallis had no TV at all in their home. What "screen time" they got was dosed out to them in Sunday visits to Grandma Wilt's place where they got to watch the weekly episode of *Lassie*. Have to say they all turned out to be smart, capable, self-sufficient people with a remarkable ability to entertain *themselves*.

When it came to disposable income, we were in the same boat as everyone at the time; we didn't have any. We took a family vacation together only once, a three-day camping trip to Davis Lake in about 1958.

Although it was a mere 60 miles away, I didn't see the Pacific Ocean until I was 18 years old and on my senior class outing.

Within that confine, and all-in-all, we enjoyed a stable American middle-class upbringing. But things were evolving. When the mill closed, a lot of the local men found work at the big Weyerhaeuser forest products complex in Springfield about 20 miles away.

For 13 years my dad was one of them. He hired on to Weyerhaeuser as a timber agent, a forester overseeing the purchase of timber and the management of timberlands. He found the bureaucracy stifling and confided to me once that his boss had dinged him in a performance review for spending too much time talking to people when he was out working.

Ugh! My dad said they didn't seem to realize that this is how he'd managed to build the kind of relationships that made it possible for the company to acquire timberlands from the people whose families had first settled them. They might have a lot of different offers for their property, but they'd end up going with Dad because they knew and trusted him to watch out for their interests.

Someday I'd get to experience the same kind of small-bore mentality at "The Office."

Anyway, my story begins as a standard-issue baby boomer growing up at a momentous time in the country's history—a small fish in a small pond, yes, but destined to have several brushes with a few of the most historic figures of the period.

CHAPTER 2

The Grittier Side of Things

I guess there was no need for Mrs. Gambill to mention in her letter to the editor about the virtues of our town that we also had three pretty busy taverns, the most prominent being the Dew Drop Inn.

It was a large white-two story building with an early-West façade—false fronts they're called—right on the main drag at the center of town. The so-called inn still had rooms upstairs but they only rented to a couple of long-timers, mostly elderly single guys working in the woods or mills. One of them was a one-legged man everyone called "Step-and-a-Half." Another one, called "Boots," referred to everyone as cousin: *"How ya doin,' Cousin?"*

The downstairs was large enough that it had a long, polished wooden bar with about 15 stools and two shuffle-board tables in addition to at least one pool table. Kids weren't allowed to go in, but if we knocked on the big glass front doors the elderly proprietor, George Carey, would come in his full-length white apron to take an order for Pepsi in the bottle. They also sold pickled pig's feet and these gross-looking boiled eggs that floated around in a five-gallon jar at the end of the bar. I never developed an appetite for either one of those.

That's all I could see from the front door. Just down the boardwalk between the Dew Drop Inn and the P.O. was Meacham's Tavern. We didn't call them boardwalks, but that's what they were. (It was a timber town and lumber was cheap.) Meacham's was owned and operated by Elmer Meacham and his wife, Jessie. I was friends with their son, Versal, when we were teenagers. The family called him "Squeaky."

The kitchen from their house opened directly into the bar. It became my first window into a side of life very unlike my own. It was in and around these establishments that the grittier side of the community came out in the form of violent fistfights in the parking lots and children doing their homework in the family car while they waited for their old man to come out of the tavern at night.

When the dads did reappear it was often just to bring the kids a pepperoni stick or a candy bar and to say they wouldn't be much longer.

Ironically, some of the families most afflicted by this kind of thing produced some of the school system's most outstanding students, and later, success stories.

One of these families had a houseful of boys and a closet full of guns. They had two sets of twins. While the parents were away—or maybe even while they were there—the boys would engage in gun fights. (And not with paint guns, either—real ones!)

Over time one of the twins shot and killed his brother. Of the remaining two twins, one shot his brother's leg off and one of them had an eye shot out with a BB gun. But except for the one who didn't escape the killing field, a bunch of them went on to graduate from college and distinguish themselves in various fields.

I've heard this called *"Hillbilly Smart."*

My beloved old next-door neighbor, Lola Harper, told me once that Marcola had *"Some of the best people and some of the worst people God ever created."*

That squares with my memory. It was, after all, a mill town; there were bound to be some toughs. They seemed to run in families. If you were advised to steer clear of one person in that family it was probably just as well to avoid the whole bunch of them. This meant their kids too. I learned this the hard way when I was about 10.

I was walking along the road following the river through town when a boy in my class from this notorious family crossed to my side of the road as he was approaching. I was always a pretty cheerful little fellow so I raised my hand and shouted, *"Hi, Douglas!"* He raised his right arm as if he were going to wave back but instead let fly a flat rock about the size of a sand dollar that hit me flat-wise in my left eye socket hard enough that it knocked me off my feet.

Before I could get up, he also yanked off one of my basketball shoes and threw it into the river. He didn't really make it clear what the point of the attack was except to just generally spread terror on behalf of his family. It worked quite effectively on me.

I was small from the time I was born until my last couple of years of high school. As a result it seemed like I was always having to dodge some bully, one of whom would tell me frequently that he was going to be waiting for me "on the railroad tracks." The tracks were between the school and my house. I don't know if he really did wait for me or not because I went *waaayy* around.

I'm not sure what the long-term effect of this kind of thing—if any—might be on a person, but I think it might have made me a little more intimidated than a lot of people when it came to dealing with some of the more difficult or aggressive people you run into once in a while at work. (Sometimes in a meeting I would just fall to the floor and pull my <u>own</u> shoes off. It was terrible.)

Seriously, I think it helped me develop an important survival skill, which was to steer clear of people like this as much as possible. Or, if I couldn't, to remember that they were the kind of people you needed to keep your guard up around. I remember thinking once, *"Oh, Lynn is likely to be at the meeting in Denver. I better have a strategy for that."*

And just by way of example I'll mention a colleague who had a nemesis in his professional circle, an individual only slightly higher than himself in the organization, who once took it upon himself to point out to others at a get-together that my friend was wearing the same shirt he'd worn the last time they'd all gotten together, implying he must only have one shirt, I guess?

What do you think would be a good strategy for dealing with a person like that? (Besides homicide, I mean.)

CHAPTER 3

Life in "Mayberry RFD"

T he Fischer Lumber Company had been the largest of more than a half-dozen sawmills that operated in the Mohawk Valley at one time. My dad worked there from about 1942 until a couple of years after it closed in 1954. The company, which had employed hundreds for decades, finally came down to just two employees: the owner, Dale Fischer, and my dad. That tells you how integral he was to the whole operation. Last man out the door.

When the mill was still running, Dad was right-hand man to the general manager, Mel Nye, and they were close. My folks were sometimes invited to the Nyes' to play canasta with Mel and his wife, Merle, while us kids slid up and down the long hardwood hallways and fed hay to a pony they kept in a grove of oak trees next to the house.

I remember during one of these visits seeing this very sizable stack of freshly-bundled U.S. currency in large bills stacked on the kitchen counter leading to the garage. The stack was about 1 1/2 feet square and about 10 inches tall. "Uncle Mel" said it was the payroll for the following day. He put it there so he wouldn't forget it on his way to work. This would have been about 1953 in "Mayberry RFD."

For many years you could set your watch to the sound of the mill whistle that told the town it was time for lunch. We could still hear a lot of noise coming from the mill site through the open windows of our nearby first-grade classroom when I started school, but they were just the sounds of it being dismantled.

A distinctive feature of the old mill remained for a period of time before it was scrapped. That was the wigwam burner. All the big sawmills had one. It was a tall, conical structure made of riveted steel panels with a cone-shaped screen covering the top, making it resemble an upside-down badminton birdy. This is where they burned sawdust and scraps from the mill. A big conveyor belt hauled the stuff up there and dumped it on the fire. The wigwam would smoke and glow all night like a lighthouse. It didn't put out that much smoke, though, due to its unique design I suppose.

I know the kilns that were used to dry lumber are still there and being used for some industrial purpose not related to kilning today.

Mud Hole Streets

As a rule, kids didn't go "to town." Instead, when you needed new shoes your mother had you stand on a sheet of copy paper while she drew a pattern around your foot. She then took this with her the next time she went to town.

In third grade, my mother took the outline of my foot into Springfield to buy me a pair of rubber boots. It'd been raining hard since school started and I was really itching to splash through the massive mud puddles that had developed between our house and the school. In the wet months, some of these side streets were little more than a series of brown ponds the length of a car.

I was so anxious to get out there that I told my mom the boots fit fine. In fact they must have been at least a size too big.

On the way home from school, I attempted to hop across one of these muddy little ponds and landed short of the shoreline. My right foot sank right down into the mud. One boot was sucked off and under in an instant. My foot came right out of it and I emerged on the other side wearing only a wet sock on one foot.

Knowing I was going to be in trouble, my loyal little friends, Eddie and Kathie, helped me try to recover the boot, but we never did. My mother was a very understanding person, but things like that could really tick her off.

Webster 363

This was so far before the digital age that for many years our phone number consisted of just three digits with a prefix of two letters—W.E., which stood for "Webster." That made our number "Webster-3-6-3."

I've heard the telephone companies put a great deal of thought into their prefix nomenclature and that some of the more famous ones, like "Murray Hill" in New York City, were chosen to convey a certain cachet. Maybe "Webster" was a code name for "End of the Road" or something. I liked it just the same and hated to give it up for the 9-3-3 prefix and four-digit number that replaced it sometime in the late 60s.

A Town of "Half-Houses"

It wasn't uncommon in Marcola for people's houses to be under construction for years. A lot of them had only tarpaper on the exterior.

This wasn't because people had a "*things-will-get-done-when-they-get-done*" kind of attitude. Far from it. It was just testament to how long it takes to build a house when you only bring home a few pieces of lumber at a time. It wasn't uncommon to see a mill worker headed for home at the end of the day holding an empty lunch bucket in one hand while steadying a couple of 2 x 6s on his shoulder with the other one. What they <u>did</u> have in that town was a "*this-will-get-done-when-we-have-the-money-and-the-time-to-do-it-ourselves*" kind of attitude.

People were always on the lookout for seconds from the mill that they could pick up for a song or take for free. I remember being at a friend's house in 7th grade. His dad worked at a plywood mill.

His mother gave us some snacks at the table in their new kitchenette. Nothing had been painted or wallpapered yet, so you clearly could see the red stamp on each sheet of plywood they'd used for the floors, walls and ceiling.

Each one had been stamped several times. They said "Reject" "Reject" "Reject."

Most houses in Marcola were small, many of them only about 850 square feet. Some of them were this size because they had first been built as more substantial company housing in the town of Wendling four miles to the northeast. When the Booth-Kelly mill there closed in the 1940s the town was razed and a lot of the houses were cut in-half so they would fit coming through the covered bridge over Mill Creek while being moved to Marcola.

Families with as many as eight kids lived in these little half-houses. Because they were heated with antiquated wood stoves and oil burners, they were also prone to catch fire and our volunteer fire department was kept hopping.

"Your House!"

The town had a 1939 White fire engine that towed a wagon with all the hoses and equipment piled up on it. It was hard to get the truck started. They actually kept it on a raised platform about three feet off the ground in an old garage across from the store. Anyone could pull the alarm handle on the outside of the building. That would activate a war-surplus military siren you could hear in the next county. It was enough to make the hair on the back of your neck stand up.

When the alarm was sounded, volunteers would rush to the fire station, throw open the doors and roll the truck down the ramp from the platform and out into the street in an attempt to compression-start it. Response time compared with today's standards must have been abysmal. I remember more than one building burning clear to the ground because they couldn't get the truck started, usually in the dead of winter.

A funny family story is the time my dad was up late working on one of his survey maps when the siren went off. He quickly put on his volunteer fireman's gear and ran to the station just as the truck was pulling away.

He hopped up on the back and shouted to the guy next to him, "*Where we going?*" The other volunteer turned to look at him, then reared back in astonishment and said "*Your house!*" Turns out that someone driving by had seen flames shooting from our chimney, which is what happens when you have a fire in the flue. Fortunately it hadn't spread to the attic or anything and they got it out right away.

The Wilt Place

You'd of thought we had more money than we did to look at our house. It was a handsome, two-story Dutch barn-style looker right on the Main Street across from the Richfield service station. It had white lap siding with green shutters upstairs and down, and a sun porch enclosed with floor-to-ceiling paned windows and a full basement.

The house had been built by Oregon's first supermarket magnate—a man named Miles McKay. He started his first store on the ground floor of the Odd Fellows hall in Marcola, prospered, then moved on. The McKay house came on the market and that's how we ended up residents of whatever address it was. (Which we'll never know, because Marcola didn't have house numbers at the time.)

Unlike the McKays, we weren't wealthy but got by because my father worked two jobs and was a good shot—venison, elk, duck, grouse and pheasant were our main sources of protein; one winter, a bear.

Meat from his hunting expeditions was stored in the freezer at McKay's market where we and just about everybody else rented a locker in the walk-in freezer. When our mothers had figured out what they wanted to put on the table that night, they'd send one of their kids down to McKay's to retrieve the necessary venison chops, frozen ducks, elk-burger or whatever from their lockers.

Imagine the owner of a store like this knowing how to cut up and package all these wild animals, which was part of what you paid for when you rented a locker from him.

The house cost my parents $5,200, a significant sum in 1950. My mother told me more than once how it was love at first sight for her. She said she knew immediately that she wanted to live—and die—in that house. I saw my mother in action enough in my own lifetime to know that she could really put her foot down, so it's no surprise that she got her way.

When I was in 5th grade the place really did catch fire—some sort of malfunction with the wood furnace. It was gutted, but they somehow got it put back together while we stayed with the Seavey family for six weeks. The Seaveys lived in the spacious former Nye residence on the west end of town that I talked about earlier. Ironically, this house burned to the ground years later when my sister, Susan, was living there with her young kids.

Our house was never totally repaired. We lived for years with a stack of particleboard panels stored in one of the downstairs rooms awaiting application. Even then, Mom lived to be 82 years old and never lived anywhere else. Dad either, for that matter.

Town Crier

As a little kid I was somewhat lost in the shuffle of our big household. My "Aunt" Louise was often my babysitter. She told me a number of years later that, *"Nobody would listen to you in that house."*

It was a different story around town where I made the rounds and visited regularly with the local population, many of them elderly women who seemed to have plenty of time on their hands and didn't mind sitting a spell.

When I was about 6, I told the aged Mrs. Savage, who lived next door to the gas station across from us, that I was *"never going to cuss, smoke or drink."* It pleased her so much that every time she had other elderly ladies over she would insist that I repeat it for them.

I would happily comply as I saw it as some sort of performance and seemed to need the attention. If I meet up with Mrs. Savage in the afterlife I'll be proud to tell her that I have Never. Ever. *Smoked.* Well, cigars.

Going from one house to another like this I also picked up a lot of information that I did not hesitate to dispense at subsequent stops. It was an important part of my emerging "career track." I loved being the bringer of news. When I was about 8 the town's water meter reader told my friend's mother, *"If you want to know what's going on in this town, ask that Donnie Wilt."*

Happy Days

You could write a television script around the long bus rides we had to take to compete with schools equally as small as ours in high school sports. Oh wait, they did. It was called "Happy Days."

These trips were pretty extensive and always accomplished in a single day—200 miles to Days Creek, 75 to Alsea, 60 or so to Triangle Lake, Eddyville and Crow—all communities like ours in remote locations surviving mostly off the timber industry.

We played in each other's primitive little gymnasiums where the crowds were right on top of you. One or two of these little towns were really hard-boiled; I remember once we had to dress down in the school's boiler room and then jog over to the gymnasium past this gauntlet of hostile adults shouting inter-regional hate-speech at you.

There were probably places where they held potlucks for the visiting team and stuff like that, but this was not our custom. Visitors were treated more like invading forces than anyone's "guest."

Coming home on the bus from night basketball games we'd harmonize on songs like *"Teen Angel"* and *"Who Put the Bop in the Bop de Bop de Bop?"* Boys doing one part, girls the other.

One night coming back from Harrisburg in a heavy fog, the driver—also the coach—missed a corner. We went off the road, through a big wooden fence and out across this field of corn stubble until the bus sank into the mud and finally came to a stop.

Nobody got hurt, or fired, or sued. No investigation either, as I recall. It was much more of a "these- things-happen" sort of society at the time.

The Corner

I should mention one more important establishment in Marcola: "The Corner." It was the former entryway to the Victory Theatre—by then closed—where during my high school years my "posse" hung out.

We'd stand around there in our letterman sweaters out of the rain and talk the night away under the street light. For a while the theatre building reopened as a small furniture factory. The new owners opened the lobby and sold soda pops out of a dispenser where the glass bottles hung from rails into ice-cold water. You could get the whole Nehi line of Orange, Lime, Grape and Root Beer, I remember that.

They also sold a nice line of candy bars—Baby Ruth, Butterfinger, Oh Henry's—and later started selling plastic model car kits. This made The Corner not just a larger attraction but the center of a movement in model-car assembly that had just about every boy in town participating—enough that we held car shows at the high school so kids should show off their plastic models.

John and Viola Wilkins had the first color television in town. Sometimes on Sunday evenings some of us would leave The Corner to creep up on their house across the street and watch *"Bonanza"* through their living-room window.

One night while we were still on our "own" side of the street, thank God, we watched as a mid-1950's model sedan came swerving down the main street. It first veered toward us, then spun out of control and straight into the front porch of the Wilkins' house.

The drunk driver managed to back out into the street and speed away crazily. The Wilkins' heavyset adult son, Harold, lived with them. I remember him running out of their house, shaking his fist and shouting, *"Park it you son-of-a-bitch!"*

The driver made it about a mile out of town before crashing into the ditch. We were there to witness his apprehension, having left our base camp at The Corner to follow the action.

I put in a fair amount of time over at The Corner. I believe that makes me one of the only people you'll ever meet who, when the time came to leave home, really did *"blow this pop stand."*

CHAPTER 4

My People, Myself

How it all Started, from What I've Been Told

I was the fourth of five children born to William Lee (b. 1916, d. 1979) and Ruth Evaline Watts Wilt (b. 1921, d. 2000). They met when she was a senior at Illinois River High School in southern Oregon. He was a tall, rugged farm boy on leave from the Oregon State College School of Forestry, there to build trails and fight wildfires for the U.S. Forest Service.

The young men of his camp created a swimming hole by blocking a branch of the Illinois River with a bulldozer blade. They invited people in the little town to come swim. On Saturday nights there was also a dance in Cave Junction.

One of the girls who came to swim and dance was 18-year-old Ruthie. One thing led to another and before the story was over they entered into a marriage in March, 1942, that lasted until his death in 1979 and produced the five of us in this order—Dennis Eugene (b. 1942), Cheryl Dawn (b. 1945, d. 2015), Susan Marcielle (b. 1947, d. 2001), Donald William (b. 1948), Darcy Varden (b. 1951, d. 2009), and then a baby girl named Rose who was born but didn't survive. Cheryl's name was pronounced with a hard "chuh." Everyone called her Cherrie (pronounced like the fruit). I've always thought that was a lovely name for a girl but you hardly ever hear it.

Our parents stood out a little bit. The picture of my dad in a black Stetson with the full beard he grew for the Oregon Centennial celebration in 1959 shows him as handsome in a Willie Nelson kind of way; Mom was an attractive and vivacious woman who didn't particularly like socializing with people outside her small social circle but still did a good job of it when she had to.

She thought she had Cherokee blood in her. If that's true, it was reflected in her wavy dark hair and flashing dark eyes. She was also—how to say this—attractive to men. None of them represented any threat whatsoever to their marriage, but it was just obvious that men enjoyed being around her. A couple of them came sniffing around after my dad died, I remember that, but to no avail.

I once said to my dad's best friend from The Illinois Valley days that it was hard for me to imagine my father romancing my mother, given his taciturn nature. He said, *"Oh, your father had very little to do with it."*

Shortly after they were married in 1942, Mom traveled to Wisconsin to meet her new husband's people. While among them she stirred up a ruckus when she persuaded one of my dad's female cousins to drive with her after dark and without benefit of a male escort to a nearby town to look for a phonograph record. They were still talking about the incident when Priscilla and I visited Wisconsin in 1973.

The Band

Both my parents were serious, sensible people but they liked to have a good time. They didn't seem to need alcohol to do it, drinking moderately and only on rare occasion. I wouldn't realize until years later that this was some good luck on the part of our family as alcoholism figured prominently on both sides of the family in their generation and wreaked its usual mayhem in other branches of the clan, but not ours.

Mom and Dad were into country music of the Jim Reeves and Patsy Cline variety. Dad had a big harmonica collection and played the instrument extremely well. He also played guitar and banjo. Mom played guitar and sang.

For a few years in the mid -'50s to '60s they had a country and western band that jammed at our house and played at least once upstairs at the Odd Fellows lodge on an important occasion. I believe it was New Year's Eve, 1960, because I remember a couple of guys in the parking lot still debating the November election between John Kennedy and Richard Nixon.

It was a big dance with a lot of people. I wasn't old enough to go upstairs, but I remember a man fell down the stairs. He lay splayed out there on the concrete floor for a few minutes with a few of his friends gathered around him asking if he could get up.

There wasn't any "landing" at the midpoint of these stairs like you usually see—they were hard wooden steps and it was just a straight shot from the coat room at the top to the street below. It appeared that intoxication was more the problem than the plummet from two stories up. Because of the alcohol involved the guy was hustled away before too long to avoid a situation.

The band had a steel guitar player and a drummer with a set of gourds he played with drum sticks. Boy, that guy could really do the "clop" "clop" "clop" of horses when the band played their cover of *"Cool Water"* by the Sons of the Pioneers.

This is where my fondness for Country and Western music first took root. One of the first things I thought I might want to be was a C&W front man. For a fourteen-year-old I did a particularly soulful cover of Elvis Presley's *"Love Me Tender,"* but never in public.

I was later disabused of this notion when my mother paid the school music teacher extra to give me lessons on the trombone. He concluded I was incapable of learning to read music and said I might be better suited for the kind of work where you wear your pants out at the knees.

You hardly ever hear that from an educator.

How I Became Who I Am

My "family values," as it were, seemed to have been in place for at least a couple of generations before mine. It's where I absorbed many of my personal values about balancing work with fun, continuous learning and pride of workmanship.

Well, that and what I picked up going to Sunday School and Vacation Bible School at the Marcola Christian Church from about 2nd or 3rd grade through 8th supplemented by participation in a series of programs for young people that also took place at the church.

Later it was the Boy Scouts. My pal Eddie and I joined the Scouts together when we were about 13. They started a troop in the old Assemblies of God Church down the street from my house. The troop had a secret signal, an ononotop of a bird call that sounded like a high-pitched *"kreeeee"..."kreeeee."*

Sometimes I'll call Ed up today—or he'll call me. When we answer, the other one says, *"kreeeee"..."kreeeee."* No mistaking who that might be.

One of the youth groups at Marcola Christian was called, appropriately enough, the "Youth Group." it was a wonderful part of our teenage years. Just about every young person in town was involved. We'd get together on Saturday evenings to go swimming, watch movies, listen to records and play games. We also enjoyed watching black-and-white films like "The Three Stooges" and everyone's favorite, "Francis the Talking Mule."

The other church group was the "King's Men," which was just for us boys when we got to be about 13. It met at the high school where we played basketball, wrestled, climbed ropes and stuff like that.

I preferred the Youth Group, but only because a night there included all the soda pop you wanted in real glass bottles pulled from a big tub of ice by the billiards table. I always went for the *Dad's* Root Beer.

I thought the young adults they sent out from Northwest Christian College to run these groups were outstanding. Often they were young married couples who set a good example. They created a wholesome environment for probably about 40 kids on any given Saturday night.

None of these people ever got real "churchy" with us. It was more a case, I think, of trying to provide a positive social experience for young people in the church environment. They didn't push it.

I enjoyed my spiritual activities enough that I maintained a spotless Sunday school attendance record all the way to 8th grade. I was thoroughly indoctrinated into the Christian way of life, which I always felt provided about as good a set of principles to live by as any.

I would say that, taken together, the things we were taught to live by—at home and in the community—hewed closely to the "Roy Rogers Rider Club Rules." I know this because I was—and continue to be—a card-carrying member of the Roy Rogers Riders Club. The rules are:

1. Be neat and clean.
2. Be courteous and polite.
3. Always obey your parents.
4. Protect the weak and help them.
5. Be brave but never take chances.
6. Study hard and learn all you can.
7. Be kind to animals and protect them.
8. Eat all your food and don't waste any.
9. Love God and go to Sunday School regularly.
10. Always respect our flag and our country.

"Be brave but never take chances." I love that one.

Bill and Ruth

My parents weren't perfect but both were capable, gifted individuals in multi-faceted ways. Overall they left indelibly positive impressions on their offspring.

As measured by the standards of the day—which were pretty high—our mom was an excellent mother who admitted to being tested pretty severely by the demands of raising five children without too much prior knowledge or instruction on how you do that. She herself had just one brother, Ned, who was younger.

But what she accomplished in the role went well beyond the meals she managed to rustle up from the wild game locker every day and helping her kids with homework. It was also evident in our school photos how much pride she took in seeing that her children went to school clean and well dressed. Our early Christmas family pictures indicate how much she enjoyed dressing us up and showing us off. Sometimes you'd have thought we were the Kennedys at Hyannis Port we looked so spiffy.

Using a timer, Dad would both take the photograph and be in it, a technique he'd perfected as a young photography student at OSC. Sometimes he was the only one in the photo whose image was blurry.

He would also develop and print his own pictures using an enlarger he made with his own two hands. I didn't know the word "autodidact" then but it's apparent to me now that he was one. He continued to acquire new skills and demonstrate his competency in new areas all the way to the end of his life.

Mom was much more than an ordinary housewife. She was in the band, as I mentioned; could sit a horse as well as anybody; and handle a rifle. Coming from Eastern Washington it would be fair to describe her as a cowgirl, an artistic cowgirl with a face for television and a voice for radio. TV didn't come along soon enough for her to cash in on, but she did perform on a radio station in Lewiston, Idaho.

Unlike Dad, who must have loved his family but was not one to verbalize it, Mom freely dispensed her affection and concern for our well-being. When we were little and needed to see Dr. Guldager for our school shots and whatnot, she had a deft way at the last second of tucking your head under her left armpit to cover your eyes and ears while the doctor did his dirty business—like a mother hen.

Then she'd give you a stick of Spearmint or whatever she had in her purse. Very comforting I'd have to say, and understanding, because injections in those days were not at all so innocuous and painless as they are today. It really was something you did not want to see coming or happening to you.

And when it came to the duties of her time my mother was a true representative of the female side of the "Greatest Generation"—a mainstay in the Marcola Mother's Club, for example, which was at the heart of a lot of good things that got done in our hometown.

When we were youngsters, word got out that doctors had ordered my friend Mike Gambill to bed. He was to be laid up for weeks. The Mothers Club brought him a present a day for the duration, most often a book. It's probably why he turned out to be so smart.

Later, in high school, when I developed an interest in writing and reporting, my mother would let me wake her up to read her anything I'd just written. I think you'd really have to love someone to let them do that, don't you? My wife would wake up for me, but when she found out why, she'd kill me.

As for my father, he was born and reared on an island in the Willamette River—Kiger Island just south of Corvallis, Oregon. That's where he and his three brothers—Stan, Joe and Neal—were born and reared during some of the country's leanest years.

As a result, you never met more resourceful people when it came to fending for themselves. They were truly "at one" with the earth and couldn't get lost in the woods if they were blindfolded. Uncle Neal told me one time that he and Dad could start out at daybreak to go deer hunting, agree on a far-distant meeting point, then walk away in different directions. They'd come face-to-face again just as it was getting dark.

I wasn't left pining for a better relationship with my father but I might have had one if I'd shown any aptitude in these arts myself. When I was helping him with one of his land surveys he'd yell to indicate which direction I was supposed to pull the 300-foot brass measuring chain.

He'd shout *"North!"* and I would just turn around and look back at him with my arms out until he would try again and shout *"Left!"* Then, a moment later, *"Your other left!"*

College Man

Dad was a first-generation professional man who grew up on the Willamette River island farm and put himself through college right in the heart of the Great Depression. He graduated from the Oregon State College School of Forestry—now OSU—and was highly skilled in timber appraisal, forestland management, road building, logging and the rest of it. He was also a registered land surveyor, a skill he used in his regular work and also to supplement his income on weekends.

My older brother sent over a bunch of our dad's old papers a while back. Going through them I came across a letter written by the head engineer of the Ostrander Railway and Timber Company of Molalla, Oregon, in January, 1945. This is where Dad first worked as a forestry engineer after he finally completed college, which took him seven years due to the Depression.

In his letter the head engineer noted that in his last year there Dad served as the resident engineer for the construction of 20 miles of main-line logging road through old-growth forest and mountain terrain. He said it made him responsible for *"plans and details for the removal of timber and the construction of roadway, bridges and overpasses on this road."* He would have been in his late 20s at the time.

I can only imagine how much someone would have to already know—and how much he learned—just on that first job. Maybe you can see why a few years after he died at age 63 a friend said to me, *"You know what I miss about your old man? When Bill Wilt was talking, you knew he knew what he was talking about."*

Most people never met anyone who knew more about the geography, geology, flora and fauna of Oregon than he did. Somebody was always stopping by the house to have him look at a map or discuss one subject or another at length.

I haven't studied it that much myself, but a fellow I used to work with who knew the Bible said there's a passage in there somewhere about the man who knows the flora and the fauna having power over them. Just Googling around a little bit, it may have been Job 12.7-10: *"Ask the animals, and they will teach you; or the birds in the sky, and they will tell you; or speak to the earth, and it will teach you, or let the fish in the sea inform you."*

He said, *"It only figures that what your dad knew about nature made him personally powerful figure in the community too."*

I don't imagine there were too many families in town that had regular visits from Dale Fischer himself, but we did. He was the owner of the sizable Fischer's Lumber Company and obviously relied a lot on my dad when it came to sourcing and operating the mill.

My dad would probably say working for Fischer's was the best job he ever had until he finally went to work for himself years later. Long after the mill was sold and gone and Dale Fischer had left forest products for the steel business, my folks received a nice Christmas gift from him every year.

He had reason to be grateful; one time my father informed him that he had come upon a piece of timberland near Veneta, Oregon, that was going up for auction. It was 250 acres of old-growth Douglas fir trees on flat ground—easy pickin's for a logging company.

But Veneta was about 35-40 miles away from the Marcola mill. Fischer said he didn't want to haul logs that far; they had plenty available where they were.

Just out of general interest and curiosity, Dad decided he'd go to the auction anyway. He showed up on the steps of the Lane County Courthouse the following Saturday morning only to discover there were just two other people there. One was his former OSC classmate and pal Chuck Foster representing the Long Bell Lumber Company. He was authorized to go no higher than $10,000. The other was a farmer who lived across the road from the acreage but didn't have the money to buy it.

The upshot was that my dad ended up buying the parcel on a bid of $10,001 dollars. That was a huge amount of money for him but he knew timber and knew it was worth a lot more than that. He could have become a rich man. That didn't happen, however, because when he told Dale Fischer the following week how the auction had come out, Fischer told him, *"Well if that's all it cost, I guess I'll take it after all."*

Dad conceded and the Fischer Lumber Company took a couple million dollars' worth of timber off the property, or 20 million dollars today.

Dad drove a dark green 1950 Willys Jeep pickup provided by Fischer's and had keys to all the gates on the company's vast Mohawk Valley timberlands. Even as a child it was apparent to me that our dad was <u>somebody</u>. He served on the school board and the water board and was clearly a very capable and responsible community leader who understood complex issues like budgeting and taxation.

My elderly neighbor, Lola Harper, told me once that one of her fondest memories of her Marcola days was of Dad and her husband, Merle, standing in front of their house under the light from their porch rehashing the issues after every meeting. Town leaders.

I'll tell you a story about my dad that says more about him than I can:

I've mentioned that the Wilt boys of the previous generation were born outdoorsmen incapable of getting lost, with no reason to fear hazards like wild animals and sudden storms. They were wired differently than most people today.

Once, when I was about 30, I was telling my dad that I planned to *go "up to Portland"* the next week. The rest of the conversation went like this:

Dad: *"Down."*

Me: *"What do you mean, 'down'?"*

Dad: *"You said you were going <u>up</u> to Portland. You mean you're going <u>down</u> to Portland."*

Me: *"No, Portland is north of here so I'm going <u>up</u> to Portland."*

Dad: *"Which way does the river flow?"*

Well, of course the Willamette River flows north. So you go <u>down</u> to Portland—as in "down river."

That, of course, is more useful and practical information to possess than lines on a piece of paper. It was what you really needed to know if you had to float your crops to market, harness the river's power, or lure food from it. As a boy reared on an island in the middle of a river he would know these things. This is the world he inhabited.

As I've said, our dad made his influence felt mostly by example, but he set a good one—of an industrious man who had a lot of responsibilities and handled them well; who never stretched the truth. He would have made a good judge.

I'm nothing like him.

"Not Going to Kill _Us_"

My dad had passed away before I went to work for Weyerhaeuser at the company's corporate headquarters in 1979. But I met a guy there named Howard Millan who didn't know him but knew of him.

Here's how that worked: it turned out that Howard and my dad had a mutual friend named Bob Gehrman, also deceased. All three were forestry school graduates working in the timber industry, cut from the same bolt of cloth.

When Howard found out about the Wilt-Gehrman connection he insisted that we lay plans to go to Central Oregon together, stay at our cabin, and hike a portion of the Cascade Crest Trail together as a way of reconnecting with Bob and my dad.

I was fine with that but we didn't get around to doing it for several years. Finally, one October day, Howard came over to my desk and said, _"Hey this might be a good time to do that hike."_ I told him I was concerned it might be a little late in the year to attempt something like that. I said, _"You know, people get caught in those early snowfalls and die out there. You read about it all the time."_

I knew Howard was channeling my father when he turned and peered out the big windows of our office as if he were assessing the weather again. Then he turned back to me and said, *"Well, a snowstorm isn't going to kill <u>us</u>...it might piss us off, but it's not gonna <u>kill</u> us!"*

I've always clung to this as an image of the kind of people we are, and I thought future members of this family should know from what kind of rock they have been chipped.

"Never a Moment that Wasn't Happy..."

Obviously, much of what I became I absorbed directly from my parents, although about the only specific rule I remember either one of them verbalizing was, *"Always leave your camp site better than you found it."* Because that can cover a lot of different situations in life I've always figured it was a good one to remember.

Our parents were more inclined to lead by example. Making yourself useful and giving it your best were a couple of the principles they lived by. These also became <u>my</u> guideposts.

My folks seemed to be pretty happy people even though I think they both deserved more from life than they got, given how much work they put into it. I will mention, though, that when Dad died I received a card from Louise Kintzley that said, *"In all the years with your father we never had a moment that wasn't happy—such a record."*

I guess you could say they made the most of things.

Anyway, they set a good example raising us up; managed to do it without any major family trauma or drama along the way; and did a good job of managing a big household on a tight budget.

For reasons I never understood, my father seemed to be highly appreciated but somewhat undervalued almost his entire professional life. And get this: do you know how much vacation he got back then? One stinking week a year. I'd be embarrassed to say how many weeks' vacation we got but it was a heck of a lot more than that and I'm not sure I could have made it with any less. It couldn't have been easy for him.

His measly week off would be spent hunting around Steens Mountain in eastern Oregon. He'd bring home venison, antelope, chukars—anything to restock the larder and start the whole year all over again. It's apparent from many photos of these outings that this is what this man would have been doing if you could get paid for what you'd be doing anyway. And he was good at it.

I remember an insight that arose for me from one of his annual hunts in eastern Oregon. I was probably about 12, hanging in the background and listening to my dad tell someone about some of the adventures they'd had on the hunt that year. He had in his hand a huge chunk of chalk—at least 18 inches long and 5 or 6 inches wide. It looked like the blocks of snow used to build igloos. He was saying how they had gone out to find this chalk mine and saw examples of how Oregon Indians had cut it into blocks thousands of years ago to build protection from the desert winds.

It was the first insight I had into what these trips were all about for a guy like my dad and the kind of friends he had; it wasn't always about the hunting. It was about exploring the world's physical wonders and whatever else they might run into. To me they represented sort of the best of manhood—both self-sufficient and cerebral. Not bad role models at all. Don't ask me why more of it didn't take.

Mom had several suitors after my dad died suddenly of a heart attack at 63 while picking up a survey map at a downtown Eugene blueprint store. But she never found anyone she thought measured up. She lived out the last 21 years of her life alone rather than settle.

I must mention one more thing about my mother, her great *resolve*. She told me several times over the last years of her life that she did not want to ever be confined to a hospital or rest home.

She remained hale and hardy until one day when she was about 80 years old my sister Susie called me in Los Angeles and said Mom had suddenly taken ill. She'd spent the day being examined at McKenzie-Willamette Valley Hospital in Springfield. She said they'd taken a number of tests and would know what's-what in the morning.

Right away I put in a call to my mother. As always, she picked up on the third or fourth ring—she couldn't have been lying down—and answered in her normal buoyant manner. I asked if she wanted me to fly up. She dismissed that as completely unnecessary. She said that she'd merely spent the day meeting *"some of the nicest people"* and expected to go back the next day to find out what they had to say. No worries.

The next call I got was from Susie again. It began with the words, *"She's gone."* She explained that Mom had learned on her return to the hospital that cancer had overtaken her entire body; she would need to be put under some kind of permanent care right away.

What? Gone? From cancer? In 24 hours? I shouldn't have been incredulous. My mother said she never wanted to be hospitalized or put in *"one of those places"*—and she never was. She died that night. Like I said, she had a lot of resolve.

These were my people. I bow down to them.

CHAPTER 5

My People's People

B y the time I came along in 1948, the Wilts were already long-time Oregonians—even as far back as when my dad was born in 1916 for that matter.

My grandfather was Albert Alford Wilt (**b.** 1880, **d.** 1938). Sometimes called Al, I was surprised to learn in researching this autobiography, he came out to Oregon from Wisconsin about 1898 when he was just 18 years old or so and began filling his purse by working in the Northwest woods during the big-log era.

Under terms of the Homestead Act, he laid claim to 160 acres in the Siletz River drainage of the Oregon coast Range, a heavily-wooded parcel of dense timber and foliage with a couple of good springs on it.

We have a black and white picture of "Al," rifle in hand, standing in front of the small cabin he built to "prove up" the place with cedar planks split from trees he felled himself. It even had a nice little covered porch and a couple of chairs. The Wilts always did like to visit.

Look closely and you can see white stakes where he put up wire to keep the deer away from his fruit tree plantings. There's probably been more than one deer or elk hunter in more modern times who stumbled upon a peach or apple tree out there deep in the woods and wondered how in the hell it got there.

One time he awoke to find a cougar on the roof trying to claw his way into the cabin. Without even getting out of bed he reached for his rifle and dispatched the lion with one blast right through the hand-split cedar shake roof.

When Priscilla and I visited Wisconsin as young marrieds in 1974, Albert's brother-in-law proudly showed us the cougar-claw key chain Albert had made and sent to all the men in his family who were still back there. They just admired the hell out of him and were still hungry for news about the Wilt family in the West.

Later, Albert would work in a sawmill in Portland to raise the money to purchase a piece of land in Benton County more suitable for farming. It was on Kiger Island in the Willamette River just south of Corvallis, reachable only by water. He spent years clearing and cultivating the property, then building a two-story frame farm house from a kit ordered out of the Sears-Roebuck catalog.

I see from a letter my father wrote to a bridge historian in the 1970s that Albert also dedicated a portion of his property to create an easement for the east end of the Kiger Island bridge and helped build it himself, which might have been part of the deal as wages were hard to find in the Great Depression. For many years it was the longest covered bridge in Oregon, so long it had to be built on a curve to accommodate the terrain.

I don't suppose any kid in America ever had a more picturesque view of his grandparents' farm than we did, rumbling across the wooden planks of the covered bridge to emerge from its tunnel-like effects into broad, river-bottom farmland. The Wilt place was first on the left. You could see the white farm house on a little knoll overlooking the great Willamette River, flanked by a grove of oak trees. Close by, a red, two-story barn with a hay-loading ramp made from heavy timbers to reach the second story.

The house had a number of fine features, including a handsome fireplace made entirely of river rock brought up from the banks of the Willamette, leaded windows, leaded book cases, a calfskin rug and a dumb waiter for bringing firewood up from the basement to the wood stove in the kitchen. Albert had a magnificent view of the river from the roll-top desk he'd had built in just off the living room.

For a farm boy from Wisconsin, Albert had a good eye for architecture and furnishings. No doubt my interest in design and houses came straight down through the generations from him to me. We both seemed to possess the same vision -- to build an exceptional house.

Albert and Alma didn't get hitched until 1915 when he was 34 and she was 30—17 years after Albert set out for Oregon to make a life for them. In the meantime, back in Wisconsin, my future grandmother wasn't exactly sitting around fanning herself, either.

Alma Wanamaker Wilt (b. 1884, d. 1973) had begun her career as a school teacher after graduating from Wisconsin State Normal School. (That would be the equivalent of a university teaching degree today.)

She started teaching in her hometown of Steuben, Wisconsin, but before too long had headed to Hope, North Dakota. There she taught in a one-room schoolhouse just eight years after North Dakota was carved out of the Minnesota Territory to become its own state. I've seen the

Dakotas in the modern era and can't imagine how remote and desolate they must have been in Alma's time.

Only eight years later she would give birth to my dad on an island in the Willamette River in Oregon. Alma always did have a lot of spunk. Once, when I was about 10 and she was in her early 80s, we were trying to follow a path down a steep gravel incline at the back of her property. I came down all right, but when I turned around I saw Grandma suddenly tip backwards, bounce onto her butt, then slide down the hill, dark blue and white polka dot dress, granny glasses and long gray hair flying out to the sides.

When she landed in a cloud of dust at the bottom, I gasped, "Grandma, are you all right?" She piped cheerfully, "Just resting!"

Alma did come out to see Albert with his sister at least once during their extraordinary and long courtship, and there may have been other visits, either in Oregon or Wisconsin as well. Albert's family would send him blocks of pure maple syrup from Wisconsin in the winter to help him stay in touch with the "Old Country." I think I would have said, "Forget the syrup; send Alma!"

Probably the most direct effect that our Grandmother Wilt had on the children in our family was to instill in them a love of reading. Every birthday and Christmas brought a book for every grandchild. Stories by Jack London -- "Call of the Wild" and "White Fang" -- anchored my personal collection. Tucked into each one like a bookmark, every time, would be a crisp one dollar bill drawn from her egg money, most likely.

Given how much pleasure reading has given to every single member of our current clan, I have to say it may have been the greatest gift that came down to us from that generation. The appreciation for education was paramount with her, and she extended it to the rest of the family.

Priscilla recently uncovered a cache of letters that provided the first insights I ever had into my father's family home on Kiger Island when he was a boy. They were written by Albert and the boys to Alma in 1933-34 when she left Kiger Island and returned to Wisconsin for a period of almost a full year. (Priscilla's genealogy research on the Wilts shows that Alma's father died in 1933 and she apparently returned home to help her mother relocate from the family farm into town).

The letters reveal a lively but well-organized household and an impressive farming operation with a half-dozen crops under cultivation at one time ("The field and sweet corn both are looking fine!"), along with a herd of dairy cows, pigs and turkeys. No wonder, then, that when he died young at age 58 Albert's obituary in the *Corvallis-Gazette Times* described him as a "prominent Kiger Island farmer."

It was also a family in which, I was surprised to learn, the boys affectionately called their father Daddy. One of them writes in a letter to Alma, "There is one thing that is bothering Daddy pretty bad and that is he could not go hunting. We tried to get him to go but he was afraid we could not get along without him.")

You can also see from the letters that it was a family in which people took pride in one another's accomplishments. (There's an entry from Albert that mentions my father, age 17, making a speech in someone's home about the Future Farmers of America. Albert wrote, "Neal and Junior went up to hear it and said it was just fine!"

It was also a household in which Bill was Bill (never Billy), Stan was Stanley (not Stan); Neal was Neal and Joe was Junior.

In the letters to their mother in Wisconsin, one of the boys wrote, "We are getting along fine now and getting used to baching. Dad is our chief cook and Neal is supposed to wash the dishes and sweep but he doesn't always do it."

The letters also reveal the emerging characters of the Wilt boys of Kiger Island, and their mother's as well. Stanley, the entrepreneur, who already had his own truck-driving business in high school, wrote to Alma requesting permission to drop out of school to get his business going. She said no way.

You could also read between the lines to see that Stanley, then 15, already had his mind on other things besides school work. One well-written letter he sent to my grandmother is single-spaced and printed on both sides of a single sheet of paper; it clearly had to have taken him at least 40 minutes to compose. It ends with the words, "Well, I see the period is about to end so I'm going to have to close."

There are no letters from my dad, Bill, who was the oldest. But the responsible and over-achieving individual he was to become is revealed in a letter from one of his younger brothers who wrote to their mother, "We have gone two weeks in our second semester of school now and I got through in all my subjects and I think Stanley did too." Then he added, "I guess you don't have to worry about Bill failing!"

A letter from the youngest of the boys, Neal, 11, mentions that "I haven't made one pie since you've been gone," which tells me that he must have known how to make one. At age 11.

Finally, the letters show a family in which everyone worked, both on and off the farm. In a passage I somehow found kind of heart-rending, Joe, 14, wrote to his mother, "This morning Grant Elgen came over and gave me a job driving his team grading the new road. I was supposed to get 20 cents per hour starting this morning, but the road boss would not let me work because I was under 18 years of age. So that let me out on that job."

So this was life for the Wilts on Kiger Island in what they called the "G.D.G.D."—The goddamned Great Depression. I only just learned about this stuff myself.

As for me and my siblings a generation later, we may have been growing up in a backwater logging town where the horizons for most of us did not extend very far, but there was never any question that my brother and I would go to college. (I'm sorry to say that the same expectation had not quite yet taken hold for girls. Neither one of my sisters did too much in the way of education after high school, smart and capable as they both were. (Cheryl, after all, was her class's salutatorian.) But Grandma tried.

The only conversation I ever had with either one of my parents about higher education was at the dinner table one night when I was about 17. I blurted out something about maybe not going to college, possibly joining the military instead. My dad only uttered one sentence by way of response and he delivered it with a kind of snort that suggested he shouldn't even have to be bothered to say it: "Of course you're going to college!"

His mother imbedded in him the importance of a good education and he imbedded it in us. It's not an unimpressive record at all that we have college graduates in every generation of the family going back five generations now. And if I asked him, my brother Dennis would no doubt say that his decision to go back to OSU and complete his engineering degree at age 74 a couple of years ago probably had something to do with our drive to never stop bettering ourselves.

Thank you, Alma Wanamaker Wilt.

My mother's family was always a little harder to pin down. Her father, Alvin Watts, seemed to be a bit of a ne'er-do-well—I suspect alcoholism was the issue although we never talked about it. He worked in construction and left the family sometime when Mom was in her teens, I believe.

By then she said she'd attended more than 20 different schools because they moved so much. Even discounting for decades of exaggeration that would have been a lot of schools. (I wouldn't have said that if I didn't think my mom would think it was funny).

Alvin was displaced from my immediate family history when my grandmother, Ethel, remarried and did much better in the bargain, making a man named Gordon Poole, for all intents and purposes, my other grandfather.

Ethel Poole (b. 1901, d. 1996) grew up during the Depression in the cow town of Spangle way out in Eastern Washington so you know she probably had some mettle.

And she must have been the spangliest girl to ever come from Spangle. Clear up into her 80s and 90s people would comment on how attractive she was. If I had to type her, I'd put her in a league with that lady who played Beaver's mother on "Leave it to Beaver." Silver hair nicely cut, pearl necklace. Dressed better than most people we knew, and looked great in those early 50's styles.

Grandma and Grandpa Poole lived in a pretty, two-story Queen Anne-style house in an area of Portland that later went to seed but is now becoming gentrified. An odd memory from staying in that house, which must have had about six bedrooms: in the morning, Grandpa Gordon would come around and collect any urine or poo we'd found it necessary to rid ourselves of in the middle of the night, which we did by going into the chamber pot left in each room. The only bathroom was on the ground floor.

Although Gordon's occupation was a humble one—bus driver for the Rose City Transit Company—they were the picture of sophistication as far as I was concerned. Ethel worked on the floor at Meir and Frank's Department Store in downtown Portland where she was paid in cash at the end of every week, handed over to her in an envelope by Mr. Frank himself.

It was probably at Meir & Frank that she acquired her exceptional sense of style, which was always evident in the way she dressed, and the way her husband looked as well, I imagine.

Funny story about Gordon: Although he died before I was 20, I'd had time to settle on him as the kind of man I'd like to be. Sort of a Spencer Tracy type, he always looked and smelled good. It was still a time when men wore hats in the fedora style and nobody ever looked better in one. I noticed how immaculately groomed he always was with his silver hair neatly parted on the side and a thin, matching mustache.

I remember once they arrived at our place after a long drive up from Mexico. I was about 13. I came around the house and ran into Grandpa Poole trying to sneak into the house unnoticed so he'd have time to shave before my mother saw him. That kind of attention to hygienic detail impressed me.

I also liked the way he treated his wife, which was with great consideration; the kind of conversations he had with his son-in-law, my dad (which I would describe as erudite); and the way he treated me frankly, which was way better than the way everyone else did.

And I liked the way Grandpa Gordon treated my mother, who utterly adored him -- and how he related to kids. He was always giving us a dime and saying, "Go get yourself a malted," even though they didn't make malteds anymore. We didn't even know what a malted was, and if we had, I'm pretty sure they would have cost more than 10 cents. In any event, he was just an all-around perfect gentleman.

And finally, I admired his intelligence. Once, he was flown to New York City to compete on a national radio quiz show sponsored by Camel Cigarettes—the kind he smoked—and won. He collected $500 in 1952, close to five grand today. Not too bad for a bus driver, I always thought.

For many years we had a record of the broadcast they sent home with him. I remember two things from it: one was that he won by correctly identifying George Eastman as the founder of the fledgling Kodak Film Company, and second, that when he advanced to the championship round, a chorus of young background singers sang a jingle whose enthusiastic and happy lyrics ended with, "Take your place in the LeMac Box!" ("LeMac" being Camel spelled backward.)

I was telling a co-worker once how I had admired and tried to emulate my Grandpa Gordon. Right after I'd mentioned all his outstanding qualities she said, "Let me guess: you didn't turn out anything like him."

I guess in truth I didn't turn out as much like him as I probably should have, but he continues to be a great inspiration to me.

In any event, these were my grandparents as I knew them with the exception of Alvin, who apparently vamoosed, and Albert, who died at 63 in 1938 of a kidney condition I'm told could have been treated not too many years later.

Whatever got him, my dad also told me that on the day before Albert died he got out of bed for the first time in several days and took his boys around the farm. He pointed out everything that needed to be done and sketched out a basic strategy for running the farm without him, which they did successfully for a long time.

I wish we knew more about both sets of grandparents, their struggles and triumphs. I'll bet they had stories to tell. And being Wilts, they probably told them well. As it is, I can't really put myself in Albert's shoes as I know so little about who he was. Only that years after he died, no one called him Al; it was always Albert. The great god Albert.

One small insight I was able to gather came from my Uncle Joe after my dad had passed away. I asked him what my grandfather was like. He said, "Oh he was a hell of a guy. Everybody liked him. Had a reputation for always being willing to lay his tools down to go have a good time."

He sounds like someone who may have been on to the whole work-life balance thing a long time before anyone was talking about it. Because, as you see from the above account, we are descended from people who were determined and resourceful; who demonstrated a strong sense of responsibility; and who set big goals in their lives and achieved them.

And who also knew how to have a good time.

These were my people's people.

This picture of my sisters, Susie (left), about 10, and Cherry, 12, tickling our dad managed to tickle me many years later. It made me happy to see him having fun with his girls. He rarely had time for this sort of thing because he worked almost every day of the week and playing with your kids was just not what men did in those days.

CHAPTER 6

I Go to School and Discover the Cookie Line

I entered first grade knowing how to spell only one word—"Indiana"-- which was printed on an apple box being used for storage that I could see from where I slept on the upstairs landing of the staircase. They'd run out of bedrooms by the time I came along except for the downstairs guest room, held in reserve for the infrequent visitor.

My pal Dennis Wooley had heard they reject you if you can't spell your name on the first day, so we got together at his house the day before to cram. But the spelling of names either never came up on Day One or there was no banishment involved for people who didn't know how.

Being outside the big family and on a new playing field brought out a much bolder me. By the time the annual Christmas play came around I was Mrs. Pierson's choice to be the announcer. She liked the way I projected.

I continued to pick up honors in the category of *Best Emcee in a School Program* all the way up to 8th grade or so when I almost fell down laughing onstage one night. It happened when a somewhat large and bumptious boy entered from up-stage so enthusiastically and delivered his line at a volume so much higher than he had in a month of rehearsals that it almost stopped the show. (I guess that's what they mean when they say you've been "upstaged.").

I couldn't stop laughing. You might have thought it would bring an end to my career, but I didn't let it stop me.

As soon as the show was over I'd beat it over to the line where they dispensed the post-performance cookies and punch. I'd discovered this was the best place to collect compliments on my "work" and I grew to gauge my performance by how things went in the cookie line.

Years later I'd relive the thrill of a good performance on the Marcola Grade School stage whenever a public speaking engagement or big work project turned out well. I'd call home and when someone in the family asked how things had gone, I'd say *Big cookie line...BIG cookie line.*

Anyway, between the budding career in show business and my established role as town crier I'd pretty much settled on a career track by the time I was in third grade; part reporter, part master of ceremonies.

Our class was among the first of the post-war baby boom, born neatly at the midpoint between 1942 and 1964, and was the largest in the town's history. There were two Donalds in the class—Donald Goldie and me. There was no confusion because I went by Donny or Donny Bill; he got Donald. (Who do you think became taller and starred in football?)

But I've let that go. I always know it's someone from my old hometown calling when I answer the phone and they say, "I was trying to get hold of Donnie Wilt."

One little girl arrived for school the first day with no shoes. She was my first desk-mate but slept through most of the first day before she was removed so her health could be addressed and I got Renee Savage instead. She was the real bossy one with Coke-bottle glasses who told the janitor off one day because water from the sprinkler had hit her on the way to school. She told him, *"You sprunked me!"*

Mr. Mauney's Spanking Machine

We were told in first grade, by the second-graders, that Mr. Mauney kept a spanking machine in his office. The message came through loud and clear: *"Whatever bad behavior you might be capable of, whatever childish impulse you might be feeling, curb it! You do not want to get sent to Mr. Mauney's office."*

No one ever told me exactly what the spanking machine looked like, but I had a picture in my 6-year-old mind of a conical device narrow at the bottom, wide at the top, and large enough to accommodate a medium-sized primary pupil.

It would have been mounted on one of those solid oak tables like they use in the electrocution rooms at state prisons, but on wheels, and kept behind the door to his office. I figured they moved it out from behind the door to administer the punishment because I'd already passed by that office a couple of times. I didn't get a real good look, but I didn't see where else they could be keeping it.

To visualize what it might have looked like, imagine the old-fashioned tabletop phonograph in the famous RCA Victor logo where the little dog is peering down into the phonograph. But bigger. The kid would have been placed into the device at the bell end, feet-first and face down with only his head and shoulders showing. At the time I imagined the buttocks would be exposed, although nothing along the lines of child abuse even entered my mind. It was just how you delivered a spanking in those days: Your dad would say, *"Turn around and drop those pants, mister!"*

Anyways, the paddle went up and down through a slit and was driven by a hand-crank that could be operated from either side. I always figured it had two cranks so the spanking could be administered by the principal himself or by the school secretary, Hazel White. She seemed nice but I'm sure she would have done whatever Mr. Mauney told her to do.

I figured he had her do it sometimes so he could lecture you at the same time: *"Did your parents (Whap!) not teach you (Whap!) to keep your hands (Whap!) off of other people's belongings (Whap!)?"*

I just thank God I never had to see the spanking machine for myself. Once informed of its existence I pretty much hewed the line for the remainder of my primary years. (Still hewing, too, I might add.)

Ina

Our first teacher was the ancient Ina Pierson. She was excellent and had me eating out of her hand by recess on the first day.

We'd been given reason to be a little apprehensive just before class started. While we were queuing up in the covered breezeway to go into our brand-new classroom for the first time, one little boy got only as far as the last support column before he wrapped himself around it and refused to go any farther.

Maybe he'd gotten wind of the holocaust or something, I don't know, but he was <u>not</u> going through those doors! Anyway, they took him on back home and the rest of us started school.

Phil Knight, the great founder and head of Nike, said in his autobiography, "*The cowards never start out. The weak die along the way. That leaves us.*"

There you have it.

Mrs. Pierson was about 60 years old, tall, and on the thin side. She wore these shoes with platform heels that laced way up and made her look like she was as tall as a basketball player. Wore her gray hair in a bun. She could have passed for Eleanor Roosevelt, and not just in appearance. All you have to do is look at her face in our first class picture to know what a sweet, kind, intelligent person she was.

Sweet, but firm.

Blanche

The teachers at Marcola Elementary were outstanding across the board—even the one everyone had learned to fear, Blanche Grafe in grade six.

Mrs. Grafe's the one who clobbered a boy in our class right in the nose with one of those big felt chalk board erasers that are only soft on one side. The throw originated from behind her desk at the front of the class but she put it right over the plate. The blow was severe enough to bloody the boy's nose but not so serious as to require medical intervention.

I got the impression that this wasn't the first time she'd done it, and it was easy to imagine her staying after class sometimes to practice. I think chewing gum had been the boy's offense. Mrs. Grafe just would not tolerate it. That and littering. She told us one time that the Kleenex tissue should be named the state flower of Oregon because you saw it everywhere.

Mrs. Grafe had two sayings that have stuck with me all these years. The first was, *"We all have an obligation to others to always look our best."* The other she reserved for when a boy needed to be sent on an errand and other boys would ask to go with him.

"No," she would say, *"because one boy is a boy; two boys is half a boy; and three boys is no boy at all."*

I don't know if it was her teaching ability or the fear factor, but people always said, *"When Mrs. Grafe teaches you something, you stay taught."* To that point, you'd be surprised at how much of what she taught us in her unit on Mexican language and customs I was able to put to use when I oversaw an important project in Monterrey, Mexico, many years later. I had stayed taught.

Myrtle

A quick mention of two more of these great teachers: One was Myrtle Sagen. She taught 4th grade and everybody adored her.

She once told my mother at a parent-teacher conference, *"If I had a nickel for every time Donnie came up to my desk to tell me a joke, I wouldn't have to teach anymore."*

I saw Mrs. Sagen at my brother's memorial service in 2009. She was 92 at the time. I hadn't seen her in more than 50 years but she grasped my hand in hers and said, *"Donnie, tell me a joke!"*

And I did—the one about the guy who goes to his doctor and the doc tells him, *"I'm afraid I don't have good news for you at all; we got your lab results back and you not only have cancer, you also have Alzheimer's."*

For a moment the guy is totally inconsolable, but then he perks up a little and says, *"Well at least I don't have cancer."*

It was great to hear her laugh again.

Neva

The other teacher I want to mention is Neva Workman—
Miss Workman. She was a spinster, about 55.

There were whispers that Miss Workman had been
engaged to be married but that her fiancé had died in
the war and she never loved again. That is entirely possible. After all, it had only been nine years since the end
of WWII. She lived with her aged and debilitated mother
in a rustic cabin part way up the side of a steep mountain
called Windy Peak.

I remember she told us once how the phone company
had come out to their place with a new experimental device
that allowed her blind old mother to use the dial telephone
in the event of an emergency. I don't know if they called
it the "key pad" then but that's basically what it was. We
thought it was pretty mind-blowing.

Miss Workman was a fairly substantial woman with
a lantern jaw who must have played some part in the war
herself—drill instructor maybe—because she carried herself much in the manner of a drill sergeant who had a lot to
accomplish and didn't want to see a lot of horsing around
while you were doing it.

She wore a large man's watch on her left wrist that further
increased her formidability and was the first hard grader
any of us had encountered. My friend Mike, who had never
gotten anything lower than an "E" (for Excellent), was dev-
astated to see on his first report card from Miss Workman
that he'd gotten an "E" in only one subject and straight "S"s
(Satisfactory) in everything else. She told him that if he

expected to get "E"s in her class, he would have to be the *"cream of the crop."*

When she was about 60 Miss Workman moved out to the high desert of Eastern Oregon to live with her sister in Fort Rock. Her sister had been married to none other than Reuben Long, "The Sage of Fort Rock," famous author and rancher.

Sometime in the early 80s Priscilla and I drove out to Fort Rock while we were on vacation to see if we could find Miss Workman and her sister. We asked at the post office where they told us "the gals" had moved into La Pine a few winters back because they didn't feel like they could hack it out there on the desert anymore. They would have been in their 80s by then.

We found their place in La Pine and Miss Workman and I had a nice chat by the fence. She remembered and asked questions by name about what had become of each of the five Wilt kids. I'm so glad I got to tell her what a great job she'd done with everyone in our family, because she did.

It made me sorry all over again that I was the one who surreptitiously moved her desk chair out from under her one time when she was lecturing us in 8th grade and sent her crashing to the floor before the class. I was astonished to learn that my lifelong friend, Kathie, actually recorded the incident in her notebook at the time. She wrote: *"Oh no! Now she's blaming it on to* <u>Donnie</u>*!"* I didn't mention this incident to Miss Workman during our fence-side chat.

Mrs. Pierson and most of the others on that staff also seemed to actually like us and want us to succeed. They brought out the best in us and I think pretty much everybody left grade school well-grounded in the basics.

The same friend who got his first "S" from Miss Workman went on to own his own highly successful forest products business. He told me that he discovered when he got to college and later in life that he never met anyone who was better schooled than himself in the Three Rs.

I'll let you in on a little secret: Reading and writing aren't the most important skills a person can possess. If they were I would have gone further in life. Perhaps you know that when Mrs. Pierson found it necessary to divide our large class into groups, I was assigned to the Bluebird Circle. That was, you know, the top one.

And don't think that just because you were in that circle you got to stay there. My lifelong pal Eddie said that he too was assigned to the Bluebirds, then sent down to the minor leagues. When his reading improved, they offered to move him back to the Bluebird Circle. He told them to go pound sand and stayed where he was. Eddie was always a very independent person.

In any event, when it came to communications work, what I picked up there turned out to be pretty useful; even advantageous. These teachers might also be one of the many reasons I was so taken with my future wife when I first met her at the University of Oregon. Priscilla herself was headed for a brilliant career as a teacher. You might say I'd seen the best and knew one when I saw one.

There wasn't so much mobility in my youth, so when the first-grade class of 1954 graduated high school 12 years later we were still pretty much intact. With the exception of a small handful of exchangees, the class was made up of the same 26 people we'd started with. Again, largest in the school's history.

Our class motto was *"This Far and Farther."* You'd be surprised how long something like that can stay with a person and even continue to inspire.

CHAPTER 7

The Gang(s) I Ran With

I first met my pal Edwin "Eddie" Head in first grade. Turned out he lived only two or three muddy streets over from us. He was painfully shy and didn't really like to play with other kids that much. Meanwhile, I wasn't allowed to go any farther than the corner in one direction and never across the street.

Consequently we didn't meet until first grade and didn't really get to know each other until we got into a playground scrap in 4th grade that drew blood. It had something to do with the game of marbles, which everyone was into then. (He turned out to be quite a bit scrappier than I'd estimated.)

I now know that the experience was traumatic for both of us and we bonded over it to become lifetime friends. He still has his marbles—really. (Some people say I lost mine a long time ago.)

I ran with a good bunch of kids and we mostly behaved ourselves. In high school we were pretty shocked when we heard it was one of our pals who had swiped the new school bus and took it for a joyride a night or two earlier. He somehow got away with it and went on to become a U.S.

Navy Seal. The service likes people who know how to get out of tight spots and he had practice.

Dual Citizenship

Eddie continued to be my main wingman clear up through high school. He was in one of the two different groups I hung out with. Later, when he was in Vietnam, I borrowed a pair of his shoes to get married in. When I went to pick them up his mother broke down because seeing me made her realize how much she longed to see her "real" son. She clutched me so hard I think Eddie must have felt it himself clear over there. Ed's dad, Sherm, had to gently pry her away, sobbing.

Mike Barr, his brother John, their neighbor Versal Meacham and I made up one of my two gangs. They were all outstanding athletes, especially Mike. He was co-captain and quarterback of the first successful football team we'd had in years. I was a freshman when he was selected to play in the East-West Shrine Game his senior year—the first athlete from our town to ever be chosen.

This "gang" of mine almost died together coming home from that game when Versal fell asleep at the wheel going 80 miles an hour. We spun around on Highway 80 somewhere west of Pendleton so many times I couldn't count before the car came to a stop. I think it was five.

I'd be surprised if anyone was wearing a seatbelt as they were just coming into common use. Luckily this was around two o'clock in the morning and there were no other cars out there to run into. Nonetheless, Versal's dad's brand-new 1964 Pontiac Grand Prix had to be totaled because it bent the frame.

I think that group revolved around a certain amount of hero worship on my part, and I suppose it was a little unusual that I was hanging with the top jocks when I wasn't one myself.

What I Brought to the Party

I was always the first to get the latest vinyl records by Bill Cosby, The Smothers Brothers, Richard Pryor and other comics of that era and I remember playing them for the gang. I would essentially assume the role of emcee in introducing these relatively fresh acts at the time so I guess you could say that was what I "brought to the party"—the party albums.

Mike Barr also had a 1941 war-surplus Jeep that we roamed around the hills in. I don't know how we survived that activity, which even then struck me as terribly dangerous. It involved trying to climb these very steep and muddy hillsides. Half the time we wouldn't make it to the top before the Jeep became starved for gas and quit running. At that point your only hope was to get down *backwards*. Plus, the brakes on those things were so terrible they barely slowed the vehicle. Just coming back down was enough of a thrill to last me a lifetime.

On one occasion I insisted on getting out because I was just sure the Jeep was going to tip over backward. Whatever public obloquy I incurred at the time was justified a few years later when a BLM crew bus carrying a half dozen men slipped off one of these muddy roads and rolled clear to the bottom of a 300-foot hillside. It killed several of them. The same thing could easily have happened to us. That old saying that God looks out for drunks and fools should be amended to include teenagers.

Comedians in Cars Getting Pepsi

As I said, Eddie was part of the other group I belonged to. We'll call it the Car Club. Its central organizing principles involved the beautification and display of our automobiles, both at home (in Marcola) and abroad (in Eugene) where we'd join what seemed like every other teenage boy in Lane County on Saturday nights dragging Willamette Street in an attempt to pick up city girls.

Every evening I can remember ended up with us at *Bob's 19-Cent Hamburgers* with no city girls to show for the expedition. Mostly we spent our time driving around and around our own town on weekend nights drinking Pepsi, telling jokes and trying to scare up whatever action there was to be scared up in a place like that. Gas cost around 25 cents a gallon at the time so you can see why driving would have been a popular pastime. Everybody still complained about the price.

There's a picture of this "gang" in the 1966 MHS yearbook. We're all assembled around Ed's classic '57 Chevy Bel Air. Funny thing is, there really was no car club in our high school. However...I happened to be editor of the yearbook. When the professional photographer came to take the various pictures of our school activities we commandeered him to take one of our gang, which then ended up in the yearbook labeled "Car Club." That's the kind of stunt we were famous for.

One of the Great Gifts to Our Generation— Cheap Mobility

Cars were unbelievably cheap when I was learning to drive. Lots of adults were buying new cars in the booming post-war economy. They'd sell their 1940's and 50's models for a song. Once, my friend Mike Gambill and I bought a dark blue 1946 Plymouth Windsor two-door coupe for $35 and ended up abandoning it in the woods above Marcola after we got it high-centered on a log. It was late Sunday after-noon and Mike had a big school paper due the next day so we just walked out and never went back.

By the time we were 16, almost every boy in school had his own car. Eddie got his before he was even old enough to drive. These weren't kids getting birthday gifts from rich parents, either. We bought our first rides with money earned in our part-time jobs, also a common thing for a boy to have.

The first one I bought was a 1955 Plymouth Savoy for $95 from my boss at the greenhouses, Bob Prickett, who told me he would not be afraid to get in that car and drive it to California that very minute.

That's something people used to say when they were sell-ing a used car. Never Idaho or Florida, always California, like it was the farthest they could imagine anyone driving. Before too long I sold the Plymouth to my friend Mike. He had to pay me $100 because I'd added slap-on whitewalls. I then picked up a beige, 1951 four-door Pontiac with a "straight eight" engine that we named "Big Otis," also for $100.

For several of our early car-driving years there were about a half-dozen abandoned cars just sitting around town on quasi-public property like the railroad right-of-way. We went to work picking parts off them to meet our own needs.

There was a 1952 Plymouth and a 1950 Chevrolet on an abandoned lot practically in Eddie's front yard. These turned out to be perfect "parts cars." We yanked all kinds of things off them—starters and brake cylinders, U-joints, water pumps—that kind of thing.

Eddie's car was a 1952 Chevy. It needed a lot of work and he started right in picking parts. Before he was done he'd carted home the bumpers, the door handles, the cigarette lighter and the seats out of the Chevy. We even discovered that the keys to his car actually fit the abandoned Chevy and we were able to get into the trunk. Oh look, a tire iron. Better get that.

The Greatest Generation Taught us how to fix our Cars

Diagnosing the problem, procuring the right parts, then reinstalling them in our own cars required a lot of guidance from Eddie's dad, Sherm. He'd had important transportation responsibilities in the war where he was a driver for a high ranking Army officer in London.

Sherm knew his way around cars and trucks and always had a pretty fancy one himself. One of my favorite pictures is the one of Eddie and me washing his dad's yellow-on-black 1958 Dodge Coronet when we were about 14. That was the one with fins so big you could mistake 'em for the dorsals on a Great White.

Better yet, Sherm not only knew how to fix cars but he also had the tools to do the job. *"You're gonna need a steering-wheel puller to get that off there,"* he'd say. *"There's one hanging on the wall right inside the door to the shop."*

Anybody who buys a car from me is lucky because I take good care of 'em, like Sherm showed us.

After I had my own family, we owned a 1983 Toyota Land Cruiser. It was a wonderful family car and we had a lot of fun in it, but it was also prone to overheating. No problem. Stand back. Use the lemonade jug to haul some water up from the creek. Pour water over the radiator cap until it's cool to the touch. Stand back some more. Slowly open the cap but only to the first click, otherwise it'll blow off there and scald you. Let it vent, then open it up and add water.

Believe it or not, if you lose the oil in your car you can actually put water in the crankcase just long enough to get yourself out of the jam. These are the kinds of things we learned at the knee of the great Sherman Head. He's the kind of guy they're talking about when they say "Greatest Generation."

I was aware even then that this wasn't just keeping our old cars going. It was also building our self-confidence and resourcefulness.

One time I'd purchased a new U-joint for Big Otis because mine was popping. I planned to go over to Sherm's so he could show me again how you replace one. It turned out to be the rare occasion when he wasn't home. That wasn't good. I waited around for a while, even got the car up on the ramps and ready for when he came back.

Time passed, still no Sherm. What was I supposed to do? I couldn't very well do it myself, could I?

Could I?

I decided to try. I knew what tools to use and how you take the drive shaft out to get at the assembly and so on. Even I was a little surprised when I actually did it, but I credit that moment with setting me on a path to greater self-reliance.

Eddie eventually graduated to his best-in-class red '57 Chevy Bel-Air. This was the car he used to woo his sweetheart, Darlene. And it worked. They've been married almost as long as we have.

We did do things like drag race a little bit and I think there may have been some minor vandalism—like the night we ran a garbage can up the flag pole at the high school in an attempt to flip it over the pole, which we should be glad we did not manage to do. I think that might have been viewed as nothing to laugh at.

What we <u>did</u> manage to do was get the can stuck way up there. That probably caused the Janitor-We-Didn't-Like a lot of headaches. That alone created a little more blowback than I was comfortable with. But for the most part I ran with a good bunch of kids. No one in our group even smoked except for the one from Arkansas who had started doing it on a chicken farm there when he was 10. He told me when he was 12 that he was hooked. His parents had promised him $50 if he could quit for 30 days but he'd never been able to do it. He's still alive at 73 if you can believe that.

St. Spud

About my senior year of high school I purchased a light blue 1951 Willys Jeep Overland station wagon, again for $100. It was in such poor condition that we hid it at Eddie's house so my folks wouldn't know we were driving around in it.

It had two-wheel drive and a four-cylinder engine that ran pretty good, but no brakes to speak of. The design was classic, but top-heavy.

The abandoned mill town of Wendling was located about four miles northeast of Marcola. It had been a thriving company town with a population of close to a thousand residents until the Booth-Kelly mill closed. The site still had a lovely park open to the public with a swimming hole, diving boards and changing rooms—one for girls on the north side of Mill Creek and another for boys on the south.

It also had a baseball diamond. Late one night Eddie and Mike and I took the Willys up there and began running the bases with it. Home-to-first, first-to-second—you get the idea. We were rounding second base for the second time when we—well, I—took it too fast and the Jeep rolled. We found ourselves upside-down with the roof torn half off.

For a few moments Mike and I were panicked to discover we were trapped. My foot was caught under the dash board. I had to wrest it free of the shoe to get out. Spilled oil was pouring over the engine, sending up a plume of acrid black smoke.

We got out all right and later marveled at how Eddie had somehow managed to leap from the vehicle and run quite a distance away where he didn't help the situation very much by yelling over and over, *"She's gonna blow!" "She's gonna blow!"*

Lucky for us, it didn't.

We walked back down Wendling Road—me with just the one shoe—until we appeared shame-faced at the door of the Janitor-We-<u>Did</u>-Like—Spud McDonald. We had to wake him up.

There was a funny story right at the end of this episode. I'll let Ed tell it in this excerpt from his own memoir:

> "After we towed the Jeep to my house, our neighbor Mr. McNeu came over and asked what happened. Donny told him he had hit a low tree limb and Mr. McNeu said, *'That happened to me one time too.'*"

Anyway, the night we rolled the Jeep good old Spud got dressed and drove us back up to the ballfield. He had known the three of us all our lives. He rescued us by using his 1949 Ford pickup to pull the Jeep back up on onto its wheels and then down to his place for the night.

Spud was just about as close to a saint as most of us will ever meet; he proved it that night. While the four of us rode back into town in the tiny cab of the old Ford, we were just crossing the covered bridge into Marcola when he turned to us and said, *"I don't see why anyone else has to know about this."*

And they never did. None of our parents ever found out what happened to that Jeep or how close we came to getting injured, killed or arrested.

We should keep a bobble-head of him on the dashboard of our cars.

St. Spud of Wendling.

The Run of the Place

We were probably held in check a little by an ever-present pair of Lane County reserve sheriff's deputies who patrolled the roads around Marcola on the weekends. They were these broad-shouldered twin brothers in Kevlar vests named Ronnie and Donnie Hanson—ranchers by day, reserve deputies by night.

The Hansons wore cowboy hats and cruised around in some kind of big Ford sedan not too much more dressed out than Andy's on the popular *Mayberry RFD* television series of the same era. They were adorable and we had a lot of fun messing with them.

Usually our encounters revolved around some dumb thing we were doing at the time, like the time they came upon us towing a car in the dark with no lights. Another time one of our gang was dragging the gut on a Saturday night in Eugene when the forward gears on his 1956 Ford went out. He ended up driving the entire 17 miles back to Marcola, then three more up Wendling Road, in reverse.

He's probably spent a fortune on chiropractors trying to get that kink out of his neck.

No matter what it was we were up to, before too long Ronnie and Donnie would come along to inquire as to what was going on. Everything always seemed to work out fine with no harm done.

We were lucky that they and the school administration never found out we had our own keys to the high school, lifted from the Janitor-We-Didn't-Like.

We'd get in at night to play H.O.R.S.E., bounce on the trampoline or try different ways of getting into the concession stand where we figured they kept the candy bars and pop. I think when we finally did get in, it turned out to be a dry hole. We later found out they kept the stuff in the little office behind the principal's office between games. I don't feel at liberty to say in what way we made use of that information, but we did.

We'd also mastered the art of signing the superintendent's signature. Sometimes we'd leave a note from her for the Janitor-We-Didn't-Like. It would say something like, *"Harvey—Girls bathroom should be cleaned again, Lucille."*

I Get a New Bro-Friend

With Eddie off in pursuit of Darlene, I began spending most of my spare time with my friend Mike Gambill, who was one year behind us in school, another friendship that has survived the years.

Mike and I were in the school band together. He was a talented cornet player with a community following. I was pretending to learn the trombone. He lived about one-half mile from me across the river. After school we'd blow our horns out the windows of our respective houses. He would blow *"Hold that Tiger!"* on his cornet and then I'd respond with that trombone thing: *Booooorrrrruuuuumph!*

I don't know how this was going over on his end but I remember at least once being asked to cool it by someone in our household.

It has not gone unnoticed by me how lucky I've been that these friendships have held up all these years. No one "gets" you like the people who were there at the time.

Mike and Ed turned out to be extraordinarily successful in their respective lines of work.

Mike may very well have been voted most likely to succeed in his class because he's done that beyond measure, but I can't remember who was voted most likely to succeed in my own graduating class, if anyone. I'll say here and now, though, that it should have been Eddie.

I say this because in thumbing through the senior edition of the school paper the year we graduated, I see he is quoted as saying that his life's ambition could be summed up thusly: *"Good car. Good home. Good gal. Plenty of money."*

He did it!

My Other Parents

My friend Eddie's Mom and dad—Sherm and Vera Head—became like surrogate parents to me. Until he was about 12, Eddie was an only child. They were delighted that he had a friend to come over and do things with him.

And because my family was so much larger, I got more direct attention at their house than I did at my own. It made for a good relationship.

The Heads also introduced me to Central Oregon by taking me with them on camping trips to places like Odell Lake, Waldo Lake and Crane Prairie. It's how I developed my love for Central Oregon and why I live here today. Thanks, Sherm and Vera.

They would sleep in a small travel trailer towed behind their red 1949 GMC pickup, which we called "The Jimmy." Eddie and I would sleep on the ground.

Once at Crane Prairie we woke up at about 3 o'clock in the morning with the earth shaking all around us. We sat up to look for the source of this big rumble. When we shone our flashlight through the jack pine trees, we saw so many deer I couldn't estimate. Okay, I will—200; 200 mule deer of all shapes and sizes running through the trees and the campgrounds.

They seemed as docile as a herd of cattle. Some of them big, five-point bucks like you see in that part of the country—and close enough to touch.

To steal a phrase from the novelist Charles Frazier, even discounting for decades of exaggeration that is a lot of deer.

I see the descendants of that migratory herd every year when they traverse the Metolius River canyon on their way down to—and coming back from—the alfalfa fields down around Paisley in southeastern Oregon.

They go down in the winter and come back in the spring.

CHAPTER 8

Eddie and the Boat

When my pal Eddie and I were about 13, we roamed for miles in every direction one summer on our heavily-customized bicycles, which we also spent hours washing, waxing and lubricating. Thanks to help from Ed's dad, Sherm, we became pretty capable bike mechanics and did all our own repairs. We rode our bikes over a thousand miles that summer. (We know this because Eddie's bike had an analog odometer, which we considered a very big deal; I remember one time pointing it out to another kid at Wayne's Market while Eddie was inside, like it was my own bike).

My ride was a standard, one-speed Schwinn but she was sharp—dark metallic green with white pin striping. We called it the *Green Hornet*. I still have the original seat to that bike because Ed found it among his possessions a few years back and sent it to me. They could add that to the list of what a true friend is: *"A friend will save a seat for you at the movies. A true friend will save your bicycle seat for you for 50 years."* (Maybe you've heard, also, that a friend will help you move; a true friend will help you move a body.)

Anyway, Eddie's bike was called *The Red Rover*. It was an "English" bike, a candy-apple red, three-speed Huffy with skinny tires and brakes on the handlebars; this was just coming into vogue at the time. And, of course, the odometer. The Red Rover was pretty tricked out. You still stopped my bike the old-fashioned way—by pushing back on the foot pedal to engage the Bendix brake.

I would later head up communications for the company that made that brake. Some coincidence, huh?

We kept ourselves in pocket money by picking up bottles while we roamed, and once came upon a safe that had been stolen from Cabels' Café in Eugene and blown apart in a quarry. My mother was furious when the story in the paper said <u>she</u> had been hunting for beer bottles with us when we made the discovery.

One of our greatest adventures was the time we were riding the county road almost all the way to the Springfield City limits about 15 miles from where we lived. Right there where the Old Mohawk Road takes off we came upon a pile of paint in gallon cans scattered in the ditch. (I think it might have been what they were lining the road with because it was a bright, nearly fluorescent yellow.)

We each took as much as we could carry on our bikes—I think it was a couple of gallons apiece—and headed for home, talking excitedly all the way about what we were going to do with all this yellow paint. Our 13-year-old-selves decided the solution was to build a boat and paint it yellow.

If it hadn't been for Sherm the project would probably never have got off the ground. But with his guidance we actually did build a boat. It was an eight-foot dinghy, which we did then paint yellow and proceed to christen "The DES-

PERATE." The inspiration for the name was the first three letters of our own names—Donnie, Eddie and Sherman.

I've thought many times what an act of pure love for his "two sons" it was for Sherm to build us a boat. He had us help with important steps like sanding and gluing, but it was mostly his doing. And of course we painted it. We had fulfilled our objective of finding something we could paint yellow. It's still my favorite color. In fact, I just bought a new sports jacket in highway-road-stripe yellow.

Setting Sail on the Mohawk

When the DESPERATE was ready to sail, Sherm hauled it down to the river behind our house in the '49 Jimmy and in she went, a really nice little boat with seats and oars and everything—entirely seaworthy with no leaks whatsoever.

A full summer of fun ensued. We could row both upstream and down that time of year. We'd hunt for crawdads, row in close to examine the rusted bodies of some of the 1930s-era automobiles that lined the river in places, and go ashore to pick blackberries and trespass on other people's back pastures.

Once, we tied the DESPERATE up on the exposed roots of a cottonwood tree and went to work building a dam across a portion of the river. We worked on the project for several days running and eventually got the dam to hold to the point where the water backed up, creating our own secluded swimming hole. I often thought in the years ahead, *"Boy, I'd like to have a job where every day you woke up and felt like I did then—how every night I went to bed thinking I couldn't wait to get back out there in the morning and get to work."*

These were the endless days of our summers. I came close to capturing that feeling in my work from time to time, but only rarely.

Close Call

Eddie and I had a close call on the Mohawk River once. It wasn't in the DESPERATE, but in a rubber raft with a hole in it that we had "plugged" with a stick. We had an air pump with us and as long as one of us pumped while the other rowed, everything was copacetic.

We had just begun drifting down the rapids coming out of Irish's swimming hole when Eddie grabbed an overhanging willow branch and was almost plucked from the boat into six or eight feet of fast-moving water. He had strong legs and managed to get himself back in the boat by towing it—and me—back to his location. I didn't learn until much later that this could have been catastrophic because Eddie hadn't yet learned to swim.

I Lose the Boat but Discover an Old Secret

Late in the summer of the year we launched the DESPERATE, the older boy I mentioned, Versal "Squeaky" Meacham, came over to my house. He wanted to borrow the boat to fish somewhere downstream of us. With no consultation of any kind with my boat partners, I said that would be fine. (It seems like I would have pressed him for confirmation that he'd bring the thing back. But he was an older boy and seemed to know what he was doing.)

Whether I pressed him or not, he did not bring the boat back. Instead, he drifted downstream about five miles and tied up at a footbridge over the river. It was getting to be the end of summer and when nobody went to retrieve it, the DESPERATE must have washed away in the first high waters or been stolen.

My mother drove me up and down the river looking for her but we never saw the DESPERATE again.

I felt guilty about losing the boat but was relieved when nothing was said about it. Before too long it seemed to be forgotten. But I couldn't forget about it; after I became a parent myself, I came to see how much Sherm must have put into that project and how thoughtless it had been of me to not make amends of some kind.

Then one day I learned that Sherm's health was failing. If I was ever going to apologize, now would be the time.

By now we were living in Washington State. I put in a call to the Heads in Marcola. Sherm and Eddie's mother, Vera, both picked up and we were able to have a nice chat about all the good times we'd had together. I finally got around to saying to the two of them, *"Hey, I want you to know how sorry I am that I lost the boat. It was so irresponsible of me. And then I made it worse by never coming over to tell you what happened."*

Almost simultaneously the two of them exclaimed, *"Oh that boat! We were so glad when you lost that boat. We just knew Eddie was going to drown in that boat!"*

Squeaky Meacham

Small footnote to this story: We decided to call the cat we have now "Squeaky Meacham," because when we first got her she didn't meow, she just squeaked.

Versal Meacham—the one they called Squeaky—died after falling from a bicycle a long time ago but I ran into his older sister Elma at my sister Susan's memorial service. I said, *"You're not going to believe this, but we have a cat named for your brother."*

She sort of screwed up her face and said, *"You have a cat named Versal?"*

CHAPTER 9

High School in an Interesting Time

Alot of momentous events took place during my high school years. One was the success of the Mohawk High School Indians football team after a dry spell that had lasted a couple of decades. That had the whole town energized.

Next came the Columbus Day Storm of 1962 that tried to level half the Northwest, then the devastating death of our own high school football hero, and not too long after that the assassination of the 35th President of the United States, John F. Kennedy.

Okay, maybe it's just wrong to put what happened in football up there with the loss of a young life and assassination of a president, but at the time it was practically an out-of-body experience for a lot of us and cannot be discounted. Our newfound success in athletics and the great positive buzz it created at our little school made what happened next all the more tragic.

After the football season ended in glory and the Indians were finding similar success on the basketball court (that's the way it was in the little schools where the same athletes played every sport), tragedy struck.

David Harley Willyard was a big man on campus and remains a big man in my memory too. I know I probably never would have made it through football as one of only two freshmen on the team—and undersized to boot—without his "protection."

Football practices in those days could be brutal affairs with few safeguards against coaches with a punitive mindset and little concern for player safety. Practicing in the late-summer heat of the Willamette Valley was not easy, and it wasn't made any easier by the fact that I wasn't much of an athlete.

We had a drill where each of us took turns trying to defend against a player attempting to catch a pass. I would be clearly outclassed by an athlete like David. The possibility of a missed assignment and the punishment that went with it—running laps in the August heat—were all too real for the poor player who got called out by the coach for messing up.

No problem.

When it was my turn to defend and David came running out in my direction, instead of juking me and going for the ball, he clutched the front of my jersey and lifted me right off the ground. He started running around with me while at the same time waving his other arm over his head shouting, *"Over here! Over here!"*

I was happy to play the straight man for his little gag as it drew all the attention to him and away from how well I was (or was not) doing at being a defender

Not surprisingly, David was going out with one of the prettiest girls in school, a cheerleader named Theresa. At our weekly pep rallies, when the student body was supposed to stand and sing the fight song, David would get out on the gym floor and interrupt the program.

He would insist that everyone first sing a popular doo-wop song by Carl Dobkins, Jr., called *"Look. Look. My Heart is an Open Book."* It was "their" song.

People loved being in the thrall of the B.M.O.C., particularly in the midst of a spectacular football campaign. And he could really rally the crowd, which is an important job for the team captain.

Seeing how well David wore the mantle of leadership while emanating a sort of high school saintliness makes me think he would have achieved a lot more in life if he'd had the chance. But he didn't. About January of that year David began feeling tired and had to quit playing basketball. Before too long the word spread: he had leukemia.

I think the entire school at one time or another went to visit him in the hospital. The 180-pound frame that made him such a formidable small-school running back had withered to half that much in just a matter of weeks. He was in terrible pain. His wrists were handcuffed to the bed rail so he wouldn't hurt himself flailing about. By March he was gone and our little campus was plunged into mourning. He was 17. I was 14.

I'm sure every boy and girl who went to Mohawk High School that year remembers this or other parts of the story just as vividly as I do.

The fall had been electric with the football team beating one Trico League opponent after another on the way to the Indians' first championship in the modern era. The district's music teacher, an Ichabod Crane-ish individual by the name of Haldeman even got into the spirit of things with his own rendition of a rousing 1950's marching tune called *"Mr. Touchdown U.S.A."* He introduced it at a pep rally in the high school gym, accompanying himself on the piano.

In the original version the schools named in the song were all colleges from the Midwest—Minnesota, Purdue, Wisconsin, Iowa, et. al. He changed them to the rival B-league Oregon schools that Mohawk had defeated on the way to the championship game:

> *Remember the day we murdered old Falls City?*
> *Remember the day we pickled old St. Paul?*
> *I'll bet those boys from Triangle Lake really have a*
> *tummy ache!*
> *We took Westfir's grey and red and turned it black and*
> *blue instead."*

That's what they call unifying the fan base today. As our fight song said, *"United we stand to back you always."* You can see how an athlete dying young must have affected us.

The principal, Lucille Dickey, put a note up on the bulletin board in the hallway the morning David died. It was the first time I had seen the word "expired." They hadn't thought up the use of grief counselors by then but we could have used a few—not just the high school, either; the whole town.

I remember we even received a note from the student body president at Westfir High School expressing its condolences *"...on the loss of your outstanding student and athlete, David Harley Willyard."*

When President Kennedy was assassinated the following fall we grieved along with the rest of the country. But for us it wasn't the first time we'd experienced something like that.

For 50 years—before a new elementary school was built on the site a while back—the big sign on Mohawk's football field identified it as *"David Harley Willyard Field."*

He lives on as a saintly figure in my memory. St. David of Mohawk.

What happened next blew everyone away—literally.

CHAPTER 10

The "Big Blow" and the Assassination of John F. Kennedy

Her Name Was Freda

I t was called the Columbus Day Storm of 1962. Talk about the mother of all storms! It knocked down half the trees in Western Oregon and when my dad and I went to cruise a timber sale in the McKenzie River Canyon out of Springfield the following summer, we walked all day without ever touching the ground—just jumped from one downed old-growth Douglas fir tree to another.

I can guarantee you everybody who experienced the Columbus Day Storm has their story. Here's mine:

Because our football field wasn't lighted, Mohawk's football games began at 3 o'clock in the afternoon. That's about the time the storm made landfall on the Oregon coast. We were about 60 miles inland. By halftime the wind was already blowing 35 to 40 miles per hour. Before it was over, a gigantic and ancient oak tree had come crashing down right on our bench.

We played the game to its conclusion, becoming one of only five pairs of schools in Western Oregon to finish our contests that day. We also became the first and last team to beat St. Paul in the regular season that year. The score was 13-2.

The "Buckaroos" got their two points when Mohawk's kicker attempted to punt the ball away from the Indians' own 30-yard line. The ball went sailing right back over his head and into the end zone for a safety and the two points that went with it.

And this is interesting: of the five high school games played that day, <u>four</u> featured safeties scored in this fashion. Crow beat Elkton 4-0 with both scores being wind-aided safeties. All 37 other games scheduled that day were either canceled or postponed, with the Monroe-Coburg game being called at 20-0 in favor of Monroe in the third quarter.

The *Eugene Register-Guard* reported that in one game, "*A punt kicked skyward ended up five yards behind the punter as the goal posts came crashing down.*" That topped our story by a little bit, but that game was called at the end of the third quarter; we kept playing to the end.

In the game between Oakland and Powers, Oakland won 14-13 in winds that hit 90 miles per hour. On the ride home the Oakland team had to get off their bus to lift trees off the highway. Good thing it was football season; the basketball team might not have been able to do it.

Just a few moments before the tree fell on our bench the assistant coach, Glenn Skinner, told the bench warmers that they might want to start thinking about getting off that bench and out into the open. Anyone sitting there when the tree came down would most certainly have been crushed. (You can credit him for the fact that I lived to tell my version of events that day because, yes, Dear Reader, I was one of those benchwarmers.)

By the time the game was over school was out. Under the terms of agreement in effect at the time it was every kid for himself. I'll never forget leaving the school on foot and walking toward home on the main road. There was this big grove of old-growth Doug firs right beside the high school. They were probably about 180 years old. Those are big trees; they would have been around 140 feet tall and nearly three feet across at a man's chest.

As I was walking down the hill toward the covered bridge, the tops of some of these trees began twisting off and going right over my head all the way to the bridge a good 100 yards or more away. They were crashing right into it. Smack! Smack! Smack!

I could see over to the right that there was already a tree down on the Nielsen's house. I can inflate a tale right along with the rest of them, but this one needs no exaggeration; I didn't know how I was going to make it down that road and through the bridge to safer ground.

I was comforted to read a while back in a book written by logger and resort owner Floyd Keeland down on the Southern Oregon coast that he saw something like this happen where he was.

"We were outside looking up at the hill and I saw the wind twist off a big old, old-growth, and it wasn't <u>blown</u>, it was <u>twisted</u> off...not just the top either, the whole length of the tree. It sailed about 300 feet airborne off our property."

Before it was over 46 people in Oregon died that day, mostly from being hit with flying objects: limbs, galvanized roofing, two-by-fours.

I didn't become one of them because, while I was standing there sizing up the situation, Mr. Skinner pulled up in his blue '54 Ford pickup and suggested I hop in the back. He gunned it and we made it through the covered bridge and out of harm's way into Marcola where I waited out the storm at home. It was the second time that day that he may have saved my life. Because he lived in Springfield 20 miles away, his "story" of what happened that day was just beginning.

Nobody had electricity for the longest time; the whole power grid in Lane County was out of commission. But in a town full of chain saws, wood furnaces, camp stoves and Coleman lanterns, life went on and was good. No school the whole time.

The storm was also called Typhoon Freda. It has gone down as the benchmark for extratropical wind storms and a contender for the most powerful cyclone recorded in the U.S. in the 20th Century.

It certainly was not ordinary. At our handsome old 1920s-era wooden school bus barn in Marcola, the wind first lofted the roof off the structure then collapsed the walls outward, sparing the bus.

The average wind speed in Lane County was close to 100 miles an hour. But up and down the state you saw gusts of 160 or better—179 at Mt. Hebo in the coast range. Most anemometers were damaged or destroyed before winds ever got to maximum velocity. It gusted to 152 in Portland before the wind gauge on top of the downtown studios of KGW Radio and TV was knocked off-line by flying debris. We'll never know how high it went at the peak but it was hellacious.

At Corvallis, a weather observer entered the words *"Abandoned Station at 4:15,"* making it the only time in history an officially recognized weather station in Oregon was abandoned due to high winds. In Seattle, people were trapped in the Space Needle during the World's Fair. Down the road at

Pt. Defiance Park and Zoo in Tacoma a cage blew open. Two lions escaped and mauled several people before being shot.

And at the original Wilt farm on Kiger Island near Corvallis, my 80-year-old grandmother, Alma, watched helplessly from the picture window of her darkened living room up the hill as the enormous two-story barn my grandfather built around 1920 came crashing down like a game of Jenga.

It was winds like these that we would have been experiencing where I lived.

For Some, a Silver Lining

When I went to work for Weyerhaeuser at global headquarters south of Seattle in 1979 I became acquainted with a man who personally benefited immensely from "The Big Blow."

In 1962 Charley Bingham was in a development assignment as the raw materials manager for the company in Longview, Washington, and in his late 20s. After the storm, it fell to him to find markets for all the downed timber on Weyerhaeuser's three million acres of timberland in Oregon and Washington.

He found them in China and Japan. The company began moving this surplus of logs over there. This not only solved the immediate problem but opened up what continues to be one of the U.S.'s most important forest products markets.

That sort of thing does not go unnoticed. By the age of 30 Bingham had been elevated to senior vice president of timberlands for the world's largest forest products company. That was one of the top four or five executive positions in the company at the time.

Charley was Ivy League-educated so it wasn't like he wasn't going places anyway. But The Big Blow blew him straight to the top.

It's been estimated that 15 billion board feet of timber were blown down that day, more than the entire annual timber harvest of Oregon and Washington combined. To quote the old logger down there in Southern Oregon again, *"The whole shiterie was on the ground."*

"For This, We Stand."

Then, a third of the way through our sophomore year, President John F. Kennedy was assassinated in Dallas, Texas. No one ever forgot that day.

I was in the high school band. We were at practice on the stage of the elementary school. We practiced behind curtains because lunch was being served in the cafeteria, which also served as our gymnasium and auditorium where the *Get-Together Club* met.

Suddenly someone appeared behind the curtain with us and spoke quietly for a moment with the band teacher, Lynn Haldeman. He then turned to us and informed us of what had happened in Dallas and that the president was dead.

Mr. Haldeman quickly told us to turn our music books to the national anthem. The curtains were pulled back and there we sat looking out on 50 or 60 of the "little" kids still sitting at tables having their lunch. They looked a little bewildered to suddenly find this stage full of "big kids" looking down on them.

Before turning around to direct the band, Mr. Haldeman said in a commanding voice to the whole of the cafeteria, *"For this, we stand!"* Boy, I hope if I'm ever put in a situation like that I can think of something that cool to say.

Anyway, they did and we began to play our dirge. When we were finished they announced that school was dismissed.

We all headed for home. It was about 11:30 on a sunny Friday morning, Nov. 22, 1963.

We didn't go back to school until the following Tuesday, after President Kennedy was laid to rest at Arlington. I don't believe anyone did much of anything except look at the television the entire time.

Being the emerging news junkie that I was, it's not surprising that while this was all happening I took frequent breaks from my job stocking the cooler and counting bottles in the back of Wayne's Market to sneak a peek at the new black and white portable television Wayne had just put up above the coolers.

That's what I was doing two days after the assassination when I saw the president's killer, Lee Harvey Oswald, being escorted through the parking garage of the Dallas Police Department. Suddenly—as anyone who was alive at the time will always remember— Dallas night club owner Jack Ruby enters the picture from the lower right of the screen and shoots Oswald right in the gut with a snub-nosed revolver.

Talk about reality TV! Today's television audiences may be accustomed to seeing just about anything on the tube, but it was all uncharted territory in those days and pretty upsetting to most people.

It still blows me away that I later would meet JFK's brother Bobby—called RFK—and come face to face with that famous Kennedy countenance and persona before he too would be assassinated.

There's an apocryphal Chinese curse: *"May you live in interesting times."* We must have been living under it from 1962 to 1966 because no one can say that our high school years were not eventful.

CHAPTER 11

When it Came to Sports

Pee Wee

When I was in third grade we played Pee-Wee basketball. Our team went off to other schools around the region to compete on Saturday mornings in the winter. I was into it mostly because on the way back we got to stop at the Big Y shopping center in Eugene where you could get a hamburger with French fries and a milkshake for 49 cents at Ron's 14-Cent Hamburgers.

I have my sweet mother to thank for pressing the two quarters I needed into my hand each week as I left for the game. Mothers didn't go to the games; dads, either.

I was still the smallest kid in my class and not very good, so when it was taking me longer to dribble around the gym at practice one day the coach blew his whistle, bringing everything to a halt. He instructed the other boys to line up against the wall while I continued dribbling around the court. He told them that when I passed by he wanted them to bow down and shout, *"Hail to the tortoise!" "Hail to the tortoise!"*

He didn't say what important athletic principle this was supposed to instill in us. Whatever it was, I'm afraid I must have missed that too because the only thing I remember taking from the episode was the feeling that they shouldn't let people like this coach Pee Wee basketball. I think his name might have been Bobby Knight.

(Oh, did you hear that after Bobby Knight left coaching he opened a furniture store? Yeah. If you buy a sofa he throws in a chair.)

The Great Uniform Shortage of 1962

In high school we played eight-man football. I was one of only a couple of freshmen on the team. When I was verifying that fact with one of my old classmates he told me, *"They were awfully hard on the freshmen that year and most of us didn't last but a day or two."*

The fact that I did was probably the result of peer pressure I'd created for myself by hanging with the jocks the rest of the year. I'm sure I went out for football more to impress them than out of any great personal desire on my part (except to belong, maybe). I weighed about 90 pounds and was virtually ignorant about how the game was played.

As the first game approached that fall, the coach had us gather around after practice one Thursday night. He informed us—like some sort of good news / bad news joke— that the new uniforms we'd been waiting for had arrived just in time for the first game. That was the good news.

The bad news was that there were only enough of them to outfit 16 of our 17 players; one of us would have to wear the old-style uni. He said he wanted the team to vote on who should get the last available uniform—me or Ricky Jones, a sophomore.

The team voted for me so I was awarded the uniform. But I thought that Ricky had worked every bit as hard as I had so I insisted that he be given the new uniform instead because he was older.

Just kidding. I kept it for myself. But I sure did feel bad for Ricky and had to wonder what kind of coach does something like that. Actually, I know the answer to that: any coach of that era, that's who.

The Meat Grinder

We had a new coach fresh out of college who demanded a lot of his players. It seemed to me that he devoted an inordinate amount of time to physical endurance drills of one kind or another. After we started the season with a loss, he told us that the next week of practice would be so hard that he'd be lucky if he had eight men left to play in the next game.

He made good on his promise with a full complement of laps and wind sprints under a blistering August sun.

I remember he had us lined up for yet another set of wind sprints late one evening that week. He'd walked just out of hearing range before he blew his whistle to initiate the drill so he didn't hear Phil Roberts, one of our veteran leaders, turn to the rest of us and issue this aside: *"All right gentlemen, let's not be setting any records here, okay?"*

Regrettably some of these early coaches provided very little in the way of instruction on how you actually play—and win—at football: What are the various positions and what are they responsible for? What are the three phases that make up the game, and where might you fit into one of them? What's our strategy for the next opponent?

And here I was, someone who had not only never played the game before, I had never even <u>seen</u> it played. As you might expect, the result was that I spent no time whatsoever thinking about how I could do better or studying up on the game myself. For me, it was mostly about getting through it with my dignity intact.

Until a new, better-rounded coach came along my senior year I don't remember ever having a session on game strategy. A friend who played quarterback told me recently that no one ever once gave him instruction on how to hold a football. We began to win, I guess, because we had some gifted athletes in our town and we probably <u>were</u> more toughened up than the opposition a lot of the time. But I wouldn't call it a true team effort as I came to know the concept later in my work career.

Despite my shortcomings I was getting a little better from one year to the next and ended up playing in every game my last couple of years. Got thrown out of a game once over at Eddyville for throwing a punch at another player, who started it.

I played center on the team and started every game at that position my senior year under the best of the three coaches I played for—Mel Nice.

What a breath of fresh air he was. Coach Nice was fresh out of the University of Oregon but he'd already spent a couple of years in the Army. We first met him when some of us walked past the high school late one summer evening. We saw him in the school basement welding on a blocking sled. We wandered on in and got acquainted.

We asked the new coach if he was going to have us practice a drill called the "Meat Grinder." He said he didn't know that one. We told him about this particularly fierce drill we'd been subjected to where one player, armed only with a plastic shield, would be put in the center of a square made up of the rest of the team. On command, other players would rush in attempting to take the dude in the middle off his feet. They would be coming from all directions. It reminded me of the ancient sport of bear-baiting and had been a favorite of our previous coaches.

Coach Nice looked a little puzzled. He said, *"I don't know why a coach would do something like that. Sounds like a good way to get people to quit football to me."* We liked him instantly.

He also took the time to educate us a little bit about the fundamentals of the game and some of the different ways a player could make a contribution. One of my assignments sometimes was to "pull," which meant that instead of blocking the opponent directly across from me, my job was to pull out of the line and run to block out a different defender. Because this maneuver involved the element of surprise it was better for an undersized player like me and allowed me to make a greater impact.

He also showed us how to down a larger opponent by basically making him fall over you. The idea is that when you're trying to tackle a larger and faster ball carrier, you don't just crash straight into him. Instead, Coach Nice showed us how to throw our bodies horizontally in front of the runner. At the same time, you grabbed him around the legs and rolled him over yourself. The runner would half-trip and half get tackled. I got pretty good at that particular technique.

"You Gotta Get Up!"

I don't want to be one of those people who brings up every little thing they ever accomplished in sports, but because I am I'll just mention that I did receive one vote for the All-League team my final year. The other linemen in the conference voted. It may not have been much, but it was one more than a lot of other people got I suppose.

Or wait, maybe it wasn't; I never really did the math. I guess it would be pretty funny if I checked it out and discovered everyone got one vote that year—like a "participant" trophy.

Funny story about Coach Nice and how small our team was: He's in his 80s now and was telling me just a few years ago that the first game he ever coached was the one we played against the Westfir Loggers. I remember the game vividly myself because Westfir was the only school in our league that had a lighted football field so the game was played at night.

The coach reminded me that at one point our strongest and best player, Donald Goldie, got injured and was lying on the field. He said at first he didn't know what he was supposed to do, but his assistant nudged him and said, *"Coach, you're supposed to go out there."*

"So," he says, *"I went out and knelt down beside him. I said, 'Donald, you gotta get up! We don't have anyone else to put in.' And he did!"*

I was at a University of Oregon football game a couple of years ago when our all-conference safety Ugochukwu Amadi went down with an injury. They worked over him for a while as the stadium grew quiet. This was happening on our end of the field. When it became apparent that he wasn't going to have to be carted, I shouted, *"Ugo, you gotta get up!"* And I kid you not—he did!

It was the only coaching I ever did but I saved the guy's career. He's in the NFL now.

Our school had so few boys that you were automatically in the draft for every team the school fielded—baseball, basketball and football. I stayed with the program until I returned to school for my sophomore year, looked at the boys around me, and realized that I was the only one who hadn't grown about a foot over the summer. I continued to play football, but that brought an end to my basketball career, which had begun with this same group of boys in the Pee Wee league.

Because I might not have another opportunity to do it, I'll use this one to point out that in 7th grade I once scored two-thirds of our team's points in a basketball game, this one also at Westfir, Oregon.

I never was one to gloat afterwards, especially since we didn't win the game. As athletes today are fond of saying, *"I don't care about my personal stats; all I care about is getting the "W."*

But just for the record, despite my efforts, I will report that we still got beat 49-3. (Two free throws, both one-and-ones in different halves of the game).

Most School Spirit—Boy

What I lacked on the field of play I more than made up for in my enthusiasm for our teams. I loved going to a school that had successful sports teams getting a lot of attention in the paper; it really brought out the school spirit in me.

My freshman year I was voted *"Most School Spirit Boy"* in a schoolwide poll. It probably didn't hurt my chances that I'd had Tom Walters cut my hair in a Mohawk. Remember, we were the *Mohawk* Indians.

It was the first haircut I ever got in an actual shop. To save money, our dad generally did the trimming around our place. Tom was under instructions from the coach at the time to cut every boy's hair the same way—in a crew cut like his.

He took the mandate so seriously that if you went in there you got that haircut whether you were on the team or not. He kept asking me, *"Are you sure the coach is going to be okay with this?"*

Tom's barbershop on the main street about halfway between our house and Wayne's market on the river side of the street was pretty much what you'd expect a small-town barbershop to be in the 1950s and '60s: all haircuts were $1.00 and it was a good place to catch up on the local news while you waited your turn.

I remember a couple of local denizens had regular chairs there, one of them being one-legged Ernie Mabe who putted down there every day in his big '53 Buick going about two miles an hour to sit around and gab. My Grandpa Gordon from Portland had a nice head of hair. He never missed a chance to get a one dollar haircut when he was in town. I'm sure they cost a good deal more by that time in Portland.

On the Warpath

Another way in which I demonstrated my outsized school spirit was to beat a drum at the Indians' basketball games—you know that menacing Boom! *Boom. Boom. Boom.* Boom! *Boom. Boom. Boom.*—that was supposed to signal the Indians were on the warpath. I can't imagine how obnoxious that must have been in that tiny gym. It must have worked a little bit, though, because we had a terrific basketball season too.

You'd be surprised how much this kind of enthusiasm and pride-in-organization carried on into my career life and, I believe, benefited both me and the organizations I worked for.

I guess you could say that's what I took from sports.

CHAPTER 12

Working in Fields and Woods

M ost teenagers where I was from were expected to earn their own money for school clothes and extras. Jobs were easy to come by and I ended up with quite a string of things I'd tried my hand at before I was ever out of school.

From about the age of 12, a lot of Marcola kids worked at H.H. Myers. This was a pole-bean farm on the McKenzie River near Springfield run by Horace Horatio Myers and his wife, Gladys. We'd catch the Myers's 1950 Ford flatbed—the "Bean Truck"—at the corner by the old theatre in Marcola at 6:30 in the morning and ride on open-air benches with no seat belts to the bean field. Horace drove the truck.

If you were a good picker, willing to take on more responsibility, and <u>male,</u> you could work your way up to pounding stakes before the season started. Stakes are the poles that green beans grow on. Picking beans paid just 2 ½ cents a pound. Pounding stakes was regular $1.50-an-hour work and highly sought-after. It probably never even occurred to most girls of my generation to go for one of these jobs, although there was no reason they couldn't have performed the work if they were strong enough.

Girls didn't pound stakes. But a few of them did work up to the position of "Bean Boy." Bean Boys drove the farm trucks, weighed beans and generally helped run the farm. Later they had both boys and girls doing this kind of work, but in the beginning that was the position description: Bean Boy.

Our nickname for Gladys Myers was "Happy Bottom." Get it? Glad Ass. Happy Bottom.

We thought this had originated with us, but an old-timer from the area told me recently that the pun actually was invented much earlier and applied to the entire family. It included Horace ("Hoar-Ass"), their daughter Lois ("Low Ass") and son Maurice ("More Ass"). Don't ask me why people would do such a thing. The Myerses were perfectly nice people.

Their right-hand man was a good-natured guy named Ernie. Together they ran a good operation. One thing that set H.H. Myers apart from other major growers was that they had hand pumps in every section of the field that brought up clean, ice-cold water. You were never far from relief in the scorching August temperatures.

Also just for the boys was the job of putting up hay. This involved "bucking" the hay bales from the field up onto flatbed trucks, then unloading them into the hay loft when we got to the barn.

Bales weighed about a hundred pounds. Some of the better-healed ranchers had a conveyor to help move these heavy bales from the ground to the truck and then from the truck up into the loft. The ones we worked for didn't have that so it was pretty demanding work under a hot summer sun.

It seemed like we were always racing to get the hay in before it rained so we had to work fast. And man, those hay lofts can get hot! I imagine it was about 125 degrees up there.

One of my aged relatives from the farm back in Wisconsin played football in college. He told me once, *"You get a few of these eastern dummies that have never been out in the country, yet they call us farm boys hicks. I got my revenge when I came off the farm and played football. I could sure show those city boys where the bear shit in the buckwheat after handling hay bales all summer."*

I somehow got a job working for Bob Prickett at Cascade Greenhouses on Wendling Road about the summer of my sophomore year in high school. It was a standard summer job that paid $1.25 an hour.

Bob was a handsome, if thin man with a kind face, dazzling smile and a nice shock of brown hair that he wore sort of Kennedy-style. He smiled a lot and generated a lot of laughter around him. I'm sure he helped shape my emerging work ethic when he commented on the fact that he could tell I was a good worker my first day because when he left me to do something it was done when he got back. That has always stuck with me as a measure of whether a person is pulling their weight.

Bob was also kind enough to put me on the payroll of Cascade Gardens in Springfield, the outlet for the products raised at his Wendling operations. It was also a full service flower shop and garden center. This was summer work that involved almost constant watering, with customer service and delivery also part of the deal.

It was laughable that one of my first jobs was delivering anything, because I had no experience driving in or even living in a city. Houses where I was from didn't have house numbers so I had no way of knowing that those in cities like Eugene corresponded to block numbers, or that houses on one side of the street were even-numbered and the others odd.

Needless to say, it took me way too long to find these addresses at first. But before too long I had it figured out. In the meantime, I have to say that Bob Prickett was one patient and forgiving man. I've always regretted that he worked so hard to create and run the whole nursery and flower shop business only to die far too young at age 38 of a brain condition.

Gyppo

If you were lucky, you might also get on with one of the "gyppo" logging outfits setting chokers—the cables they wrap around a log so it can be pulled up out of the woods. Gyppos were independent loggers not associated with the big timber companies. They often went in to salvage trees left by the larger companies which only wanted certain species. Gyppos paid well but didn't provide things like medical care and retirement benefits. Unions and their organized workers took a dim view of gyppos.

I did this kind of labor the summer of my sophomore year in college, working for my Uncle Stan's logging company on a cutting unit high above the McKenzie River. We were building an access road to reach trees the company had purchased in a U.S.F.S. timber sale. This meant that we not only had to fell the big Doug firs that were in the way, but remove them entirely, including the stumps.

I was a powder monkey. My job was to dig holes and carry the sacks of blasting powder and the sticks of dynamite for the blaster, a heavyset older guy with a lot of grey stubble and a thick Scottish accent. His name, of course, was Scotty. He'd say things like, *"It 'us so warm last night I had to sidetrack me kivers,"* by which he meant he had to remove some of his blankets. My dad and uncle thought he was hilarious but he and I never clicked.

One thing no one liked about this job was that when you handled dynamite the glycerin got on your hands. The first time you wiped your brow—which was always early in the morning because it was hard work—you'd immediately have a headache that lasted all day.

Scotty had been complaining for some time that he needed a better chain saw. One morning my dad showed up with a new Homelite for him that he'd just picked up at the shop. I think they said it cost $450, which is more than one would cost today.

After he'd exclaimed over it a little bit, Scotty set the saw on a big Doug-fir stump and proceeded to set the charges for the next blast.

We were taking out a series of about six big stumps at a time so it required a big charge involving multiple sticks of dynamite. Following Scotty's instructions, I retreated behind some tall standing timber about 30 yards uphill and waited for him to shout *"Fire in the hole!"* Then he'd depress the plunger to send an electric current to the fuse and detonate the dynamite beneath the stumps.

It was from this vantage point that I saw, first, one of these enormous stumps weighing at least a ton and a half and trailing rocks and roots and a trail of dust like a comet fly 80 feet in the air right over my head.

That was impressive. But what caught my eye was not the stump but the new chain saw that had been sitting on it. Even after the stump began to lose altitude and crash back to earth, that blue and white Homelite was still glistening in the sun high above the trees.

My dad went after it. Being the great woodsman that he was, he located it and dragged it back. The 36-inch bar was bent at a 90 degree angle, the chain had somehow flung off and the housing, made of steel in those days, was crushed like a pop can.

I heard Uncle Stanley was pretty mad about it but my dad thought it was funny and he told the story many times in his remaining years.

This kind of work did not appeal to me at the time and I'm sure I embarrassed my dad by not trying any harder than I did. I felt trapped all day with this old Scotsman who was no fun at all as far as I was concerned. He didn't like to talk. How do you think that went over with me, Mr. Conviviality?

It probably didn't help that we both had headaches from the dynamite, but I know I could have tried harder because Scotty kept comparing me with my older brother who had worked with him when <u>he</u> was in college. Denny was a superstar—a real stud when it came to logging—and I heard several times about how he had moved an entire logging "show" by himself one weekend when he could have just sat and watched for fires, our "night job."

A "show" is all the cables and pulleys and everything needed to set up a logging operation, so he would have had to do a lot of heavy lifting and climbing in rough terrain to do it. But Denny is that kind of guy. Sadly, I was not. This was partly because I couldn't even have carried one of those steel cables if I'd wanted to and partly because I didn't want to.

By this time I had met and fallen in love with Priscilla. She was in Eugene. I really did not like the fact that my work schedule gave me exactly one half of each Saturday and Sunday a week to see her; even then I had to take care of everything else like groceries, laundry, etc., before I headed back up the hill.

The situation led to an unfortunate incident involving the company's emergency fire telephone, kept under the bench in the travel trailer where I slept. When Uncle Neal pulled the cushion off to show me where it was kept, I'm sure I was supposed to be thinking, *"Okay, this is where I go if I ever spot a fire and have to call it in."*

But I'm afraid it was more like, *"Hey, now I can call my girlfriend!"*

And that's just what I did the first chance I got. We kept up our nightly calls for about three nights before the battery went dead.

Idea: get the jumper cables and hook them up to Uncle Neal's new Ford pickup and then to the battery for the phone.

Bad idea: Connect the cables to the wrong poles of the truck's battery and burn up the alternator on the truck.

I probably should have been fired over something like this, but family's family. In any event, I only worked that job one summer. I don't suppose it broke their hearts later that year when I took a .job at a service station in Eugene and left the life of a powder monkey.

Having lunch one day at the Marie Callendar's in San Pedro, California, I overheard a family at a large table talking about plans for the summer. It became apparent that they owned a family jewelry store. One of the girls said her brother planned to work at the counter that summer.

However, the woman I took to be the grandmother said to all of them that she wouldn't allow it. She said, *"Boys that age need to have jobs where they use their hands for a few years."* She said, *"They need to learn how to do things."*

And I did—things like how you know when your hay is ready to be cut, how to use a chainsaw, drive a tractor, set a choker on a log and put out a wild fire.

It's given me a lot of pleasure in life to be able to apply these skills to bringing in my own fire wood, helping out a neighbor or working on the various improvement projects that come up in the community. It also gives a person an identity beyond who they "were" in their working years, and that's always a good thing.

There's a retired Forest Service guy here in town who works so hard at finding and bringing in his own firewood that they call him "Benny the Beaver."

If that nickname had not been taken I would like to have had it.

CHAPTER 13

The Kalitan

C asting about for an activity I could more likely "own," I was naturally drawn to the school newspaper and somehow became editor. The paper was called the *"Kalitan."*

Kalitan, you may be interested to know, is a Chinook Indian word for *"Arrow."* I don't think it had anything to do with the Mohawk Indians, to whom we were "mascotted." But you'd have to admit that was some pretty nice symbolism: Fast as an arrow. Sharp as an arrow. Straight as an arrow.

Sadly, we were none of these. The *Kalitan* was a silly little rag. But I liked having a hand in its manufacture and enjoyed what little status accrued from being its editor.

For reasons that will become more apparent later in the story, I'll note that the paper probably didn't get any better on my watch, but it did get bigger. Trying, no doubt, to leave my mark I set out to produce the largest edition of the *Kalitan* in history—and succeeded.

Working only with a girl I'll call Celeste Brown, who I was hoping would become my girlfriend, we put out a whopping 54-page edition to commemorate the graduating class of 1966. The cover carried the paper's nameplate and the words "Senior Edition." It also featured a nice pencil etching of an Indian on horseback drawn by my talented sister, Susie.

I wish I could say that the additional pages added more than mere bulk, but that wouldn't be true. We just ran more of what the paper had always contained—profiles of the graduating seniors with their lists of favorite foods, favorite movies and plans for the future; a senior class "will;" and sports results. Only a little real news—"School Robbed"—under headlines drawn by hand. Photographs only rarely.

I edited the *Kalitan* in its 36th and 37th years of publication. Given the rewarding newspapering, teaching and corporate paths it opened up to me, I now understand this was a great gift.

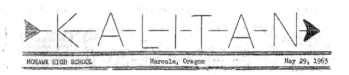

MOHAWK HIGH SCHOOL   Marcola, Oregon   May 29, 1963

Wayne Warner

I'd been responsible for about a dozen issues of the paper when I got a letter at school one day from a man named Wayne Warner, managing editor of *The Mackinaw Valley News* in Minier, Illinois. It turned out that he was a graduate of Mohawk High School himself, class of 1951, who had also worked on the *Kalitan*.

He was looking to lay his hands on some current issues and wanted to know a little bit about the current editor (me). We began to correspond, and the following summer Wayne came to see me on a trip to Oregon.

I remember him parking his car at Art Moran's Richfield service station and walking across Marcola Road to shake my hand. I didn't fully understand who he was or what he did, but I somehow heard the faint sound of opportunity knocking. Thus ensued a couple of years of correspondence between my high school-age self and the first real journalist I ever knew.

Wayne is nearly 90 now. He was digging through his files a while back and came upon our correspondence from that period. At first I was terrified to think what might be on those pages, and there's a cringe-worthy moment or two in there to be sure.

But for the most part, the correspondence with Wayne depicts the thinking of a 17-year-old hick from the sticks just beginning to ideate about a career in journalism. The letters were written in a passable hand on lined tablet paper—a small misspelling or two, but otherwise correct and cogent.

At one point I explain to him that I'm unable to provide a copy of the latest issue of the *Kalitan* as he'd requested because, *"One of the girls at Mohawk, and definitely the best writer on my staff, died Sunday of complications from the flu."*

I'd have to say that was a pretty solid excuse for not getting around to doing something; plus, as one of my old bosses used to say, *"It had the additional benefit of being true."*

The girl was Leo and Lois Paschelke's freshman daughter, Laney. She'd gone with a group of girls—maybe from the church—to a swimming party at a new heated pool in Springfield. She died afterwards in the night from breathing complications. Her mother came into the garden center where I worked to order flowers. She was inconsolable.

Anyway, I was amused to see that I'd also added a postscript to one of my handwritten letters to Wayne that said, *"I can type, but between school homework and sports I have very little time in the school building where they keep the typewriters."*

In another I asked him what kinds of jobs might be available to someone with my interests. He responded by sending me the classified ads from *Editor & Publisher* magazine: Sportswriter, News Editor, Photographer.

My next letter reveals the extent to which I really had no clue how you actually do any of these jobs. At one point I asked Wayne if he thought I needed to bother with college. Couldn't I just jump right in there as, say, a sports editor?

His response was avuncular: *"Sounds like you are anxious to get your feet wet in journalism. You asked me what I thought about going into the field without college. My advice would be for you to go on to college because future advancement, as I see it, still hinges a whole lot on journalism degrees. What I have learned has been on the job and it would have been much easier if there had been classroom preparation."*

I must have thought it was pretty good advice because by that fall I was enrolled in journalism classes at the brand-new Lane Community College in Eugene.

Robert Fulghum wrote a popular best-seller in the 80s called, *"All I Really Need to Know I Learned in Kindergarten."* The foundation for everything I would do with the rest of my life would be laid down in the four years after I graduated from high school, began studying journalism and went to work in newspapering.

P.S. Did you hear about the young reporter who said to the publisher, *"Sir, I would like to marry your daughter...that is, if you have one."*

"I Do Know He's Quite Wealthy"

Funny story about that old flame, Celeste, with whom I worked on the *Kalitan*. To appreciate it you need to know two things: one is that I'm far from being wealthy; the other is that my sister, Susan, remained a small-town girl for the rest of her life and didn't have much perspective on that kind of thing.

Anyway, Susie says to me on the phone one day during our middle years, *"I've been going to the Valley Hospital for my cancer treatments and guess who I see there?"*

Turns out that Celeste had become a nurse. I couldn't resist asking if they ever talked about me and was delighted to hear Susie say, *"Well, she asked me what you do for a living. I told her I wasn't really sure, but that I do know you're quite wealthy."*

I realize that not even money would have resulted in the lovely Celeste Brown thinking I was the catch that got away, but it's funny to think that Susie made it sound that way. (It wouldn't have worked out anyway. When it comes to women, I like mine a little more "Priscilla-like.")

CHAPTER 14

Off to College and into Newspapering

There was an unspoken expectation in our family that I would go to college, but the idea that I would study journalism and then teach it was entirely my idea.

It was also totally endorsed by the administration at my little high school. A couple of years ago a couple we know called to say they were having cocktails at a resort in Mexico and had run into a woman who claimed to be my first journalism teacher. I said, *"If it's Kathy Downing, she's right."* It was.

Mrs. Downing was the typing teacher who served as advisor to the student newspaper and really got behind the idea of me going into journalism education. Journalism was taught as part of the typing class and simultaneous with three other subjects in the same classroom: shorthand, stenography, and the use of calculators. There were only two journalism students and we were responsible for putting out the paper.

So the extent of my journalism experience when I started college was being editor of the *Kalitan*. But I apparently thought I was a stud because with nothing more to show for myself than this and the fact that I was enrolled in journalism classes at Lane Community College, I went right into the offices of the *Eugene Register-Guard* and got a job. It was a job in the circulation department, so I guess my "credentials" didn't have all that much to do with it. But still.

I Get Torched

Going to community college instead of the U of O my first year was probably just what I needed to make the transition from high school in the hinterlands to a big university. Lane had an excellent journalism teacher by the name of Larry Romine who taught the transfer courses *Journalism I and II* and was also advisor to the student paper, *The Torch*.

Romine's classes were responsible for producing the paper so it was on the staff of *The Torch* that I first cut my teeth in legitimate newspapering. I benefited not just from his journalism classes and writing for the paper, but also because he set up a paid summer internship for two students in his class at *The Springfield News* and I managed to secure one of them.

That's where I was when Neil Armstrong first set foot on the moon. The publisher, John Nelson, kept a small black and white television with rabbit ears in his office. He brought it out and sat it on the counter so everyone in the newsroom could watch the event as it happened. (It was pretty grainy, like it might be being faked in a sound studio in Phoenix, which I guess is what really happened. But that's another story.)

Anyway, the internship led to continuous employment at the *News* for the duration of my college years, which pretty much paid for my education.

Also, by taking the early reporting classes at LCC I was spared the ordeal of taking them from the notoriously demanding professor Warren C. Price at the U of O who might very likely have sent the likes of me packing.

I owe a lot to Larry Romine. And all praise to community colleges.

The Guard

The *Register-Guard* was a highly decorated daily newspaper with a circulation of more than 80,000 subscribers, which is a pretty good-sized paper. Its coverage area was immense, reaching all way from the Pacific Ocean 50 miles west of Eugene to the peak of the Cascade Mountains even farther to the east; it also covered an area more than 50 miles in length from north to south. It had an outstanding staff that included a Pulitzer Prize-winning art director. The *R-G's* sports writing and coverage were venerated all up and down the West Coast in particular.

My first job there—the one in Circulation—was to handle calls from people who hadn't gotten their papers. Every once in a while we'd get a "complaint" from U of O dorm boys with too much time on their hands. They'd ask us to write down names like *"Ben Dover"* and *"Pat Myaz."*

That job ended at 9 p.m., which was right when the action was picking up over in the sports department. I made it a habit to wander over there and get friendly with the high school sports editor, Paul Harvey III. By Christmas I had a job in Sports too.

In fact, on my office wall here above the desk I have mounted the first check I ever received for writing from the *R-G*, along with a copy of a basketball story headlined, *"Churchill Falls Big After Close First Half."* It's by-lined *"By*

Don Wilt for The Register-Guard." The check is dated Dec. 29th, 1966, the same year I graduated from high school.

I owe a huge debt of gratitude to Paul Harvey and the other sportswriters and editors who took me into their fold with so little to recommend me for the job.

Unfortunately, I wasn't able at first to count among them the long-time assistant sports editor, Pete Cornacchia.

Pete was late middle-aged by then. I'd been told to look him up because he'd lived in Marcola as a youth and, like me, graduated from Mohawk High School. His given name was Marcel. That's what people in Marcola called him. And they pronounced the last name *"Kuh-Nar-Chee."*

The family had dedicated some land there that was still being used as a summer day camp for girls. It had a sign over the gate that read *"Camp Kinarchy."*

One of his old high school friends would always tell me, *"If you ever run into Marcel Kinarchy down there at the paper tell him I said 'hi.'"* The same individual enjoyed telling me how Marcel, when he was in high school and just beginning to be interested in sports journalism, used to walk the sidelines of MHS football games calling the game into a stick he held in his hand like a microphone.

Well, as it turned out, these were not memories that he wished to relive with anyone, and certainly not with me. I couldn't have gotten off to a worse start with him if I'd tried. I sat down in a chair across from him at his desk one afternoon, extended my hand, and said, *"You must be Mr. Kinarchy."*

To which he acidly replied, *"It's pronounced 'Kor-Knock-Ee-Uh.' It's Italian."*

He later told me when we became more friendly that his parents had been first-generation immigrants. He said they'd been hurt when people "Americanized" their last name. He said his family had reminded him frequently that he was not to object to people pronouncing their name incorrectly, but that he was not to forget it either. I believe converting from Marcel to Pete was his own idea.

What I earned at the *R-G* jobs supplemented what I earned at *The Springfield News* and together they were sufficient to pay all my university expenses, which just weren't all that much at the time. I believe tuition was $127 a quarter term with typically no more than an additional $80 for books.

I went to cash my check from *The Springfield News* at a supermarket in Eugene once. The clerk said that she'd never heard of it. I said, *"It's a tri-weekly in Springfield."* She said, *"Oh. We have one here in town that tries daily."*

Over the next few chapters I'll fill you in on what my own "trying" amounted to in these years.

CHAPTER 15

Getting Paid for My Real Schooling

The Paper Chase

During my undergraduate years I operated very much in a mode where the object of going to college was less about learning than it was about satisfying the requirements for a diploma. Journalism school was more back-drop to the newspaper work I was already engaged in than preparation for it.

But because my ambition was to become a high school journalism teacher, I took a great interest in my journalism classes, if nothing else.

Instructors in the J-School were almost all good teachers; more importantly, they were also demonstrated professionals in their various fields, some of them come home from WWII. One had been prominent on Madison Avenue; others were accomplished reporters and editors.

Willis "Bill" Winter headed an advertising segment that sent scores of Oregon J-School students to the top of the profession. Two of them—Dan Weiden and David Kennedy—founded Weiden+Kennedy in Portland and grew it into one of the largest and most imaginative advertising agencies in the world. They're the ones who came up with the slogan *"Just Do It"* for Nike.

They still have the Nike account and Dan Weiden owns his own magnificent 60-acre mountain lake just a few miles from here so deep and blue it's known as "The Crater Lake of the Central Cascades."

Thanks a Lot, Bunky

I was making a pretty good living going to college. I had my own apartment in an old house off-campus and not one good job, but two—the one at the *Springfield News* and the other at the *Register-Guard*. The pay at the *R-G* was union scale at first; so-called "news trainees" like myself earned $4.50 an hour. That was a pretty handsome wage at the time, even if you were a head of household.

About my third year at the *Guard* a new boy by the name of Tony Baker (later to become publisher) came to work as a news trainee. His father happened to be the publisher, Alton "Bunky" Baker. When his son brought home his first paycheck, the elder Baker supposedly took one look at it and said something like, *"Holy cow! How much are we paying you down there?"* Shortly thereafter we all got reassigned from news trainees to "stringers" and our pay reduced by about a buck an hour.

I probably should have been paying them given how little I actually knew about sports writing. One thing I didn't know at first was that the Oregon State Beavers are also called "Aggies" because they were one of the original land-grant agricultural colleges. I found that out the first time someone called into the paper and asked, *"How'd the*

Aggies do?" I must have sounded like an Aggie myself when I didn't know what in the hell they were talking about.

Still, I guess I got with it quickly enough that before very long I was working more hours in the sports department than any other part-timer with the exception of the bald and bespectacled sports nut Jack Hall, a department institution. He worked at the *Guard* to supplement his income as a junior high school social studies teacher at Pleasant Hill Jr. High. He'd been around there a long time before I got there and was there for a long time after I was gone—one of the really great pals from my newspaper days.

Jack was the first person to ever give me any fatherly advice as concerns women. Respect when you're talking about them to others was very big with him. I could see he enjoyed an excellent relationship with his spouse, Nona, and found what he had to say worth listening to.

Bonanza 303

My main job in the sports department at first was to collect scores and stats from high school basketball games played around the state. Coaches were paid to report their scores, so by 11 p.m. we usually had heard from all of them. If we hadn't, we'd start calling around to see if we could get the results someplace else. The paper rarely went to bed without a score.

One night we were having trouble getting results from Bonanza, a little school in southern Oregon. When I couldn't reach the coach at home or at the school, I told Paul Harvey III the problem. He said, *"they must have won"* and told me to try calling the tavern.

Bingo! Or maybe I should say Bonanza! I got the score just in time to make the deadline. And I got it directly from the winning coach with a quote. He apologized profusely for forgetting to call. He said he'd gotten caught up in the excitement, which was evident in the background. There's a small town for you.

I remember this episode for another reason too: the phone numbers I was dialing in Bonanza were still only three digits at the time. To reach them you dialed the letters B and O (for Bonanza), then the number. I remember the number to the tavern was *Bonanza* 303. That would be a good hip name for the place today if it's still around.

Boy, I'll tell you; if you like to be where the happenin's happenin', the sports department around deadline would have been the place for you. The tension grew as the evening unfolded. Issues inevitably arose as stories were held up or you waited to hear back from an A.D. or coach somewhere. One night I saw an assistant sports editor kick a chair almost the entire length of the sports department out of frustration. And he was the golf writer!

We were a morning paper so all the writing, headlines and editing had to be done around midnight or 1:00 in the morning. If everything was on schedule, we'd have time to pore over proofs sent up from the composing room so we could take one last look at what we'd written before it went on the presses. This was the last chance to catch that misspelled headline or yank one of the two identical paragraphs the Linotype guys had accidentally produced and set into type.

The atmosphere was electric. It appealed to me, but it also intimidated me a little bit, particularly the need not to just write well but to write fast. As much as I learned in the job, I didn't pursue a newspaper career any further because I didn't think I had what it took in that department. I was probably wrong, but I'm glad I didn't go in that direction because newspapers pretty much died on my watch.

Out Where the Action Was

From here I worked my way up to covering, first, B-League basketball and baseball games in the smaller Lane County towns, then games at some of the bigger schools in Eugene and Springfield. My competition for assignments came mostly from other J-school stringers like myself. They were almost always "big city" kids who had it all over me when it came to knowing their way around both newspapers and athletics. One was the son of the head football coach at the University of Oregon; another one's mother was a well-known section editor at the *Journal* in Portland.

Obviously, I had a lot to learn to compete with these jocks, but I know I could spell better and had better manners than some of them.

After the circulation department closed at night, the phones would occasionally roll over to us in Sports with people complaining about not getting their papers. Because I'd worked in Circulation I knew they kept one "shorts" runner on the clock late into the evening and I was always glad to help these people get their papers.

But this one particularly surly jock-journalist I worked with was sitting there at a desk one evening with that day's *Guard* spread out in front of him. Pretty soon the phone on his desk rang. It was a man calling to say he didn't get his paper.

What the jock did was to put the phone on speaker, then noisily unfold the pages out before him before snarling at the caller, *"Okay, go ahead; whadja wanna know about?"*

Another one I worked with at *The Springfield News* got a call from a reader who complained that her daughter's tennis team had not received appropriate coverage after their big win. They only discussed it for about a minute before I heard him shout into the receiver, *"We're the News. We decide!"* before he slammed it down.

I once covered a three-day state championship wrestling tournament at Willamette High School, recording the scores of each match and working up a box score to appear in "agate" type in the next day's sports pages. Agate is the really tiny stuff they set box scores and death notices in.

Tournament results could run to pages and pages of copy because of the different weight classifications and the number of schools and wrestlers involved. I'd just finished typing up all the results and was getting ready to send them to the back shop for typesetting. There was another part-timer there that evening who had a reputation for doing dumb things. He rolled all the pages of copy paper up and put them into the pneumatic tube that was to whisk them to the composing room.

That was fine. What was not fine was that he forgot to put them in the plastic cylinder you were supposed to use for sending copy. Consequently the pages were instantly sucked into the tube and shredded like a roll of toilet paper. And, like a roll of toilet paper, they "clogged the pipe."

Fortunately we had carbon copies so we made the deadline, but the pneumatic tube had to be dismantled to get all that stuff out of there.

When Oregon's football team went to Shrevesport, Louisiana, for the Independence Bowl in 1983 I met up with the old sports department gang at some of the pre-game parties. I asked one of the regulars why they'd been so welcoming and helpful to me when I had so little to offer. He said, *"There was just never anyone like you who ever came through the place."*

I know he meant this in the nicest way and I was flattered. They liked me. They really liked me.

It might have helped that—as dumb as I was—there was that other, highly gullible fellow trainee who provided most of the amusement for the older hands. I came into the office one afternoon to find him crawling around under the desks trying to find the "crank" someone had told him you needed to start the electric radio so we could listen to the World Series.

Joe Frazier and the Fraternity of Journalism

I want to mention here someone I gained a great deal from knowing, but only for a short time. His name is Joe Frazier.

Joe was a successful young reporter in his own right and also the son of the legendary editorial page editor of the *R-G*, Bob Frazier. His dad was still working there at the time. I have a collection of his columns on my bookshelf, *"Bob Frazier of Oregon."*

Joe came into the department one night right after I started working in Sports. I was waiting for the phones to start ringing with basketball results. He knew from experience that I wouldn't be needed for a little while. He said, *"Come on, I'll show you around."*

He explained what happens in the newsroom, how the Teletype machines work, and so on. He took me over to the morgue—that's the newspaper's library—and showed me what you do when you need to retrieve something from it, like back issues.

Then down the stairs to the press room which was nearly a block long and contained the enormous two-story printing press. When it was running you couldn't hear a thing anyone else was saying. Joe pointed out that, for this very reason, the *R-G* employed deaf people to run the presses because they were conversant in sign language.

Then it was over to the composing room past these big pots of boiling lead. Every once in a while one of these pots would erupt a little bit, like a mud pot at Yellowstone. If you were anywhere near it those little droplets would hurt like hell when they landed on your skin.

One night, a well-known dufus I won't name here came in from the parking lot and shook off his raincoat right in front of the lead kettles. When the cold water hit those pots boiling lead went *everywhere*.

It was only funny later.

That's how they made up the newspaper then. Every story had to be converted into lead type by a Linotype operator. That's where the bubbling lead came in; it was used to make a casting of each letter typed and then inserted into a frame for reproduction after it cooled. After the paper was printed, the lead type would be melted down and used all over again the next day.

It's too complicated to go into here, but Joe gave me about as good an understanding of how a newspaper gets made as anyone could hope to get. He later became Latin America bureau chief for the Associated Press.

Some of the most enduring relationships of my life were forged on the newspapers—Don Mack and Ann Baker from the *Guard*, Bob Caldwell of the *Springfield News*, who later became editorial page editor of the Oregonian, where he won a Pulitzer; Fred Westerlund from the *Springfield News*, and Les Zaitz from the *McNary Piper* to name a few.

Newspapering is like logging—you create a lot of memorable experiences doing it. I always thought it was a great privilege to be part of a fraternity like this if only for a few years.

When I graduated right on schedule in 1970, the editor Paul Harvey III offered to write a letter of recommendation for my job search. It said I'd come into the department as a novice but was leaving as a dependable high school sportswriter.

That would have been almost pure hyperbole, but it was greatly appreciated on my part. He also said some nice things about my potential as a journalism teacher, which was even more greatly appreciated because that was my first ambition upon leaving school.

That part was actually true...thanks to people like him.

CHAPTER 16

That Girl

Who Did I Think I was?

The fact that I rode onto the campus of the University of Oregon in the fall of 1967 and managed to cut one swell little filly out of the herd was just about the best and most important thing that ever happened to this cowboy. If Priscilla goes before I do I'm going to feel like an old man I sat next to on an airplane once who told me his wife had just died. He said, *"We were married 52 years and it wasn't enough."*

I first laid eyes on Priscilla Claire Beistel when we were both ducking—to the extent we were allowed—the U of O's physical education requirement. We were in the "classroom" of legendary professional bowler and instructor Lou Bellisimo, an eight-lane bowling alley in the basement of the Erb Memorial Union. Taking his class would put us one credit closer to satisfying the six you needed to graduate and help us avoid some of the more rigorous P.E. offerings like swimming, soccer, rugby and basketball.

The class was divided into four groups of four. Lucky me, we were assigned to the same team. I'm not sure if that would have made any difference in the end; once I laid eyes on her I'm pretty sure I would have found some other way to get closer to that girl.

My old friend Ray Nash used to say that when he first saw his great love, Betty, in the lunch line at Concordia College, he knew immediately that he wanted to marry her. Then he would add, *"It never even occurred to me that someday I might actually want to talk to her."*

So it was sort of like that in my case too, although it became evident pretty quickly that this girl had a lot more going for her than looks. She was smart and on her way to really doing something with her life. And with a good sense of humor on top of it all.

I'd already picked up on her name, which she told the group was "Pris." That was a new one on me so she explained that it was short for "Priscilla."

After a few class sessions we were pretty friendly and did a lot of talking between our turns. I was all about making her laugh. I didn't have that many recognizable strengths to play to so I guess I thought funny was the way to go.

One of the things that she liked to talk about was the fact that I had yet to outscore her in any of the countless games we bowled as part of the class. And I never did. I never have. She turned out to be just as good at Ping Pong.

I'd already gotten a few of her vitals: she was a Eugene girl who grew up just a few blocks south of campus and graduated from South Eugene High School. Her family was well-known in Eugene where her dad and uncles all held prominent jobs.

Her Uncle Paul was the superintendent of parks for Lane County; Uncle Henry was a big man with the Eugene Water and Electric Board; and her dad was a top guy for one of the first big rural power cooperatives. I only recently learned that her Uncle Dean, before he died young, was a member of the "Willamette Valley Contenation of Hoo-Hoos." They were all somebodies in the timber industry. You can look it up.

I'd also learned she was majoring in elementary school education and was one year ahead of me.

Also, that she belonged to Gamma Phi Beta and lived at a sorority house on Hilyard Street. When it came to getting her <u>last</u> name, though, she tried to throw me off the scent by making up some cock-and-bull story about the name being *"Grumschwartz."*

"You know," she said, *"of the Grumschwartz and Grumschwartz Furniture Company? That's my dad."*

She didn't really sell it though. It was an attempt at humor that only endeared her to me even more—as if I needed any other reason to be enamored. Five-feet, two inches tall with the most astonishingly beautiful blue eyes. I can't see how any boy wouldn't have felt the same way.

How I extracted her phone number I don't remember, but I did. I wrote it in large black numbers on one of my Pee Chees with a Sharpie: 345-6306.

First Date Not a Date

The best way to describe how Pris looked at this age is to refer you to one of those glamorous photographs of Audrey Hepburn taken in Paris for *LIFE Magazine* in the 1960s. She liked to wear this cream colored, ribbed fisherman's sweater with a canoe collar and her hair was styled in what I guess you'd call a pixie cut with some kind of red highlighting. It went well with her pixie-ish sense of humor.

She also wore a Navy-blue pea coat with a matching beret sometimes. Very *au courant*. Look up "Cute Co-Ed. 1960s" in your Webster's sometime and see if it doesn't say "Priscilla Beistel at 20."

Let's just say that bowling became my favorite class even though it involved regular beat-downs by a cute girl in a beret I barely knew.

I really don't know who I thought I was, asking her out, since you would think we had nothing in common. In fact, the way she tells it I had *Hicksville* written all over me. This included carrying a brief case that my mother had gotten for me in the mistaken belief that that's what university students carried around their paperwork in. I was probably the only one of 15,000 students who actually did, and it wasn't for very long.

I'd be too embarrassed to tell you how long I'd been on campus before someone suggested I go to the library. I said, *"Where's that?"* Let's just say it wasn't the first week.

Oh, *Here's* Who I Thought I Was

It would have been easy for me to just decide that this girl was out of my league because there was no getting around the fact that she was. But I'll tell you something about growing up in a small town: it may have its shortcomings, but one of them is not the lack of opportunity to build your self-esteem. The Mohawk High School fight song says, *"High esteem we'll never lack,"* and apparently I didn't.

Pris may have been part of her society's aristocracy, but so was I where I came from. My dad was an educated man with big responsibilities as well. My older brother was valedictorian of his graduating class, my eldest sister salutatorian of hers; all of us held positions in student government. I'd lettered in football and was editor of the school paper, as dubious as that honor was. The fact was that I actually had it in my head that the way we lived was not _inferior_ to people in the big city, but _superior_. I guess you could say that I thought more of myself than I had any real right to.

Further complicating matters was that she already had a boyfriend in the army. She turned me down a couple of times before I finally persuaded her to go bowling with me at Empire Lanes off Highway 99 out in west Eugene one night. This would have been our first date, although I think she did not really regard it as such—more just a friend thing. A "Not-Date."

Just like in Lou Bellisimo's bowling class, she beat me again.

Basketball Stories

There probably wasn't a better college job to be found than working for the papers, but it had its problems; one was the difficulty of _dating_ when your every weekend night was occupied with putting out a morning newspaper. In both football and basketball seasons we'd work Friday and Saturday nights until about 2 o'clock in the morning, sometimes 3:00. I worked every weekend they needed me.

I solved the problem by inviting Priscilla along with me to the games I was assigned to cover for the paper. Jack Hall at the _R-G_ had shown me how sportswriters keep a running account of a game and I taught Pris how to do it.

You began by drawing a vertical line down the middle of a yellow legal pad. You'd then label one side with the name of the home team and the other side with the visitors'. Every time the score changed hands you'd immediately enter the home team's points on one side of the ledger and the visitors' on the other side adjacent to each other. Then—on the appropriate side of the paper—you'd briefly note the time and make a brief entry as to what occurred to affect the score.

You'd note the name or number of the player and a brief reference to the play—"FG" for field goal, "FT" for free throw and so on. The code continued with "AST" for an assist, "RB" for rebound, etc. There was no such thing as a three-point basket then.

Later you could glance at the summary and instantly see how the score changed as the game proceeded and what the big plays or turning points had been. For example you could quickly see if a team went on a run, exactly when it started and ended, and how many points they put up in that period.

Things like that became candidates for your "lede" paragraph. It's the first thing you have to come up with when you write a news story. Very important to have this already taking shape in your mind as you sit down to write on deadline.

The summary would also allow you to quickly tally the top scorers and defenders for each team, how many times the score changed hands, when a key player may have fouled out and the other facts that make up a story.

As soon as the game was over, we'd hop in my '56 Chevy and speed back to the Gamma Phi Beta house to drop Pris off. Then I'd head back to the *R-G* just a few blocks over. By the time I got to the office I'd already have a pretty good idea of what I intended to write. All I needed was to pull the key facts from her running account of the game. This allowed me to add details like this:

"With just 10 seconds remaining on the clock and down by one, Harrisburg coach Al Rollins called time out and quickly drew up a plan to get the ball to senior center Andy Nelson. It turned out to be a good one as the six-foot, two-inch Nelson took the ball on a running bounce pass from point guard Eddy Sorenson and chucked in a floater with his left hand from the top of the key to seal it for the Eagles 62-61 as time expired."

If only. My stuff at the time was really much more prosaic than this. In fact, our style was proscribed by the *R-G's* requirement that every story include five facts in the lede: the score, who was playing, when the game took place, where it was played, and what sport it was. I wish they would hew to this today—sometimes I don't know whether I'm reading about women's basketball or men's until the third or fourth paragraph down. I have to read until they use a pronoun.

Not-Dates and Deadlines

I got my first lesson on how inviolable a newspaper deadline is one night when I was just a keystroke or two away from finishing my story. Paul Harvey III came by the desk and ripped the paper right out of my typewriter. *"Times up,"* he said, without even looking back. Yanking the paper out like that created a "zing" sound that hung in the air for several seconds after he was gone.

If I hadn't had my future wife's help in preparing to write the story, I might not have made those deadlines and probably would have fallen out of my chosen career before it ever got started.

I think these early "Not-Dates" with Pris gave me a chance to impress her as a possible life-mate. Sometimes I flatter myself by thinking what she might have been saying back at the sorority about this boy she kept going out on Not-Dates with: *"Oh, he's in J-School. He's a sportswriter for the Register- Guard, and also a reporter at the Springfield News. He just had a front page story on Bobby Kennedy,"* she might have said. *"But he's not my boyfriend."*

Or, I don't know, maybe she just said, *"A funny dork from my bowling class."*

Whatever it was, it was exciting and I happily dumped my friend Mike to start doing more things with Pris. He and I went way back and had been inseparable for a long time. He told me many years later that all I could talk about was <u>that</u> girl and that I started spending all my time doing things with her instead of him.

Yeah, I can see that now. But what was I supposed to do?

Besides, I made up for it later when I lined him up with another cute girl I'd met at the first Taco Bell restaurant in Eugene. She was a dead ringer for Sally Fields in her role as the Flying Nun, and you gotta admit, Sally Fields made a pretty cute nun! This time things worked out better and they ended up married.

CHAPTER 17

"Grab Her Quick"

Winter turned into spring and Pris and I were still hanging out. We added new activities like borrowing my dad's pickup to go spotlighting deer in the hills above Marcola and driving over to the coast to climb the sand dunes in the moonlight before heading back to Eugene, sometimes as late as 2:00 or 3:00 in the morning. Once, she got locked out of her sorority house because we came back too late.

I was still playing the funny angle as the way to her heart. That usually took the form of re-telling the entire contents of recently-released albums by comedians like Bill Cosby, Bob Newhart or Richard Pryor. Sometimes I gave them credit and sometimes I claimed the stories for my own.

We almost always ended up at Bob's 19-Cent Hamburgers on Coburg Road where I'd go in and order cheeseburgers while she waited in the Bel-Air. I noticed when I looked around that when it came to other couples at the drive-in, it was usually the <u>girl</u> who went up to get the food, or they did it together. Pris made it clear from the beginning that if I was expecting to have a life with her, it would be one of servitude. But I wasn't complaining.

We enjoyed taking my sister's little girl and boy, Marcy and Reese, on some of our outings. They were about 4 and 2 at the time and clearly saw us as a couple even if that wasn't what we officially were. They always used one word—"UncleDonnyandPris"—when they referenced either one of us and I think they still might.

By the next summer I took it as a given when Pris needed a date for the sorority's annual dinner dance and invited me. It was a luau that year. I was more surprised to learn that they were calling the event "Kamonawona" and Pris said some of the girls were adding "laya" at the end, making it "Kamonawonalaya."

I just came across the picture of us sitting for the photographer "Indian-style" in beach shirts and shorts with the "Kamonawona" banner hanging above us. I remember thinking at the time that it could very well have been a thought balloon coming out my head, but I kept that to myself.

Sometime in here I took Pris by the Cascade Gardens nursery to show her off to my beloved old boss Bob Prickett. While she was off looking at something in his nice gift shop, Bob pinched my bicep and said, *"Grab her quick before she gets away!"* I didn't need his affirmation to know that I was on to a good thing, but it was nice to have someone I admired so much say it just the same.

How we moved from "No-mance" to "Ro-mance" and ended up getting married still baffles me a little bit. I would describe it as more evolutionary than precipitate. But somehow that's what happened.

On August 23rd, 1969, we took our vows at the United Methodist Church on Olive Street in Eugene and started our life together in a cute little white 1940's bungalow at

850 W. 8th Avenue in Eugene. I had gotten on to the house when one of my co-workers at the service station where I worked during the summer vacated it. We ended up renting the place for $110 a month from a nice old man who lived next door named Bart Plunkett.

Pris had just graduated in education and was about to start her first teaching job at Lowell, a small town near Lookout Reservoir on the Willamette River southeast of Eugene. I was 20 years old and still a senior in college. It had been just a few weeks shy of two years since I first laid eyes on <u>that</u> girl and now we had the same last name.

I had no way of knowing, even then, that Pris would turn out to be just about as good a wife and mother and life partner as a person can be, so in that respect I either got immensely lucky or I have that certain gene that tells a person, *"this is the one."*

There's an old character in a book we both like who says, *"I had two wives in my lifetime and both of them was a danged marvel."*

I've only had this one, but I can tell you that she, too, is a danged marvel.

CHAPTER 18

Newspaper Stories

The Night Life Ain't No Good Life, But it was My Life

Because I was working at the *Register-Guard* until the paper was put to bed on weekend nights, just about the only opportunity I had for social engagement was going out with some of the guys from the paper to one of the two Chinese joints in Eugene that stayed open until 4:00 in the morning. Either that or go over to a place called Lil' Sambo's with my pal from the paper, Jack Hall. It's where he introduced me to something I'd never had before, an *omelet*.

Lil' Sambo's name derived from a popular children's book called Little Black Sambo that had been around for 50 years or so, but the racial overtones forced it to begin experimenting with alternative names. In Eugene, as I recall, they first removed the "Lil'" to make it just "Sambo's" and painted over the images of the little dark-skinned hero of the story.

It wasn't too long after that that the chain went out of business altogether and that part of my social life went bye-bye too.

A Plane Goes Down and 25 Years Later I Learn Why

It seems like some of the things I've experienced had a "Forrest Gump" quality to them. I wasn't really involved in certain events, but just happened to be there when whatever happened was happening. Let me tell you about one.

By the beginning of my freshman year in college I'd started the job in Circulation at the *R-G* but all I knew about the newsroom was what I could see from the other side of the floor. However, I was becoming familiar enough with the place to be comfortable wandering around over there once in a while.

On the evening of Oct. 1, 1966, I was taking a break over that way when all the wire service teletype machines began ringing. The high school sports editor, Paul Harvey III, came over to the Teletypewriters to see what was going on. He's the one who informed me that the maiden flight of jet service out of Eugene's Mahlon-Sweet Airport had just crashed on its way to Portland.

West Coast Airlines Flight 956 was a Douglas DC-9 with 13 passengers and five crew members aboard. It departed Eugene at 7:52 p.m. and was on the ground in the Cascade Mountains east of town by 8:09. Nobody survived.

I went back to my job in Circulation so I can't relate any heroic actions on my part, like pulling on my Jimmy Olson hat and rushing to the scene of the accident. As I said, I was just sort of passing by when it all happened. The reporters and editors on duty must have really been scrambling to cover the story but I wouldn't have known about it. I did not then—and do not now—have a *"Nose for News."*

Oddly, 25 years later, when I was working in the aerospace industry, I learned quite a lot about what must have happened that night. It would have been categorized as a "CFIT" accident—"Controlled Flight into Terrain," the number one cause of aircraft fatalities in the world. I know this now because it was my company that invented the radar system that eliminated that category of accidents on airplanes so equipped. I interviewed the aeronautical electrical engineer who invented it, Don Bateman. Very humble. Not an easy interview.

Assigned to Cover Bobby Kennedy

Before my years with *The Springfield News* were over, I'd written any number of feature stories. One was on my own older brother, Dennis, when he came home from serving with the Peace Corps in Africa. Another one on Bill Llewellyn, the new superintendent of schools in Springfield, would lead to an excellent job offer as the district's communications coordinator a few years later.

But in the spring of my sophomore year, a story came along that topped them all and turned out to be about as big as anything I'd ever accomplish in real newspapering. The assignment was to cover a portion of Robert F. Kennedy's presidential primary campaign swing through Oregon in 1968.

I had met the girl I'd eventually marry right after I started attending the University of Oregon the previous fall and by this time we were seeing a lot of each other. I was crazy about her, and we were both crazy about Bobby Kennedy.

We had waited until 2 or 3 o'clock in the morning to see him disembark from his plane at the Eugene airport just a couple of weeks before I covered him. He came and went from the area more than once during the primary campaign, which shows you how critical the state was to his chances.

The first time Pris and I saw RFK he was just coming back from a float trip on the Colorado River. He was tanned and his hair was sun-bleached. He was wearing a powder-blue sports jacket that fit him beautifully and a white dress shirt open at the collar. He looked stunning—more stunning than a *Kardashian*. The real thing.

It had been drizzling all night, but when Kennedy stepped to the door of his airplane it was as if someone had turned a spotlight on him and only him. (Or imagine one of those black and white photos in which only one person has been colorized.)

We have a picture taken by Wayne Eastburn of the *Register-Guard* from that night. I saw it in the developing tray the next day in the darkroom at the *R-G* and he printed a copy for me. It shows the candidate walking along a low chain link fence chatting and shaking hands like they do.

Look closely in the lower right quadrant of the photo. You'll see a young feminine hand being extended toward the candidate inside the cuff of a distinctive light brown raincoat with pink and dark brown polka dots. That is my future wife's hand. Boy, she was really cute in that raincoat. I'm surprised Kennedy didn't stop and kiss her. That's what I would have done.

Looking back, it sounds a little like a Beatles Moment. I suppose it was. There were several thousand people there doing the same thing. I wasn't working, so I wasn't really worrying about any objectivity issues. So like I say, we swooned along with everyone else.

It was partly out of this idolatry for the younger brother of President Kennedy that I came to snag the assignment to cover him. I'd learned that part of RFK's visit would include a tour of logging operations on Weyerhaeuser Company timberlands in the Mohawk Valley.

John Nelson was the publisher of *The Springfield News*. I persuaded him that I was the logical reporter for the assignment because of my familiarity with the area—I mean, you had to drive right through my hometown to get there.

He said okay and told me to bring the story directly to him.

Bob (If I can Call You Bob), Who's Your Running Mate Going to Be?

To my credit, I did somewhat grasp the significance of an assignment like this, and by way of preparation went past the J- School to visit with a couple of my professors about it. One of them recommended that I ask Kennedy who his running mate was going to be if he got the nomination.

In the end I didn't ask him that question. I thought it was impertinent. I figured Robert F. Kennedy would not be choosing a part-time reporter for a little newspaper in Springfield, Oregon, to break this news to the world.

Running With the Camels

An element of covering RFK that I'd somewhat anticipated, since I'd seen it at the airport a few nights before, was the animalistic behavior of the national media that accompanies a presidential candidate. They came from news outlets all over the world: big papers like the *New York Times* and *Washington Post;* the "Big Three" of network television— NBC, ABC, CBS; and *Reuters.* No CNN at that time.

They were really aggressive, particularly the network cameramen. Most of us weren't yet familiar with the term "paparazzi," but that's what their behavior most resembled— very pushy, even provocative.

The size and bulk of their equipment made them seem even more formidable. The cameras all had these enormous dual-magazine film canisters mounted on top, and the cameramen carried the whole apparatus on their shoulders. They looked like a herd of camels lumbering down this muddy logging road after the candidate.

It had rained the night before and those logging roads can go all to hell. At one point, one of the leaders of the pack took a face plant. His camera and everything crashed right down into the mud and he was completely splayed out there on the ground feeling for his glasses.

Some of these beasts streamed right past and over him. It was like the *Running of the Camels.* Welcome to big-time news coverage. As the morning progressed, I got muscled out of position a couple of times but otherwise held my own pretty well against the horde.

I Said Get Down, Whoever's Dog You Are

The *Register-Guard's* story about the event was written by the popular columnist Don Bishoff. He was one of their best and most experienced writers.

You can see the gap between my story and his in details like this: in my account I reported that, *"Muddy paw prints appeared on the front of the senator's navy blue suit as someone's sad-eyed cocker spaniel appealed to the New York senator for attention despite his calm order for the dog to 'Get down, boy, get down'."*

My more talented and experienced competitor wrote pretty much the same thing except that his story mentioned that the animal I'd referred to as *"someone's sad-eyed cocker spaniel"* was actually the senator's own dog, *Freckles.* (I think it might also have been a Springer.)

Still, the story came out all right and John Nelson made it better with some last-minute edits before we went to press. The story appeared with my byline on the front page of the paper under the headline *"Kennedy in Whirlwind Visit to Springfield."*

I sometimes tend to remember only the things I wish had gone better in my work. There must have been enough of them in this instance that I didn't even save a copy of the Kennedy story at the time. But when my childhood friend, Kathie, sent me the April 17, 1968, copy of *the Springfield News* a while back I was pleasantly surprised to see that it actually held up pretty well.

It becomes plain as you read the story that I'd obviously held my own and was close enough to both pick up and—this is very important—write down some of Kennedy's best quotes from the day. When the senator asked how much timber the company takes off their land each year, the Weyerhaeuser representative told him it was about 150 million board feet.

It says in my story that Kennedy quipped, *"How many Time magazines is that?"* Later someone explained to Kennedy that loggers have a lot of respect for the person who climbs the spar pole trees to cut off the tops. Kennedy asked, *"If I do it, will I win the primary?"*

For the Reader, a Cringe-worthy Moment

The well-known writer and columnist Bob Welch counseled us in his work shop on memoir-writing that when it comes to personal narratives, what people really want to hear can sometimes be the things you'd least like to talk about. So if that's what you want, here's one for you.

At one point in my conversation with Kennedy I found myself volunteering that this would be my first vote in a presidential election and that he would get it. He thanked me. I tossed it off like, *"for what it's worth, you've got my vote."* But I said it just the same.

Aside from the total disregard for even a semblance of objectivity, there was another little problem with this; namely, it wasn't true. I wouldn't have been casting my vote for him or anyone else. I'd just turned 20 two days before; you had to be 21 to vote.

What to say here? What I did appears reprehensible, of course; I felt terrible about it for a long time. But in fact, my true motivation had been only to buck the guy up. Things hadn't been looking that good for Kennedy that spring and he did eventually lose the Oregon primary by a whisker to Senator Gene McCarthy. I thought he looked a little down, like when someone is doing something out of a sense of obligation rather than because they want to.

My humanitarian impulses must have overwhelmed whatever nascent journalistic principles were there. Some time back I decided to remember my misdeed as the little white lie it was intended to be and stop feeling guilty about it. Now I can just feel dumb and unprofessional.

Happy now?

How You Speak Oregon

One of my more vivid and personal memories of the morning with RFK occurred on the crew bus after everyone else in our group had gotten off at the landing. They were outside milling around, waiting for Kennedy to get out to make his speech.

I lingered on the bus and watched while Kennedy and his small entourage moved to the back of the crummy. They gathered around him and together helped him practice how to correctly pronounce the word "Oregon." He would say in his Massachusetts accent *"Orry-Gone."* They'd all say, *"No. No. Orey-Gun!"* Then Kennedy would say "<u>Orry-Gone</u>" again and the chorus would all shout "OREY-<u>GUN</u>!"

I don't remember how Kennedy pronounced the name of our state after he got out there, but I do remember that the term "to stump for office" was not just a metaphor that day. Kennedy scrambled up onto a big Douglas fir stump and talked for about 20 minutes to the choker setters and truck drivers and others who get involved in a big logging operation like that.

The audience may have been a little heavy on management, because anybody with any pull in the company had probably found a reason to be in that neck of the woods that morning to get a glimpse of a possible future president, or at least the brother of a former, sainted one.

You Want Some Charisma with That?

I've done enough reading about RFK in the years since to know he had a lot of sharp edges about him, but these weren't on display that day. I think pretty much everybody found him to be worthy of the public's veneration. And Kennedy really was venerated; at the 1964 Democratic Nominating Convention in Atlanta he'd received a 22-minute standing ovation just for appearing at the podium.

At the same time he seemed to be a completely different kind of politician than you generally see today. He certainly didn't appear to be testing the wind before he said what he had to say.

I suppose he could have been talking to a national audience instead of the people in front of him, but it didn't come off that way. I think most of the people who heard him up there on that stump left feeling he was a pretty square-shooter.

According to my account in the paper, *"Kennedy drew applause with his declaration that no one should be denied his rights because of the color of their skin,"* and to his references about the war in Vietnam and the search for peace.

> *"In the last analysis, we have to say to the South Vietnamese that they have to win this war,"* he said. *"The deep-seated corruption and the long delay of the South Vietnamese in drafting their own 18-year-olds for service ought not to be acceptable to us."*

I can also confirm that the legendary Kennedy charisma is a thing; it was palpable and everyone—the logging crew and the media alike—had a hard time resisting it.

In the end, I didn't include in my story the part about watching him practice how to pronounce "Oregon." It didn't seem appropriate. That was a reasonable enough view for a small-town newspaper to take at the time, if not very progressive.

But Hunter S. Thompson wouldn't have left it out. And Don Bishoff might not have either—if he'd been lucky enough to hear it. He might even have made it his lede.

Lucky for me, he didn't; otherwise his story would have been even that much better than my own.

In Which I Single-Handedly Bring Justice to the Newspaper Frontier

Right after we launched my section *"Teen Scene"* in *The Springfield News*, the much larger *Eugene Register-Guard* introduced a new section for young people. They called theirs *"Teen Scene"* too.

I was in the newsroom of the *R-G* a few days later so I went by the news desk and informed Don Bishoff—then the city editor—that they were using a name already taken. I showed him a dated copy of *The Springfield News* to prove it.

He looked up and deadpanned, *"Well, can't you just change yours?"*

Read Those Headlines Closely

Between J-School and working at the papers, I learned to write a good headline. A few years later I met one of the more memorable characters from my newspaper days who had turned it into a fine art.

His name was Conrad Prange. He worked as a writer and editor for the *Oregon Statesman* in Salem. He was a long-timer there and just so damned likable that he never feared for his job. Thus, he wasn't afraid of getting caught at a little game he played when he was working nights on the copy desk.

The way it worked was that he would write double *entendrees* into his headlines and then award himself 10 points to start. He would then deduct one point for each complaint the paper received. It was just a little game he played to amuse himself and the handful of people who *"got it."*

Of his many, I had two favorites. The first was *"Teen Pregnancies a Mounting Problem in State."* The other appeared in the *Statesman* after a man was arrested for going around the Meir & Frank Department store with a cane that had a small mirror attached to it. He used it to look up women's dresses.

Conrad's headline on that story read, *"Man Arrested for Possession of Rear View Mirror."*

The 49 Photos I <u>Didn't</u> Take
of Bobby Kennedy

One of the great "tragi-com-dramatic" events of my life occurred the day I spent with Robert F. Kennedy. Up until the time I started working there, the *Springfield News* had a staff photographer. But with the common adoption of the new, supposedly easy-to-use 35 millimeter cameras, small papers like ours began to require that reporters take their own pictures.

To tell you the truth, these new cameras weren't all that easy to use. What <u>was</u> easy, was to muff it and come back from an assignment with no pictures—or at least that's what I could see happening for any number of reasons: Wrong exposure. Wrong F-stop. Forgetting to take the cap off the lens. Any of those will do it.

My greatest concern on the RFK assignment was that I wouldn't be able to replace the film in the camera without exposing it to sunlight. In my opinion, Nikon had made this harder than it needed to be.

Out of an abundance of caution, our darkroom attendant—a tall, *Doonesbury*-looking guy named Larry—eliminated the need for me to change the film at all by rolling what he called a "fatty." A film canister would usually contain enough film for 36 exposures at the most. He made this one more like 50. I left his darkroom with no worries. Who needs more than 50 pictures, right?

Well, here's what happened. As we were walking

up to the log landing with Kennedy, I snapped my first photo. It showed the former attorney general and his hunting dog alone with just the muddy logging road laid out in front of them.

It was a good shot and similar to an iconic image of RFK taken by professional photographer Burton Berinsky somewhere around Baker City a month later. We've had his picture hanging in our main hallway for decades.

But my picture was the only one I got before everything went to hell. When I went to advance the film it wouldn't "go." I knew I should stop and try to figure out a solution to the dilemma, but at the same time I worried that I'd fall behind the media entourage. Out of impatience, I forced the lever to advance the film and that was that—the film ripped in-half inside the camera. I never got another picture that day.

Our coverage included some excellent pictures of Kennedy at various events around the area—two on the front page and four more on the jump page—only one of them mine, for obvious reasons. I knew after that that I was going to have to get much more comfortable with the Nikon.

The Story of the Local Publisher and the Dead Fisherman

There's a story that says a lot about the publisher, John Nelson. When I was about 19 and in my early days at *The Springfield News,* I was the only reporter in the newsroom one Friday afternoon. Everyone else had left for lunch. The paper had been put to bed but the presses weren't yet rolling.

Suddenly John comes bursting in through the front door and says, *"There's a police helicopter flying up and down the river. Call the sheriff's department and find out what's going on!"*

I got hold of the Lane County Sheriff's Department right away. They told me that a body had been sighted floating in the nearby Willamette River. John said to me, *"Call the photographer and get out there! I'll go hold the presses."*

So I got hold of the photog and started getting ready to roll when John suddenly reappeared in the doorway between the newsroom and the back shop.

He was a tall, heavily-built guy about 65 with a grey buzz cut and wire-rim glasses. He usually wore a short-sleeved white dress shirt, probably from J.C. Penney, with a tie held in place with a Rotary Club tie bar. People used to say that as far as John Nelson was concerned, *"If it didn't happen in Springfield, it didn't happen."*

Anyway, he puts his hands on either side of the door, sort of leans into the newsroom and says, *"Now that I'm thinking about it, by the time they fish that guy out of the river he's gonna be all the way down to Harrisburg. Let's just put something in the police log on Monday."*

The poor dead fisherman's final indignity was that he had floated out of our coverage area.

John and Ina and Jack

Being part of the media horde covering one of the great political figures of our time was one of the more memorable adventures of my life.

For Bobby Kennedy, it was on to the next election where just a few weeks later he took the big prize in the '68 primaries—California, making him a good bet to be the next president of the U.S. That same night he was gunned down by a twisted Palestinian-American named Sirhan Sirhan in the kitchen of the Ambassador hotel in Los Angeles at only 48 years of age.

I was living in LA when they tore the Ambassador down to make room for a new high school. A portion of the building was preserved within the new structure to commemorate its place in history.

I have *The Springfield News* and its publishers—first John and Ida Nelson and then their son, Jack—to thank for this brush with history, and quite a lot more. Because of them I became knowledgeable enough about how to put together a newspaper that they entrusted me with creating a monthly section for young adult readers.

I would handle every phase of production from writing the stories and taking the pictures to working out the headlines, laying out the pages and pasting them up for printing. Sometimes Pris—my "not-quite-girlfriend"—would come in with me at night and help with the paste-up.

My journalism "education" went so far as helping—along with the publishers and everyone else—to wrap bundles as papers came off the press. My youthful arrogance led me to resent this last duty as somehow "beneath" me.

I don't see it that way now. This end-to-end view of the publishing process would prove invaluable when I went out to teach journalism and even later when I was managing publishing contracts for the various big organizations I worked for.

CHAPTER 19

What I Didn't Do in the War

The backdrop to my college years was the Vietnam War and the attendant protest movement. Eugene, like Berkeley, was a hotbed for every form of antiwar protest and social activism. This included classroom takeovers, university buildings being occupied and blown up, and the Black Panthers taking potshots at the Eugene Police in their patrol cars.

This had all gotten totally out of hand as far as I was concerned. At my brother-in-law's graduation from the University of Oregon Law School in June, 1969, acting president Charles Johnson was attempting to address the gathering in Autzen Stadium. Suddenly a well-known black activist by the name of Ray Eaglin came onto the stage and insisted on taking over the microphone.

This was just one of a long series of clashes with protestors that Johnson had endured in his interim role. People had also taken over the administration building to conduct sit-ins and camped out on the lawn of his home.

Johnson was a genteel academician from the ranchlands of Wyoming, unaccustomed to this kind of confrontation.

It came out later in a book titled, appropriately enough, *"Confrontation"* by U of O journalism professor Ken Metzler, that Johnson had been despondent for months and felt trapped in an unmanageable situation.

When he conceded to let Eaglin make an unscheduled speech on racism at the commencement, it looked to many like Johnson had turned the asylum over to the inmates. Criticism rained down on him.

One morning two days later Johnson got into his 1965 Volkswagen Beetle and drove east toward the Cascade Mountains on the McKenzie Highway. Somewhere around the town of Nimrod he swerved the Bug into the opposing lane and into the path of a loaded log truck weighing over 36 tons, killing him instantly.

Even though this kind of mayhem was happening all around me, I didn't pay much attention to it, or to the war itself for that matter.

The Eugene Hotel was situated just one block over from the *Register-Guard* offices in Eugene. The hotel had installed a Times Square-like electronic message board on top of the hotel which broadcast news headlines, sports results and stock market updates in large illuminated letters that raced around the four sides of the hotel's finial.

Coming and going from the paper I could look up and see the day's headlines. Many of them pertained to the war. It reminded me daily that a war was going on and made me glad that I wasn't in it, but I didn't give it too much more thought than that.

Then, sometime in 1968, my friend Jim Sellers and I both got notices to report for our U.S. Army induction physicals. We drove to Portland together where we stayed at the YMCA. Years later I read an autobiography by a man from the Southern Oregon coast who said his semi-literate neighbor had done the same thing, only he had referred to it as the "UMCA Hotel," which he'd mistaken for the word "Umpqua" like the river where he was from.

In any event, Jim and I both came back classified as available for military service but not under present conditions. They said they'd call us if something changed. We stopped at an Elmer's Pancake House in Salem on the way back and celebrated our good fortune with a fried chicken dinner.

I probably shouldn't tell this story, but the timing was so exquisite that I have to give someone who shall go unnamed credit for that. We were talking about what happened to us in that period. When I told him that I was classified a "1-Y," he gave it the mandatory three beats before he said, *"That's the one where you're gay, right?"*

Vietnam was the first time a lottery had been used to determine the call to military service since 1942. Every male between the ages of 19 and 26 was subject to the draft, so we all had a stake in the lottery.

For those of us who were born on April 15th, the number chosen was 273.

There were several different drawings held as part of the lottery, two of which either hit right on or went past that number all the way up to 305. So I, no doubt, would have been drafted if not for an unfavorable physical exam.

My deferral from the military was not a total surprise. The summer I got out of high school I'd been thrilled to land a good-paying job on the green chain at Weyerhaeuser to earn money for college. It was a physically demanding job that required a full physical examination. I was allowed to begin working before the results came back.

One day the company physician came out to the chain and asked me to accompany him over to the medical department. He informed me that X-rays from my physical exam showed I had a condition called Spondylolisthesis. That's where one vertebra in your spine slides forward over the bone below it. In my case it was the tail bone.

This was apparently caused by a blow I'd taken sometime earlier in my life. It probably happened in high school football, although there was also the time I ran to jump into a rubber raft floating in shallow water and landed on my back right on top of a rock. Could have been that he said.

I was crying the blues to the company physician about how disappointed I was to lose the income. I told him I was counting on it for college tuition. Poor me. He told me, *"Look on the bright side. It'll keep you out of the Army."* And darned if it didn't. So that's as close as I came to serving in uniform.

The Weyerhaeuser doc said I should avoid activities like diving or jobs that required me to do a lot of lifting or swinging my arms. I've done a lot of things that required those kinds of motions over the years so I'm sure I could have served in Vietnam as well as anybody else. For that I do feel remorse.

In retirement I was the go-to guy for the local Band of Brothers for a while. I helped them when they needed write-ups in the paper for their various good works and fund-raising activities.

Some of these guys came home from Vietnam with battleground experience, but mostly they reflect the fact that the majority of people who go to war wind up working in kitchens and offices or performing other mundane activities far from the front. I had a good friend at work who pounded a typewriter over there for a couple of years and another one who was on the staff of the military newspaper, *Stars and Stripes*.

Most likely this would have been my experience too. I've always been grateful I didn't have to find out for myself because I never met anyone who had anything very good to say about going to Vietnam.

A sense of having somehow failed to perform one's duty does nag at a lot of us who didn't go to Vietnam. As it was, I may have been the only *pro-war* student roaming the campus at that time. I supported what the U.S. was trying to do there as I understood it and I didn't think it helped anything that all these people back home were strengthening North Vietnam's hand by giving them hope that people in our own country would make us go away, which is what eventually happened.

I've read enough history since then to know that this is the way it always goes. As far back as the Revolutionary and Indian Wars, sympathizers made it difficult to prosecute the war and heartened the enemy. Of course it didn't help that the Vietnam war itself was not well-managed.

In any event, I guess my opinion shouldn't count for very much when it comes to Vietnam as I had virtually nothing to do with it one way or the other.

*Albert Wilt in front of cabin he built on his donation land claim
in Siletz River Canyon of Oregon. This is where, from his bed,
he shot and killed a cougar trying to claw through roof. He later
lamented, "You could have knocked."*

In this picture of the Kiger Island farmstead, Albert and Alma Wilt look out over their rich, river-bottom farmland from the front porch of the newly-completed house Albert ordered from Sears-Roebuck. Woman at right might be one of Alma's friends from Wisconsin. Circa 1915.

My Uncle Neal Wilt as a U.S. Navy Seabee on Guam at the end of WWII. The island was supposedly pacified when he and some others went out to hunt deer. They came upon a Japanese campfire with a cup of tea, still warm. These were Japanese soldiers who hadn't yet learned the war was over and were probably watching from concealed caves. They left them there for someone better equipped to deal with the situation.

Don Wilt

Here we are, all 26 members of the largest first grade class
in Marcola history. That's dear old Mrs. Pierson; she looked
a little like Eleanor Roosevelt and was just as kind-hearted.
That's me holding the sign. I emerged as the kind of person who
should hold the sign quite early. My first "boy" friend, Eddie,
far upper right, was not happy about it. He wanted to do it
but was too shy to ask. I apparently was not. He only told
me this six decades later.

This picture of my family (absent my older brother Dennis for some reason) was taken beside the first house my parents owned in Marcola on Murdoch Lane. The occasion could be Easter as my grandparents have come all dressed up from Portland. From left, my mother holding me, Susie, Grandpa Gordon Poole, Cherry, Grandma Ethel Poole, her son (my uncle) Ned and his first wife, Barbara. My dad, Bill Wilt, is standing on the end because that's where he always stood when he was taking the photo and had to get back in-frame before the shutter went off.

The manse on Main Street where the Wilts took up residence in 1950 when I was 2. This would have been in the big snow of 1964. That's our beloved labrador, Abner, at right. Dad trained him to retrieve ducks using his decoys. On their first outing, Abner retrieved all the decoys Dad had set out before the sun came up. No decoys, no ducks.

My brother Dennis in Micronesia with U.S. VISTA after serving in President Kennedy's Peace Corps in Africa. He was excellent role model for me as a youngster. When I was a freshman in college he wrote me a check to help with expenses, purposely leaving the amount blank. This little lapse in judgment set him back almost $70. I call him the family's "Wriggler in Chief" because he keeps his nose pointed upstream and his tail a' wrigglin'.

　　　　　　Don Wilt

*My friend Eddie Head's dad, Sherm,
always had a neat car. Here we are washing his
1958 yellow and black Dodge Coronet at their house in
Marcola around age 13. Behind me on left is the 1949 "Jimmy."
Just visible is the tiny gravel-floor garage where Sherm
conducted mechanics classes for us on a regular basis.*

My high school and lifelong pal Mike Gambill standing between "Big Otis," my 1951 Pontiac, on right, and the 1956 Chevrolet Bel-Air I drove through college. Mike's on crutches here because he was working his part-time job at Chase Gardens when he fell through the roof of a glass greenhouse. It took more than 250 stitches to suture his wounds, 1967.

*Mohawk High School at Marcola, Oregon,
before it was destroyed by arsonist.
This picture was taken by journalism
mentor Wayne Warner around 1960.
He and I both worked on the
Kalitan newspaper here.*

*A typical load of Douglas fir logs passing daily through
my hometown on railroad built by Uncle Stanley Wilt's
construction company, circa 1965.*

Don Wilt

Wigwam burners like this were used at sawmills to deal with wood waste. Today logging and milling refuse is used for biofuel and no longer considered "waste."

Brother Darcy with cougar tracked by hounds.
He felt he should have been born in an earlier time
as he thought of himself as a mountain man and
liked the moniker, "The Wild Man of Marcola."

With my birthday twin, Kathie Kintzley,
high school graduation 1966

*Senator Robert F. Kennedy and his dog Freckles
in the Mohawk Valley, Oregon. This is only picture
I got of RFK the day I covered his presidential primary
campaign due to a malfunction involving the camera
(namely, the operator didn't how to use it).*

Professor Dean Rea in retirement.
He was my mentor when I went into teaching
journalism and later inspired this memoir.

*Priscilla by my '56 Chevy in front of her parents'
house at 2460 Kincaid Street in Eugene during the
big snow of 1969 shortly after we were married.*

Don Wilt

The author and his sweetheart in college.

Priscilla with E. Adeline Curtis, circa 1969.

The kids helped build the Original No. 8: A) Kami wields a level on construction of original deck; B) Cooper learns to pound a nail; C) Mike supervises from the aerie where kids were not allowed to be (Hah!—try to keep them out of there).

First visit to the original No. 8 and ready for a swim, summer 1985. Clockwise from upper left—Priscilla, Kami, M.J, Coop.

Small Cabin—Front view of the Original No. 8
just after completion to the weather-tight stage
by builder and neighbor Chuck Newport in 1985,
design by Lanny Schreiner.

*Les Zaitz, editor of the McNary Piper the first year
I taught high school journalism. He went on to become Oregon's
most storied newsman with little help from me. Now publisher
of the Malheur Enterprise, he was just named a fellow of
the Society of Professional Journalists—the very top of the
profession where he joined a roster that includes Edward R.
Murrow, Walter Cronkite, and Bob Woodward.*

CHAPTER 20

High Octane Romance

N ot all of my college jobs were in newspapering. I had the summer job as a powder monkey that I've already mentioned, and I also ran a service station on the night shift one summer between my sophomore and junior years.

I worked at the Union 76 station on Franklin Boulevard just a few blocks west of campus. I loved that job and had romanticized thoughts about owning my own station sometimes when working in the big organizations was testing my limits. I liked the fact that you could see tangible results coming from your efforts. I was the only one on duty from about 10 o'clock at night until the owner, Norris Jorgeson, came in at 6:00 in the morning.

Norris was a big Norwegian guy, very tall and well-built with blonde hair that he kept neatly trimmed. He dressed in the same uniform the rest of us wore—blue work pants, a crisp white shirt with his name and the Union 76 logo on the pocket, and a bow tie topped off by a dark blue U.S. Air Force-style folding cap. On him it looked like a Luftwaffe pilot's uniform.

If you ever saw one of those old Texaco commercials with the theme, *"You Can Trust Your Car to the Man Who Wears the Star,"* you know what we looked like in our uniforms, but for Union 76.

I don't know if it was Norris's idea or something he was required by the oil company to do, but he had every new employee watch a "film strip" that spelled out the duties of a service station attendant.

This involved a lot more than just pumping gas. There was every expectation that you would also *"catch that windshield"* and check the oil, the water, brake fluid and tire pressure. According to the orientation script, the attendant was also to ask customers if they would like to have their car swept out. The picture showed a young Union 76 attendant kneeling beside the passenger side door of a 1950's model sedan with a whisk broom and dust pan in his hand.

I don't think we took it that far.

There was a dirty little secret associated with all this service: It wasn't only to keep your car in good operating order; it was also a way to sell you things.

We were instructed to always check the oil level. If it was low, offer to refill it. If a radiator hose felt soft, recommend that the customer replace it. Same with a loose-fitting radiator cap, worn tires or windshield wipers. We got a commission for moving these parts, so there was an incentive for us to give the car a good once-over while the pump was running.

Funny thing is, I don't remember ever selling anything to anybody unless they drove in already intending to buy it.

There was a camera above the door at the station with a sign that said *"Camera No. 3."* I think there was really just the one camera and the sign was there to give prospective troublemakers the willies. However many there were, it was enough for Norris to catch one of the guys who covered the night shift when I wasn't on duty replacing a customer's tire and pocketing the money.

Norris said the secret to making money was to have someone else earning it for you while you slept and I did my best to help him prosper. Most people have probably never pulled into a better-run service station than the Union 76 on Franklin when I was on duty.

The graveyard shift tended to be slow so I took great pride in hosing down the lot every night, sweeping out the lube room, cleaning the bathrooms, restocking the vending machines and totaling up the receipts in time for Norris to see how much wealth I'd accumulated for him while he was asleep.

Just to further set the scene, I would be doing all this on a hot summer evening while songs like *"Hey Jude"* by the Beatles were coming over the station's loud speakers. Totally 1960s, man.

One additional benefit to the Union 76 job was that my heart throb would come by to see me when she got off her shift sorting green beans at the Diamond A Cannery just a short walk away. This would have been about 2 o'clock in the morning.

Pris had to wear a powder-blue uniform that she wasn't crazy about but I liked it because it showed off her vivid blue eyes...and breasts. The song *"Five Foot Two, Eyes of Blue"* comes to mind. That was her.

She was also required to wear a tiara-like headdress with netting that said *"Diamond A"* on it. Damn she looked cute in that uni.

Traffic was slow in the early morning hours. She'd keep me company and help me total the receipts before going back to her folks' place where she stayed during the summer.

I suppose this "Take Your Girlfriend to Work" plan made for an unusual courtship, but apparently a pretty effective one, If I do say so myself.

CHAPTER 21

Juking My Way through J-School with the Journalism All Stars

There's a Mark Twain quote about not letting your schooling interfere with your education. That's sort of how I played it.

I transferred to the University of Oregon and into a very fine journalism school at the start of my sophomore year. How I knew it was good before I got there I can't remember, but something argued for me to go to the U of O even though the "family college" was Oregon State University 40 miles up the road in Corvallis.

My dad graduated from Oregon State and so did my older brother, Dennis; he was just a few hours short of earning his degree in 1967 when he left to go into the Peace Corps. Then, just a couple of years ago, he got it in his head to finish up and get his diploma.

He was 74 when he walked across the stage at Reser Stadium to become the oldest of more than 4,000 students who graduated that day.

Driven by Alma

Besides being an extraordinary accomplishment, Denny's belated graduation from OSU is also testimony to the value our family has always placed on education. Our grandmother, Alma Wanamaker Wilt, graduated from college clear back around the turn of the century; she as much as anybody imbued in all of us a drive to educate ourselves. This is what propelled my brother, I'm sure.

In my case, I'm lucky I took from my classes as much as I did because my real focus was on what I was doing at the newspapers. This was also around the time I discovered Priscilla, so there went a lot of my attention.

To begin, my entry into the School of Journalism was very much to my liking, which is to say it was entirely too easy. And in hindsight not wholly to my advantage.

Here's what happened: I'd already completed Reporting I and II at LCC and was holding down jobs at both local papers. I think this gave the J-School the impression I was a little more advanced than I actually was. In any event, the powers-that-be let me waive a couple of pretty important news-writing and editing classes that I very much could have used.

I ended up having to learn a lot of things in the school of hard knocks that I should have learned in the reporting and editing labs.

Still, I got a pretty well-rounded journalism education. I see looking over my official transcript that my course of instruction—insofar as the School of Journalism was involved—included the introductory reporting classes plus *Principals of Advertising; Mechanics of Publishing; Principles of Public Relations; History of Journalism; Journalism and*

Public Opinion; Theories of Mass Communication; Magazine Design and Production; Radio and Television Reporting; Supervising Scholastic Publications; Critical Reviewing; Newspaper Editing; Law and The Press; one week as part of a reporting team investigating issues at Jefferson High School in Portland as part of a *Reporting Urban Problems* class; and one term of student teaching.

I was a barely organized, undisciplined student. If they hadn't begun to give grades away by this time, things probably would have turned out different for me education-wise.

As an undergraduate my GPA hovered just below a 3.0 even though I had all A's or B's in my journalism classes. But that doesn't mean I wasn't paying attention. In fact, it's fairly astonishing how useful all the stuff I picked up in J-School turned out to be just in general, if not professionally. The rest of it I either didn't learn in the first place, or have since forgotten.

But I'd have to say that what I learned in journalism school and my part-time newspaper jobs gave me a leg up in life and a set of skills that kept me employed through some of the worst economic times in history for people in my field. For that alone I'll always be grateful.

The Faculty All-Stars

The faculty of the U of O School of Journalism was a constellation of stars led by John Hulteng, seen everywhere as the dean of deans among the nation's journalism schools. His book "The Messenger's Motives" was the first to address ethics in journalism and is still a staple in J-school classrooms.

Some of the others had owned their own firms or otherwise been players on Madison Avenue, or in big-city newsrooms around the country. Some of the best members of the faculty were proven reporters and editors with outstanding reputations for their work. My photography professor—Bernard "Bernie" Freemesser—palled around with the likes of Ansel Adams and Edmund Weston.

There were also what we'll call the faculty "all-stars." Let me dwell on a few of them here, beginning with one who's been particularly inspiring to me, first at the time and more recently in getting me to write this autobiography. This would be the legendary Professor Dean Rea. More than 500 people showed up at a big *soiree* for him when the School of Journalism inducted him into its Hall of Fame a few years ago.

The legend grew primarily from the experience—some would say ordeal—he put his students through. Rea taught the earliest classes you were required to take in the school of journalism—like Reporting I—along with upper-level editing classes. If you were really a glutton for punishment, you could come back for a master's degree and take his class on press law like I did.

It's hard to imagine Professor Rea as anything other than the blue collar newspaperman he was at heart.

He actually got his start as a printer's devil for a small newspaper in Ozark, Missouri, when he was still an adolescent. You can't start any lower in the business than a printer's devil. It was basically an apprentice responsible for putting lead type back in the proper cases, running errands and sweeping up.

He went on to graduate from the University of Missouri School of Journalism. You don't get much better than that as far as academic credentials are concerned. He then distinguished himself in different newsrooms around the country before turning his talents to the classroom.

Professor Rea was tall and lanky with a countenance and disposition that seemed to make others *want* to produce for him. I've only seen this quality in a couple of other individuals in my lifetime, but it's a powerful gift. Someone like this can push people to their limits and they lap it up.

He also had a stentorian voice that he used to command his classroom and a custom of wearing bright red socks that revealed his inner showman. He probably would have made a good evangelist.

In any event, Professor Rea brought a deep conviction to his mission of turning out graduates who knew how to gather information, organize it, write under the pressure of deadline and get the details right. *"Fair. Complete. Accurate. And on time."* That was his mantra.

Rea had perfected his editing skills in several newsrooms and they were razor sharp. One guy who worked for him as a reporter told me, *"That man could take a hundred words out of the Declaration of Independence and no one would miss them."*

He used a red pen to correct papers. A term some students used to describe what their papers looked like when they got them back was "bloody."

Was Dean Rea tough? Yes, I would say people thought so. His own son took one of his classes once and gave up journalism as a career. In his introductory journalism courses he exhibited a number of ways of driving home the principles of punctuality, speed and accuracy; some of them were, shall we say, a little unorthodox.

His son recalls going to one of his classes with him as a youngster. Students had been told they were to file their out-of-class assignments by the time class started at 8 a.m. As they arrived, each added his or her own paper to the stack on the table and took a seat. When 8 a.m. came around, Professor Rea picked up the stack, stuffed it into his briefcase and began the lecture.

Students who arrived *after* the class began still went up and put their papers on the table. By a quarter after 8:00 about seven or eight of them lay loosely stacked on the table in front of him. His son said he watched as his dad paced past the table—still lecturing—and without even looking down reached out with his arm and swept all the remaining papers into a metal wastebasket placed strategically at the end of it.

The small collection of bound papers made a significant "clang" when they hit bottom. Only after he had completed whatever point he'd been making did he pause by the waste basket, point his long index finger down at it, and say, *"That's too bad, but meeting a deadline is important in this business."*

Rea also liked to catch students napping by messing ever-so-slightly with the information he provided them for assignments, or even on his tests—just to see if they were paying attention.

Here's an example: the press law class required either a position paper or a 10-question True-False quiz every Friday. One question went something like this: *"In Near vs. State of Minnesota (1931), the U.S. Supreme Court ruled that 'prior restraints on publication of newspapers with malicious, scandalous and defamatory content violated the First Amendment,' as applied to the states by the 15th amendment. True or False?"*

Well, duh. We'd been talking all week in class about the importance of this Supreme Court case when it comes to First Amendment law. So, yeah, true. Right?

Bronk! I wasn't the only one who missed that one.

Wah! How can it not be true?

Well, because it's the 14th amendment the case was based on, not the 15th.

You're probably thinking, *"Oh, come on!"* But wait, what did Dean Rea say he was going to teach us back there in Reporting I? Pay attention to the details. Be sure it's right. Check your facts. Ask the right questions. Just because it wasn't reporting class anymore didn't mean the requirements had changed. You had to be on your toes to get past this guy.

A good question would be how somebody like this came to be called "the beloved Professor Rea" as he was described in the invitation to his induction. Well, that requires that you know the rest of the story.

About the time most of us were giving up hope of pulling anything better than a "C" from Dean Rea, if you went to see him he would tell you, *"Relax. The purpose of the test is to determine what I have not yet succeeded in teaching you so I can be sure you know it before you leave here."*

He also hosted a study session in his home after the tests where he went over the answer to each question. And he allowed one retake, like traffic school. To our great relief, in the final analysis Professor Rea's philosophy was the same as his first J-school dean who told him, *"If you err in assigning a grade, err in favor of the student."*

One class session of Rea's that would be hard to forget was the one dealing with the legal principles of slander, libel and defamation.

There was an older learner in the class, a woman about 40 years old. I don't think I was the only one who thought she made a nuisance of herself. She sat in the front row and never missed a chance to interject her thoughts. Asked a lot of off-the-subject questions as I recall.

She had one particularly annoying habit of asking a question right when the dismissal bell was about to ring so we'd all be sitting there tapping our toes instead of getting over to our next class.

On this particular morning, though, she took a distinctly different angle and began interrupting Professor Rea, even talking over him. She said, *"All you're doing is reading to us what you already assigned us to read"* and, *"We paid good money to take your class and all we're getting is a stale presentation that you apparently just pulled out of your lecture file this morning."*

Then she got up and stormed out. The class was stunned. Professor Rea himself looked like he had been knocked back on his heels a little bit. He stood there, speechless, for a while, staring at the door.

Finally, he turned back to us, leaned into the lectern and began to speak. But now his voice and manner were subdued. He started by apologizing to us if we thought that the irate student was right to complain. Then he began to tear up a little. He took off his glasses and wiped them with his handkerchief, or maybe his sleeve. Everybody felt terrible for him.

He went on muttering. *"You know, I've tried to do my best with this class. I don't just pull the same lesson plan out of the file. I prepare for every class . . ."* He went on like this for a little while before beginning to pull himself together. He stopped talking and just looked around the classroom. There wasn't a sound. Nobody knew what to do.

Finally he put his glasses back on, straightened up and shuffled the papers on the lectern back into order. Then suddenly he looked up at us and asked in his normal booming voice, *"So, what do you think? Was I defamed?"*

Now it's all *Ha Ha* and the student complainant comes waltzing back into the classroom to take a bow and hug her fellow performer. The adult learner was a plant and it was all a big set-up. The outburst. The tears. Everything just a big act.

But it sure made you think: *was* he defamed? Rea says in his own autobiography that he would *"be fired and jailed today"* for some of the incidents he staged in the classroom. He put great emphasis on making the learning experience immediate, challenging, interesting and real. That created a stimulating learning environment and one I tried to emulate when I began teaching myself.

Professor Rea and I have stayed in touch by long distance over the years and we correspond. He's 90 years old now. I told him once that more of his former students would probably write to him if they didn't still fear the "bloody" pen.

I also liked the journalism history course taught by Roy Halverson. He did an excellent job of laying out America's journalistic past and all its colorful characters—people like Ernie Pyle and Henry Luce.

He emphasized the heroic role that newspapers had played in major historical events like WWII but didn't leave out the big blunders they'd made either. *"Dewey Defeats Truman"*—that was a good one.

Another graduate of the Oregon J-School said that Halvorson liked to disparage a newspaper from someplace in Tennessee that he considered the absolute worst he'd ever seen. He said it once ran a headline that was supposed to read, *"Governor's Pen is Poised,"* except they'd left out an important space between words. Subscribers opened their newspapers that morning to the headline *"Governor's Penis Poised."*

Then he'd always say, *"And if you can believe it, they discovered the error <u>before</u> the presses started to roll but decided to go ahead and print it anyway."*

Professor Halvorson always had a good story to go along with whatever his subject matter was. In his section on how headline writing had evolved, he always included some examples from his "favorites" collection.

I remember one from a newspaper near the town of Sandwich, New Hampshire, that read, *"Man Found Dead in Sandwich."* Another was from a story in the *Register Guard* about men in the city's public works department who get up at 2 o'clock in the morning to shovel sand from the back of dump trucks when the roads freeze over: "A *Chilling Tale About Men With Grit."*

There was one other mentionable class called *Media and Mass Communications,* taught by Dr. James Lemert. I got the impression that I may have been one of the only people to ever come through Professor Lemert's door who appreciated what he had to teach.

A lot of students couldn't see what application the subject matter might have in their careers. To me, though, some of the principles introduced in his class were indelible; a good one being that people will respond differently to a message depending on only a few variables. Change any one of them and you get a different effect.

This turned out to be gold when my job responsibilities in the big corporations evolved to include how the company should be communicating with its 40,000, 60,000 or even 120,000 employees. It was, after all, a matter of *mass communications.*

Just having that context for making decisions in the planning stages of a major company communications campaign provided me an edge over a lot of other communication professionals working in the industry at the time.

You Said to Write When I Got Work

I'd have to say that I probably left the tutelage of these individuals about as well-prepared to teach high school journalism as a person could be—or as a high school principal looking for a journalism teacher could hope to find for that matter.

Almost no one advising a high school publication at the time was doing it because they wanted to. More typically it was just something they were doing to add a few hundred dollars to their teaching contract. So, to be honest, there probably wasn't that much competition for the job I ended up getting.

Looking back on how everything turned out, though, I can see now that it was a situation ripe for the plucking. I just happened to be the lucky—and, yes, well-prepared—individual who came along to pluck it.

I had to carry 27 credit hours my last quarter of college and use a lot of the same material from one class in another to do it (I guess you're not supposed to do that), but in June, 1970, I graduated and began applying for teaching jobs.

It was a good time to enter the job market. The economy was booming and I had two other job offers at smaller schools before I accepted one at the second-largest high school in Oregon—Charles McNary Senior High in the state capitol, Salem.

My 1956 Chevrolet was being overhauled at the time so my mother, bless her heart, drove me to two interviews on the same day. The first was in Gervais, a farm community outside of Salem which would have been a nice place to begin teaching. It was a moderate-sized school, like the third possibility in the town of Silverton just one town over.

The interview at McNary was in the afternoon. The principal, an Aristotle Onassis look-alike with the unusual name of Gurnee Fleischer offered me the job before I left his office. He was even able to promise that he would line up an elementary school teaching position for Priscilla, which he did, at Kennedy Elementary not too far away from McNary. Precisely how far it is on foot figures prominently into another story from that era that I will get to later.

I liked the idea that McNary was the biggest job available. After the interview I came out to the car. When I got in, I told my mother, *"Well, that's where I'm going to teach journalism."*

A small-town girl herself, she looked at the big, two-story concrete structure and said, *"But it's so big!"*

I looked back at her with a big smile and said, *"I know!"*

Up to now everything I'd done had been baby steps on the way to the career I envisioned for myself. Actually landing a job teaching high school journalism represented the attainment of the first major career goal of my life.

From now on I would be at the head of the class instead of in it.

Professor Lemert

Funny story about my journalism professor, Jim Lemert: He seemed to be a nice enough guy, but fairly introverted and hard to have a casual conversation with.

He invited all of his grad students to his house for a barbecue one evening. A young lady in the class attempted to draw him out. She said, *"So what do you do in your spare time?"* Lemert responded that he enjoyed reading research papers on mass communications.

She tried again: *"But don't you have any other interests?"*

This time he said, *"Well, I'm also a hypochondriac and that takes up a lot of my time."*

CHAPTER 22

All the News That's Fit to Pipe and My Best "Hire"

McNary

M cNary High School had been built only a few years before I began teaching there and still had a new-school feel to it. It'd been built to ease the student overload at Salem's other two high schools which were so full that one of them had been operating on a double shift. McNary was the state's second-largest high school with several thousand students.

The school was named in honor of Oregon Senator Charles L. McNary who represented Oregon in the U.S. Senate for 27 years and was once nominated for vice president in an election against Franklin D. Roosevelt. Other names were considered for the school with the dumbest being North Salem High School.

Dumb because that had been the name of one of the two existing high schools in town since 1954. They were going to change the name of the first one to Capitol High. I have to admit that would have been a pretty good name for a high school, but I can't imagine how much confusion and animosity it would have caused if that plan had been allowed to go forward.

The school adopted a theme consistent with Sen. McNary's Scottish heritage. This explains how the school paper came to be called the *Piper*. Its slogan was *"All the News That's Fit to Pipe,"* a lift off the New York Times's famous slogan *"All the News That's Fit to Print."*

This was a good time to be in teaching at the secondary level. Kids were generally respectful of their teachers but not afraid to let their personalities out. They responded well to opportunities to get involved in school activities, and McNary was making a name for itself in lots of different areas besides sports, including drama, debate and even automotive trouble-shooting competitions. My friend Ron Muggerud started teaching there the same year I did and ran a metals working program second to none.

The success of these various entities led to a high level of school spirit and equally high expectations. It fell to me to be sure that the school paper did its part to bring glory to the school and provide an exceptional learning experience for kids who signed up to be on the staff.

Teaching high school journalism turned out to be a glorious experience. It even ended up exceeding my own expectations, which were pretty high to begin with, and propelled my career along in ways that no one could have imagined.

The *Piper* had been around a few years before I got there, but there was a feeling on the part of the administration that we could do better.

Until I became advisor, all a kid had to do to be on the staff was enroll in journalism. I felt that if the paper was going to be special, then getting to work on it should be seen as something special as well. The general-enrollment journalism classes went on as usual and those kids continued to contribute to the paper's content, but you had to <u>apply</u> for the various editor positions and other key staff roles.

A few years ago my former student, celebrated Oregon reporter and publisher Les Zaitz, sent me a copy of the letter he received from me in April of his sophomore year. The letter was on McNary High School letterhead. It read as follows:

McNary High School

Dear Les:
As I informed you in our recent interview, you have been accepted for work on the 1971-72 McNary Piper.
Your background in the field of journalism should be most helpful to the successful operation of our staff. I hope the experience will be just as beneficial for you.
Your primary area of concern will be news-editorial so I suggest you begin planning now for ways in which we can improve our paper.
Plan to meet with the new staff in the near future to discuss these ideas.

Congratulations!
Mr. Wilt

Les was nice enough to tell me a few years ago that this letter meant a great deal to him and that he had kept it all these years. The boys and girls accepted for other key assignments received similar letters. Our launch as an outstanding high school newspaper had begun.

A Born Newsman

The letter to Les is a little laughable in hindsight because he really came to me almost fully-formed as a newspaperman. His father, Clarence, was the long-time capitol bureau chief for United Press International, one of the two big news services in the country at the time.

If that weren't enough to give Les a leg up when it came to newspapering, the Zaitz family also owned the local weekly, the *Keizer Times*. It's still in the family.

Like Dean Rea, Les had been a printer's devil for his old man. They might not have called it that by his time; let's just say he knew his way around a newspaper, having performed every job they had at the *Keizer Times* except editor, including some reporting, before he ever came under my influence.

Unlike the other kids who got their letters and awaited further instructions, Les fired one right back. It basically said that we were already behind schedule and outlined an eight-point plan to bring everything together in time for school.

Remember, this is a junior in high school. I hardly knew this 17-year-old boy but I remember telling my wife, *"This kid is either going to be a godsend or he's going to be a real pain in the ass."*

At his retirement party a couple of years ago I told people that I turned out to be right on both counts. Not really; it was always good with Les, and when his dad took a job in California in Les's senior year, Pris and I were more than happy to have him come live with us for the balance of the school year.

Needless to say, I appointed him editor of the *Piper*. That had to be right up there with the best "hires" I would ever make. To be honest, everything we accomplished with the *Piper* was as much Les's doing as anybody's. For all intents and purposes he was already a professional-caliber newsman with nascent but clearly visible leadership abilities.

All those pictures you see of the great *Washington Post* editor Bill Bradlee standing in front of his staff with one leg up on a chair? That's exactly the image that remains in my memory of Les taking charge of his newsroom.

He was a tall, lean-limbed boy with a mop top that was sort of a cross between a Beatles cut and a mullet. I want to say he had a big nose but only so I could then add *"and an even bigger nose for news."* (His actual nose, while a prominent part of his long face, was not that outsized.)

In an earlier time he would have been an unlikely candidate for BMOC. But the times they were a'changing, and Les came along just in time to catch the wave. It was the same one that artists like Bob Dylan and Mick Jagger rode to displace the likes of Frank Sinatra and Tony Bennett as what we thought of when we imagined a popular male vocalist.

Athletic stardom may have still been an important attribute in high school society but a new appreciation was emerging for kids who excelled in activities like student government, debate and journalism. Les excelled at all of them. To top it off, he had a personality that drew people to him and led to his election as student body president his senior year.

If he'd been interested in government instead of journalism Les was the type who would have angled for an appointment as a senate page in Washington, D.C., where, somebody once said, *"The whole town is made up of former high school student body presidents."*

But he stuck with journalism. Those of us who "knew him when" were not surprised when Les went on to distinguish himself like he did, first building a reputation as one of the state's best general assignment reporters and later as the chief investigative reporter for the state's largest newspaper, the *Oregonian.*

The Bruce Baer Award is Oregon's highest honor for investigative journalism. It's presented annually by the Greater Oregon Society of Professional Journalists. Before he retired from the *Oregonian* a year or so back, Les had won the Baer Award a record <u>five</u> times. He'd also been a finalist for the Pulitzer Prize in Journalism twice.

He was responsible for an almost endless series of blockbuster stories going all the way back to the 1970s that included the eruption of Mt Helens in 1980. His bylined front-page stories on the eruption were displayed in super-graphics on the exterior wall of the Oregonian's big printing plant in downtown Portland. That's almost better than having a sandwich named after you like they used to do for the big-name journalists in New York and Chicago.

Les also led the Oregonian's coverage of the Rahjneeshees, a religious cult that invaded the state in 1981 before morphing into a terrorist group. They were led by an Indian mystic by the name of Baghwan Shree Rajneesh. His followers wore red robes like monks and showered their leader with gifts that included <u>93</u> Rolls Royce automobiles.

The Rajneeshees had bought up a massive ranch out in Wasco County on the eastern side of the state called "The Big Muddy" and incorporated it as a city called Rahjneeshpuram. The population at the ranch swelled to 7,000, which allowed them to gain political control over the nearby historic town of Antelope, which they promptly renamed "Rahjneesh." This gave them almost complete control over decisions affecting their development activities in the region.

Almost. When the county denied them the necessary building permits for their grand plans, they decided that they would also have to take political control of that jurisdiction. That's what led them to the main population center in the county, the town of The Dalles. There they sprinkled the bacteria that cause Salmonella on salad bars at 10 restaurants around town. The poisoning sickened more than 750 people, sending half of them to the hospital.

Their intent was to incapacitate the voting population of the city so that their own candidates would win the 1984 elections in Wasco County, handing them controlling seats on the Wasco County Circuit Court and the sheriff's department. The incident is considered the first and single largest bioterrorist attack in United States history. In the end, a number of Rajneeshees went to jail and the Baghwan was deported.

Les's reporting helped uncover a lot of the cult's nefarious activities, including their plans to knock off a long list of state and local leaders. After the group's various plots were exposed, it turned out that his reporting had landed him on their assassination list as well.

Les's success went far beyond filing a good story. Over time he established a long and distinguished record by challenging one state or municipal bureaucracy after another for withholding public information by pleading exception to the state's disclosure laws. They always said you knew it was going to be a bad day when you came to work in the morning and Les Zaitz was sitting outside your door. He himself called it *"Getting Zaitzed."*

The Enterprise

When Les retired from the *Oregonian* he was quoted as saying, *"I have no more journalistic mountains to climb."* I don't know what he was thinking, but this turned out to be complete fiction.

Within the first year after retiring he was back at it. He and his wife, Scotta, took over ownership of the 110-year-old *Malheur Enterprise*, a weekly paper in the eastern Oregon town of Vale. Almost instantly he found himself in a battle to force the state's Psychiatric Security Review Board to release records pertaining to the release of a dangerous patient named Anthony Montwheeler from the nearby state mental hospital.

Montwheeler had been institutionalized for 20 years since murdering his first wife and their son in Salem. He pled insanity in that case which earned him a relatively pleasant existence living in a cottage on the grounds of the state hospital at taxpayer expense. He'd even persuaded the staff to let him out during the day so he could pick up a few bucks at a job across the border in Idaho.

When Montwheeler finally admitted that he'd been faking his insanity, the state Psychiatric Security Review Board just let him out even though one psychiatrist on the staff warned that he would very likely kill again and that it would most probably be a close family member when he did.

This turned out to be just about the only thing anybody involved in his release got right. Within the month he'd kidnapped and stabbed his third wife to death in a car outside a mini-mart in Vale. He was trying to escape with his dead wife's body in the car when he intentionally rammed another car head-on at highway speed, killing yet another person who was just trying to get to work.

The *Enterprise* sued to get the public records explaining how such a lethal bungle could have occurred but the hospital refused on the grounds that it would invade Montwheeler's privacy, if you can believe that. Sure, patient privacy is a real thing; but in this instance it surely was outweighed by the public's right to know.

Instead of releasing the records, the PSRB turned around and filed a countersuit against the *Enterprise*. They even went so far as to make it public that they'd hired a big-city law firm to prosecute their case. The lead lawyer alone would be paid $400 per hour with no limit on how big a bill they could run up. In other words, the state made it clear that if the *Enterprise* did not back off they would put it out of business.

But they didn't succeed. Backed by the Oregon Newspaper Publishers Association, Les reached out for support by establishing the *Enterprise Defense Fund* to *"hold those in power accountable for what they do."*

Support poured in. More important, papers across the state and the nation took up the cause. Before it was over Oregon's governor had ordered that the state's suit be dropped and the records turned over to the *Malheur Enterprise*, Les Zaitz Publisher.

In 2017 The *Enterprise* was presented an award called the Frank McCulloch Award for Courage in Journalism. It honors journalists who *"demonstrate courage in resisting intimidation, whether from use of a political or corporate power or physical threats."*

Winning the Courage award put the *Malheur Enterprise* in the same league with *The Los Angeles Times* and the *New York Times,* the previous two papers to pick up the award. At the request of the governor, Les now sits on a state task force overseeing the reform of the state's public records law which still contains more than 500 exceptions.

I mention all this only because I've watched as his contributions to the field of journalism—real, grassroots journalism—have mounted; I don't think there's anyone in the country who is doing more to keep journalism alive and to develop the next generation of journalists.

You can never be sure someone like this and what he's accomplished is going to be appropriately remembered; I wanted to be sure it was, somewhere. It really makes me proud to include Les's accomplishments as part of the story of the *McNary Piper*—or maybe I should say the *McNary Piper* as part of <u>his</u> story.

I don't want to diminish the contribution of other students on the *Piper* staff since there were many who made enormous contributions to the paper's success; but even they would agree that Les was the star.

For him to come to McNary and be on the *Piper* was something akin to the college football coach who lands the nation's number one quarterback prospect. He was definitely a "Five-Star" recruit and helped to put out one hell of a good little newspaper. That made me, of course, "Coach of the Year."

CHAPTER 23

Room 144 Becomes the Place to Be

Camp Piper

I went into the classroom my first year without any real idea about how you actually teach anybody anything. None of the handful of courses I'd been required to take in college dealt with practical matters like lesson-planning or classroom management. (I probably ducked those too somehow.)

I'd had one term of student teaching at Springfield High School under a competent journalism teacher named Ken Fenter. He ran a relaxed classroom where kids were generally free to carry out their assignments as they saw fit. Ken was available to help deal with problems as they arose, but otherwise it was like working at Google.

I guess you could say that the style I adopted at the outset of teaching was a cross between his and the more demanding Dean Rea's. The kids knew we could have a good time, but when it was came to getting the paper out it was all business.

I really loved journalism and wanted the students to love it too. I put up quotations from some of the great leaders in journalism history around the room to impress upon them that they were taking part in something great—*"The Purpose of a Newspaper is to Comfort the Afflicted and Afflict the Comfortable"* and *"Journalism is the First Draft of History"*—that sort of thing. I told them that they were going to get to do something most people will never do—put out a newspaper.

I discovered that kids this age are eager for guidance. If you're passionate about something, they become passionate about it too. Several people from these two classes went on to successful careers in writing, newspapers and television.

One thing I did right away to help the group bond around a shared vision and plan was to arrange for a *Piper* retreat before the school year even began. We found a rustic place called Whitewater Camp about 60 miles east of Salem in the foothills of the Cascade Mountains. Everybody who had won a staff position participated, bringing the group to about a dozen.

We'd sit around the campfire and kick around story ideas and production issues. Before the weekend was over we'd have a pretty good idea of how we were going to make a run at being the best paper in the country. On one level this couldn't have been a better idea, and it worked to perfection. Kids formed bonds and bought into the vision just as I'd hoped. Good for me.

Not so good was the total disregard for any kind of school district approval and the absence of other adult chaperones. No permission slips. No discussion with somebody downtown about legal concerns or liabilities. I just wasn't aware as a person ought to have been about doing things by the book.

This is not to say that there was any great expectation out there either. After all, the kids' parents all allowed them to go without asking any questions. It was just a more relaxed time.

It's just lucky nothing went wrong. We did have an incident where two girls fell into Whitewater Creek, a fast glacier-fed stream that couldn't have been any colder if it had been frozen. They got themselves out, but that could have turned out badly.

Room 144

We operated out of Room 144, a large classroom near the back of the school that looked out on the courtyard. The photography darkroom was down the hall. I'd persuaded the department head to spring for a super-duper IBM Selectric Pro typewriter that we used to compose the paper and the other stuff needed to produce headlines and paste up the paper.

Room 144 went from being an ordinary classroom to several other things at once: a journalism lab, a newsroom, and a composing room—all with a sort of "Journalism Club" atmosphere. In time it very much became the place to be.

The strategy of making the *Piper* staff more selective had worked to perfection; many more people now wanted to be in this group of individuals they saw wearing "Piper Hats," of the flat and tweedy "Newsboy" variety. And people already on the staff were trying hard to outdo one another from one issue to the next with their writing and photography.

How important Room 144 became to me and the kids both was driven home at Les Zaitz's retirement soiree at a big golf club south of Portland a few years ago. Several of the former *Piper* staff were present and without any prompting from me talked excitedly about the time they spent there.

We structured the program so that I would act as publisher of the newspaper while the student editor ran the operation with the help of sub-editors for sports, student government and other beats.

A funny thing caught on quite early in the year and prevailed for the next two years I was the advisor. The sports editor was a delightful boy named Ed Hermann. He was from a large Catholic family in south Salem and was as respectful of his current instructors as he'd been of the nuns who brought him up. Whenever he was arguing his point of view on something, he would politely but emphatically say to me, "But _Sir_! But _Sir_!"

Before too long he had everyone on the staff doing it too and I became, to the denizens of Room 144, "_Sir_ Wilt." It's not like I was Sydney Poitier in "_To Sir with Love_" but it did imply that we enjoyed something beyond the average teacher-student relationship and I've always cherished it.

Ed also introduced another important expression to the _Piper_ lexicon: "_to Fluke._" When he was explaining that a certain story from his department was late or missing or poorly done, he'd say somebody had "fluked" it. He was always warning his sportswriters to avoid fluking, or assuring the rest of the staff, "_Don't worry. We won't fluke it._"

They made fluking something you just did not do on the _Piper_.

It became a sort of red badge of courage to show up for the after-school final paste-ups before the paper was ready to go to the printer. We always had a full crew when it came to getting the paper out and those late-night work sessions remain in my memory as more like a bi-weekly party for those of us who loved being part of it all.

If we'd had to turn to a professional print shop to set the type, create headlines, take and print pictures and do the paste-up there's no way the school could have afforded a paper the size and frequency of the *Piper*.

We could set the Selectric Pro to "justify" the type, which means to make each line come out even. You could have a nice straight column of type the exact length needed. We had the light tables, waxing machines and everything else you need to put out a paper except for the printing press. I mention our ability to do all this because it factors into one of the *Piper's* most important achievements, which I'm going to describe in more detail later.

But first, a really outrageous story, and one that was *"on me."*

A Journalism Teacher's Wife's Life

The story of the *Piper* wouldn't be complete without this one because, as they say, *"Behind every successful man there is a woman."*

Working on any student publication can involve some late nights; the *Piper* was no exception. Once everybody got into it and understood the deadline situation, they'd throw themselves into it with such a fury that time stood still, or seemed to.

Alas, time does not stand still. One evening it raced right past the time that I was supposed to pick Priscilla up at her school. I think we'd agreed on 5 p.m. Like everyone else, neither one of us had a cell phone in those times.

Taking only one car was not our usual routine. Typically we'd drive ourselves to and from work. For that reason, what happened next could probably have been predicted: I got so wrapped up in the rush to deadline that I forgot all about her over there waiting for me. It was like those poor parents who forget it's their day to take the baby to the sitter and end up leaving them to die in their car seat.

Okay, okay it wasn't that. But it was still pretty bad. When we finally came out the side door of the school about 10 o'clock that night, I was startled to discover someone asleep under a towel in the backseat of my Malibu. Guess who?

Pris had tried to call the high school from her school when I didn't show up, but with no results. She waited an hour before starting to walk the mile between her school and McNary, which required her to cross a very busy and dangerous four-lane Keizer Boulevard in the dark.

Then, after she got to the high school, nobody responded to her knocks on those big metal doors with the little square wire mesh windows at the end of each hallway. We were having too much fun in Room 144. She had no choice but to sit it out in the car, which she did for several more hours before finally crawling into the back seat and going to sleep.

Pris wasn't very happy about it, but I give her a lot of credit for taking the incident in stride. Some women make good coach's wives. Priscilla was a good journalism teacher's wife.

Her name lives forever in the annals of Room 144.

CHAPTER 24

The News Room

Looking back on the *Piper* today makes me pretty proud. Maybe it <u>was</u> the best student paper in the country. As I flip through the pages, I see in the masthead the various honors the paper had accumulated after just one year—The All-American Award from the National Scholastic Press Association, a First Class ranking from the Columbia Scholastic Press Association, and the coveted George H. Gallup Award from the International Honor Society for High School Journalists.

Every one of these was the highest ranking available. Along with them came written remarks from the judges that included comments like *"Thoroughly excellent professional-caliber writing"* and, *"You make excellent use of your extensive news space; your paper's size would be the envy of many other schools."*

Calling the *Piper* *"an outstanding, attractive package,"* judges awarded the paper marks of distinction for content and coverage, writing and editing, physical appearance and photography.

A story in the *Oregon Statesman* newspaper that year said, *"McNary had never won an honor rating from the*

National Society of Publishers before. In doing so, the Piper becomes the first Salem high school to gain such distinction in recent history."

A New Editor and some All-American Fun

By my second year of teaching, Les Zaitz had gone on to his student government activities but had been succeeded by a capable new editor named Jim Reed. Jim did a great job in the big chair and we never lost a step in the transition.

I really pulled a good one on Jim after we'd submitted the first batch of *Pipers* produced under his direction to the Columbia Scholastic Press Association for rating against papers across the country. Under Les the paper had never received anything lower than "All American"—the highest ranking. Next came "First Class," then "Award of Merit." I knew that if he got anything lower than All-American it would be a terrible blow to Jim.

When I went to check my mailbox one day, there was the envelope from the CSPA containing the *Piper's* results. I opened it and was pleased to see that the paper had retained its All-American ranking.

But as I was going back to Room 144, I noticed that the envelope the award came in was marked "First Class" by the U.S. Postal Service. The words were in pretty large type and even underlined.

I couldn't help myself. I went over to where Jim was sitting on the edge of a table and said, *"I don't suppose you'd be interested in knowing how your paper scored in the Columbia Scholastic Press Association competition."*

Jim was a round-shouldered boy with an expressive face and a Bohemian style. He had a mess of curly brown hair and had already begun to sprout an equally-unmaintained growth of facial hair. If you had put a pork pie hat and sunglasses on him you might have thought you were looking at John Belushi.

I had his attention immediately.

With great fanfare, I brought the envelope up from behind my back and held it out for him to see. Then I pointed to the postal code on the outside of the envelope and said, *"Look, you got First Class."*

His whole body sank. He started to shake his head back and forth slowly. Then he looked up at me like he wanted to say, *"God, what does it take?"* I didn't make him suffer too much longer though. Even though he said he didn't want to look at the certificate, I encouraged him to take it out of the envelope so the others could see it.

When it became clear that the All-American ranking had been preserved, everyone began to clap and Jim was rewarded with the recognition he'd earned. I'm sure he still looks back at his time as editor of the *Piper* with a lot of pride. He should.

The paper wasn't just excelling editorially, either. A natural-born salesperson named Ione Darras served as business manager and carried out her duties with a certain bombast that went well with her fiery-red locks. It's apparent when you look at the volume of paid advertising she was generating. I count more than 35 separate ads in one issue alone. That's enough to make a lot of newspapers lick their chops even today.

Her accounts covered the waterfront in Salem. They included all the usual suspects like local drive-ins and record stores, but managed to also pull money from more unconventional sources like country clubs, car dealers and lumber yards. The revenue generated went into the school's general fund to offset our relatively high operating costs, so advertising revenues were no small matter.

When another go-getter also chose to sell ads, he had a business card produced on his own initiative that identified him as a sales representative for "*The McNary Piper*— Oregon's No. 1 H.S. Newspaper."

Kids excelled in the other departments too—news and sports writing, editorials, columns, features and design of the paper itself. I'm reminded as I go through these past issues that we even had a political analyst—two, actually, and political cartoons. This was not the *Kalitan*[1], if you get my drift.

Gosh, I'm proud of those kids. And I'm glad I had the opportunity at Les Zaitz's retirement to look a few of them in the eye 40 years later and say, "*You were all great kids. It was a pleasure to have you in my class.*"

Funny story about our chief features writer, Al Riske. He was a slender, fairly introverted boy who looked a lot like one of *The Monkees*—the tall one. He clearly had the makings of a professional writer but could still be a little awkward around those of his own kind—you know, humans.

One night, again working late on the final paste-ups, people were chattering up and down the line when Al turned to me and said, "*What do you think, Don?*" Now, nobody had ever called me Don. It was always Mr. Wilt or "Sir."

There was nothing entirely out of line about it in those days, but nobody expected this informality to come out of Al's mouth, especially Al. So going back to the top of the conversation, here's how the dialogue unfolded:

Al: "What do you think, Don?"
(Long, awkward pause)
Al Again: "Wilt."

---

1   The school paper at Mohawk High School, which I first edited

The whole "newsroom" cracked up. Makes me laugh just to think about those times.

For the most part, all the sports writers were athletes themselves. They did a terrific job of covering that front. I hope I had something to do with inspiring them to look beyond the obvious to find the real heart of the story because they did an outstanding job.

One that stands out after all these years was a story with the headline "*Job of Manager a Thankless One*" by sportswriter Paul Duckworth. He went behind the scenes to describe what a high school sports equipment manager does.

"*In their own way,*" he reported, "*managers play every game. As does the athlete, the manager wins or loses too.*" I teared up reading such sensitive writing from a high school kid all these years later.

Going through these back issues of the *Piper* I'm struck by how many different angles the kids found to cover the high school scene. In a periodic update we learned that Lincoln High in Portland had installed driving simulators to replace real driver trainer cars, and that in Medford, Oregon, the high school there was going online with its own radio station. Talk about all the news that's fit to pipe—the *Piper* was even covering events at <u>other</u> schools.

Speaking Snark to Power

This might be a good place to mention that these kids (to borrow a phrase from my friend Pat Hughey) had no trouble speaking snark to power either. I noticed in one issue the editorial staff had worked up an opinion piece that took on one of the top scholastic publication organizations in the country.

The point they felt they had to dispute was a minor criticism the rating organization had made about the issue of the

Piper they'd reviewed and otherwise found to be at the very highest level of their ranking system. It had brought McNary no small amount of public and school-wide attention.

But, they said, the *Piper* shouldn't have run the classic story from the *Boston Sun*, "*Yes Virginia There Is a Santa Claus.*" They said it had been reprinted so many times that it was painful to subject readers to it again.

The *Piper* waited a full year before running another editorial the following Christmas that basically said, "*Hey Great Big National Scholastic Publication Ranking People, thanks for your feedback and now here for the second year is our reprint of the timeless classic 'Yes, Virginia There Is a Santa Claus'.*"

It was like the winner at the Westminster Dog Show peeing on the judge's shoe.

Looking back I'm impressed that the school administration didn't express more concerns. I think the youth movement was far enough underway at the time that schools were learning they were going to have to get more relaxed about things and not take them personally—another great blessing for me because I didn't want to get caught up in a culture war or something.

The epiphany I took from my teaching years was that the success of any group effort will almost always come down to effort and leadership, whether it's a profitable company, a winning football team or, yes, a good newspaper.

I would equate it with being the coach of a championship sports team—maybe the *Piper* staff couldn't have done it without you, but you sure as hell couldn't have done it without them either.

Now I'm going into coach speak and will stop.

CHAPTER 25

The Big Scoop

An earlier scoop (that the locally legendary Bob's Nineteen Cent Hamburgers would be raising its price to 24 cents), carried to us by a 17-year-old student who flipped burgers there, paled by comparison with the heroics of the Piper staff in the late fall and early winter of 1972-73. That's when the paper pulled off a scoop that led Oregon's governor to declare that, *"No other high school in the United States has shown the enterprise of The McNary Piper."*

Here's what happened:

President Richard Nixon had pledged to get us out of the war in Vietnam when he was elected in 1970. But things had dragged on despite years of secret negotiations in Paris between Secretary of State Henry Kissinger and his North Vietnamese counterpart.

Finally, on October 26th, 1972, Kissinger uttered the words, *"We believe peace is at hand."* He said that it would probably take only one or two more sessions to finalize what they were calling the Paris Peace Accords. The official title was *"Agreement on Ending the War and Restoring Peace in Vietnam."*

The *Piper* sprang into action. While everyone in the country waited for the official announcement that the war was over, Jim Reed mobilized the staff and began collaborating on how the *Piper* might play a role in the historic occasion when it arrived. The decision was made to put together a special edition of the *Piper* just as the newspapers of old used to print "Extras."

It turned out the kids had plenty of time; it would be another three months before the agreement was finalized. They put it to good use. The former editor and now student body president, Les Zaitz, came back to write a major piece on the tortured path that the peace talks had taken and to generally help plan and execute the undertaking.

Together they proceeded to create an eight-page special tabloid edition about the war well before Nixon finally went on national television to say that an agreement had been reached. All they needed to complete the edition was one final front-page story.

Above the nameplate on the front page of the special edition were the words **"EXTRA * SPECIAL * EXTRA"** in 64-point boldface type. Below, a four-deck headline in even larger type reads, *"Cease-fire Declared in Vietnam."*

Some of the headlines inside provide a pretty good picture of what the issue covered—"Peace Announced—U.S.—North Viets Sign," "War's End Prompts Quiet Faculty Relief," and, 'It's About Time' Common Reaction From Students."

And then the *piece de resistance*: a guest editorial from Oregon's legendary governor and former television newsman, Tom McCall, headlined, *"Governor Expresses Hope."*

The governor's contribution, along with reactions from Oregon Senator Mark Hatfield and several other members of Oregon's congressional delegation, had been gathered in advance with the understanding that if the settlement didn't come to pass, their comments would never see the light of day. The same was true for members of the faculty and students who responded to "man-on-the-street" interviews in advance.

Then everybody waited. And waited. And waited some more until finally, at 7:01 p.m. Pacific Time on Jan. 23, 1973, President Nixon went on television from the Oval Office to announce the end of hostilities between North Vietnam and U.S.

By this time Les Zaitz was living with us while he finished out his senior year. The two of us jumped into my '70 Malibu and took off for the high school and Room 144. As planned, the current editor, Jim Reed, also headed to Room 144 and several other staffers arrived to take part in the final push.

Because the *Piper* had its own composing equipment, it was no time at all before Les had finished the final, front-page story with the details of what had transpired. Another student proceeded to put it into type using the *Selectric*.

Not even an hour had passed since the news broke and the *Piper* was already ready to go to press. The one regret I've always had is that we did not take time to change out the placeholder used in place of the date on each page of the paper; instead of Jan. 23rd, 1968, it reads *"Peace in Vietnam Day, 1968."* That was unfortunate because it meant the paper didn't bear the actual historical date.

We immediately drove the few miles over the Willamette River Bridge to West Salem where we'd arranged with a 24-hour printing company called BME Web Press to print the special. We were a pretty good customer, working with them every-other week when the regular issues of the *Piper* came out.

They got into the spirit of things and only 30 minutes later we left BME with a trunk full of "Extras" hot off the press.

By now other *Piper* staff members had been alerted and were waiting at the school to begin distribution. They started in the gymnasium where several hundred people were watching a McNary Celtics basketball game, making them the first people in the entire United States to read the news about a cease fire in Vietnam.

Later, some of the kids took a bundle of *Pipers* down to the joint offices of the *Oregon Statesman* and *Capitol Journal*. They laid a copy on every desk in the building.

Imagine coming to work the next day and discovering your paper has been scooped by a bunch of high school kids. I have to concede that that was showboating but, try as I might, I've never been able to work up much regret over it.

Later the same week, the *Piper* issued its regular edition with a story that told about the scoop. I'm including it here in its entirety:

Piper Scoops State; Peace Told In Extra
By Jim Reed
Piper Editor-in-Chief

The McNary Piper has carved a permanent place for itself in the annals of scholastic journalism in the United States by becoming one of, if not the, first newspapers in the country to carry the news of the peace agreement between U.S. and North Vietnam.

In an 8-page special edition printed and dis-
tributed within two hours of Pres. Nixon's Tuesday
night announcement, The Piper told of the formal
settlement to be signed Saturday in Paris. The special
was distributed during the closing minutes of the
McNary-Crescent Valley basketball game and many
of the fans first learned of the agreement through the
historic edition.

The appearance of the Piper shocked many of
those gathered in the gym. As one observer described
it, "It was almost like there was no basketball game—
you could look around and everybody was reading
the Piper."

The special drew attention from many quarters
including local newspapers and television stations,
the Associated Press and state legislators.

Governor Tom McCall, when presented with a
copy of the special, said, "As a former newsman, I
feel confident I can assure you no other high school
newspaper in the United States has shown the enter-
prise of the McNary Piper. A great job!"

The governor wasn't the only one who thought so. Over
the following days the *Oregon Statesman* newspaper would
credit *the Piper* with having produced the first "extra" in
the City of Salem since the end of World War II. The mayor
of Salem went so far as to come to the school to present
the staff with an award from the city and a few days later
declared it "McNary Piper Day in the City of Salem."

Just for comparison, I recently printed out the front page
of *The New York Times* which announced the historic news
of the war's ending in a triple-decker headline that read:

VIETNAM ACCORD IS REACHED
CEASE-FIRE BEGINS SATURDAY
P.O.W.'S TO BE RELEASED IN 60 DAYS

The paper is dated Jan. 24th, 1973—the day after the *Piper* had already printed the news. In these days of social media and the instantaneous news coverage it allows, it would be no big deal to scoop *The New York Times*. But in 1973 it was a remarkable achievement.

Another indicator of that was that the school made room in the hallway trophy cabinets, normally reserved only for athletic achievements, to display some of the plaques and trophies the paper had been awarded along with a copy of the extra edition and some of the news coverage it generated.

When I went back to visit the school a year or so ago I searched the trophy cases to see if this part of the school's history was still on display. But all that's in there today are trophies from the school's good years in football, baseball, basketball and other sports. The *Piper* stuff had all been removed and there was no longer any evidence for today's students to see how once, long ago, the *McNary Piper* had scooped the world.

I had taken the McNary job with hopes of the *Piper* becoming an outstanding student newspaper, but all this exceeded even my own expectations.

Even before the special edition, the Salem School District devoted the entire front and back pages of one issue of its weekly staff publication to the McNary journalism program. The *Piper* even made the cover of *Quill & Scroll* magazine, the leading publication for scholastic journalism in the U.S.

Neither of these was like getting our picture on the cover of *The Rolling Stone. But* it might as well have been in terms of what it did for me personally. I'll tell you why next.

CHAPTER 26

In Which I Get not <u>A</u> Better Offer but <u>Two</u>, and Abandon the *Piper*

ronically, it was the success of the *Piper* that led me to leave teaching journalism at the end of my second year and head for what I perceived to be even greener pastures. I've said that my life story might not defy the imagination but that it's bumped up against the laws of probability once in a while. What happened next is a good example.

Not too long after the *Piper* had attracted state and national attention with the special edition, I got a call at school one day from the State Superintendent of Public Instruction, Dr. Dale Parnell. He was considered the father of Oregon's community college system and a good bet to be Oregon's next governor.

Dr. Parnell told me he'd been impressed with what he saw in the news about the *Piper.* He wondered if I'd be interested in coming over to the Department of Education to, *"Do for me what you've been doing there at McNary."*

I was flattered and excited about the opportunity, but he wanted me to start right away. I didn't want to just walk out on the *Piper* and, besides, I was under contract to teach through the end of the school year, still four months away. Parnell said not to worry about that; he would talk to the new Salem Schools superintendent, Dr. Bill Kendrick, and work something out. Doctor to Doctor.

But before I even had time to digest the first offer, I got another one. This time the call was from Dr. Kendrick. He told me that Parnell had called about hiring me and he wanted to suggest an altogether different arrangement; instead of going over to the Department of Education, I would go downtown to work for him. He offered me a little more money.

This time I had to say, *"Well that's a nice offer but I've already told Dr. Parnell that I would go to work for him."* Kendrick said, *"Don't worry about that. I'll talk to him. He'll understand."*

I hope he did, because I finished up the school year and then moved downtown to the district office where I had a nice view of the city and a sign on my door that said "Coordinator of Communications." I regretted abandoning the kids who had signed on to the *Piper* for the coming year but I found myself unable to resist the siren song of more money and a higher position. So abandon them I did.

I would teach again, first as an adjunct professor in the School of Journalism at Oregon while I was working for the Springfield School District and then again at Pacific Lutheran University in Tacoma while I was working for Weyerhaeuser. But for all intents and purposes I'd moved on to a career in an emerging field that really didn't have a commonly-recognized name at the time—"Organizational Communications."

Because of the promotion I received as a result of the *Piper's* success, I got in on the ground floor of what has become one of the most important functions in just about any large organization today, particularly the big companies.

I heard a historian say once that, *"The United States has always been a great country for self-promotion."* The *Piper* and I were proof of that. Several people got launched out of Room 144 and into successful careers, but nobody benefitted more than I. Whatever else it accomplished, The *Piper* drew a lot of positive attention and propelled my career along in ways that none of us could have imagined.

Going "downtown" was not without its risks. I had to prove myself on a whole new playing field, about which I'd thought very little. Fortunately, I was being hired primarily to put out publications so that was where I concentrated my efforts.

Apparently my predecessor's publications weren't quite hitting the mark as far as the superintendent was concerned. Ours <u>did</u> hit the mark and were both well-received and recognized right away, so that turned out to be a good year.

However, almost exactly at the end of one year I took a phone call that changed everything. The call was from Bill Llewellyn, the superintendent of schools in Springfield. He said he needed somebody to help him deal with the community and the press.

The job paid about the same as I was then making, but the offer included the opportunity to begin work on my master's degree at the University of Oregon; that was something I'd set my sights on and so justified the move.

So it was back to the upper Willamette Valley again for us.

CHAPTER 27

Before the Kids Came Along and Ruined Everything

There's a regular feature in the *Oregonian* we like called *"Love Stories."* It interviews couples who've been married more than 50 years about what's made their marriages last. They almost always talk about the importance of communicating with one another, supporting each other's interests and not letting the sun go down on your anger.

I can say Pris and I got off to an awfully good start. We didn't have our first baby until we'd been married more than six years. This gave us time to sort out the kind of things that allowed us to reach a peaceful co-existence.

Neither one of us knew before we got married and started cohabitating that I could be so impossibly impatient, or that when it came to making decisions I didn't really feel any great need to consult anyone else—my spouse included.

It was this latter trait that led to us owning a 375-horsepower muscle car for a while that we did not need or even want. Actually, that one also involved a big dollop of consumer gullibility on my part.

What happened was that not too long after I graduated from college, I got the itch to buy a new car. The '70 Chevrolet Malibu had caught my eye. I started checking them out at Joe Romania Chevrolet and decided on my own to purchase a dark maroon, two-door model with a black vinyl top, black vinyl bucket seats, and "four-on-the-floor" for $4,300. It sported a V-8 engine but still was within the "normal" range for a passenger car as far as power was concerned.

The salesman turned out to be a disgraced city official I vaguely recognized who now found himself selling cars for a living. We'll call him "John." Honest John.

Honest John had found his true calling as a car salesman and had no trouble sizing me up. "First-time Buyer" would have been the words that flashed through his mind when he saw me come through the door. And he did see me coming.

The problem started a couple of days after I placed the order when "John" called to say that, unfortunately, they were unable to find that model in the same color combination I'd ordered. He said they'd found one without the vinyl roof at a lot in Medford that they could get in a couple of days if I wanted. Same engine. I said okay.

Before too long John was calling again to say the car they found in Medford had been sold, but that another Malibu in a different color and a little bigger engine was still available. He said it was the Super Sport edition—*"It's a little more money, but you'll like it."* This one was a color called "Gobi," like the desert.

So finally the car comes in. I go down to the lot to pick it up. John accompanies me to the back lot where the cars are prepped for delivery. He says, *"What do you think?"*

Well, this was not all what I expected. First of all the paint job included two wide black racing stripes down the hood in the front and down the trunk in the back. I asked if those could be removed. Sadly, John said, that would be impossible.

I queried him on what the situation would be if I didn't take the car after all. He implied it wouldn't be easy to get out of it since they'd gone to all the trouble to get it there. Of course this was their problem, not mine. But for reasons I can only attribute to youthful idiocy, I went through with the purchase.

I hated this car and when I got home Pris hated it even more. She wanted me to take it back, but I just couldn't bring myself to even try. It had this big honking 396cc engine with cowl induction. When you stomped on the accelerator the cowl flap in front of the windshield would open up and you'd get this big roar from the carburetors as it sucked in oxygen. Teenage boys loved it.

The muscle car fiasco would have to serve as Exhibit A in a pattern of doing things without listening to my wife. Trust me, I'm completely over that today but this was not the only time I would do something like it over the next number of years.

We only had the Super Sport Malibu for about 10 months before I knew it had to go. It just wasn't us. Plus, four of the days we owned it were spent stranded in a little village on a trip to British Columbia so a push rod could be replaced. Saw a nice pod of Orca whales while we there though.

Already, the car was not worth near what I'd paid for it. I ended up listing it in the classifieds and letting it go at about a $1500 loss.

One day a few months later I was driving by Bob Cochran's Auto Sales on Franklin Boulevard when I spotted a 1970 Chevelle Malibu. Maroon with black vinyl top, black bucket seats, four-speed transmission and the more modest 350cc engine. It was identical to the one I'd originally set out to buy at Romania's. For all I know it <u>was</u> that car. I happily drove it for the next 10 years.

Adeline

Although we didn't have kids at first, we did have a little black kitty-cat with three white paws and an L-shaped tail. We adopted her from the Green Hill Humane Society about a year before we got married and kept her in my apartment. Pris named her for E. Adeline Curtis, one of the founders of Gama Phi Beta. We just called her Adeline, or Addy.

Adeline was a piece of work, and in very little time had pretty much taken control of the household. It was like Bill Murray's movie *"What About Bob?"* In our instance it took the form of asking ourselves, before we made arrangements to do anything, *"What about Adeline?"*

It was seriously important that we do this because this cat had an uncanny sense for detecting when we were planning to go somewhere and would disappear at the precise moment we had to leave. Pris ended up devising this contraption she used to lure her out from whatever hiding spot she'd selected to make trouble from. Once, she disappeared into the heating system of my parents' house; we had a devil of a time luring her out of there.

She pulled this little stunt in a campground on a day trip to the Oregon coast once and we ended up having to come home without her and then drive all the way back over there the next day to retrieve her.

And don't say, *"Well you should have left her home."* We tried that once when we were living on Chemeketa Street in Salem. We left her home alone while we went to Central Oregon for the weekend.

We'd just begun spoiling her with a fancy new kind of cat food that came in these sleek little aluminum-wrapped packages. Apparently she'd been planning on going with us and was none too happy to see us drive away without her.

When we did get home, two days later, it was to discover that even though we'd left plenty of available food and water, Adeline had found it necessary to get up onto the kitchen counter, then up to the cabinet where we kept the new cat food.

From there it was only a matter of dragging the box out of the cupboard and onto the floor where she systematically went through it, opening and scattering each individual package around the kitchen. She didn't eat it, just scattered it.

That was pretty bad, but not as bad it got. After the mess in the kitchen had been cleaned up, I went into the spare bedroom we used for an office to discover that—just to be sure she'd made her point—Adeline had also left a large deposit of you-know-what right in the middle of my desk.

After that, whenever we asked ourselves *"What about Adeline?"* we'd quickly reach the same conclusion: *"Better take her with us."*

CHAPTER 28

Henry Fonda Gave Me a Ride in His Car

Sometimes a Great Notion

After we were married, Pris continued to go along with me on some of my reporting assignments. That's how she happened to be with me the time I met the godlike movie star Henry Fonda in the summer of 1970. We'd only been married about six months and I was still going to school and working part-time at the *Springfield News*.

I'd been working on a story about the making of the movie *"Sometimes A Great Notion"* based on the novel by the famous Oregon author Ken Kesey. It was being filmed near the town of Kernville on the Oregon coast. The local angle was that Kesey lived on his family's dairy farm at Pleasant Hill not far from Springfield.

"Notion" is the story of a hardheaded and independent gyppo logging family in the fictional town of Wakonda, Oregon. They're at war with the union for supplying the local sawmill with logs while the union is striking it for higher wages.

I'd had trouble persuading Kesey to sit for an interview or let us come out to the farm to take pictures, although I did talk to him on the phone a couple of times. His number was listed in the phone book.

Kesey was friendly enough, but declined the interview the first time I called. He said he was trying to avoid *"that old American trick"* where, as authors become better known, everyone wants a piece of them. *"They take pictures,"* he told me, *"and they interview you until you're distracted."*

So it was without his blessing that I set out for the Oregon coast one Saturday with the same 35-millimeter Nikon I'd first used on the Bobby Kennedy assignment. The mission was to take photographs for the paper of the film's all-star cast and the movie as it was being made.

And all-star it was: Henry Fonda in the role of Henry Stamper, the grizzled logger at the head of the family; Paul Newman and Richard Jaeckel as his two handsome sons; and the beautiful Lee Remick as Viv, Hank Stamper's wife.

Fonda had already been nominated for an Oscar for best actor a couple of times and later won it for his part in the film *"On Golden Pond"* with Katharine Hepburn. It'd be hard to say which of them was the bigger box office draw—Fonda or Newman, fresh from his roles in the wildly popular films *"Cool Hand Luke"* and *"Butch Cassidy and the Sundance Kid"* with Robert Redford. I know there was no one bigger at the time.

I had yet to grasp the importance of preparation and research for a story like this so I was very much flying by the seat of my pants when I parked my 1956 Chevy at a logging gate along the Coast Highway one day and hiked a couple of miles into the set on a dirt logging road.

I'd found time to have one brief conversation with the publicity firm in Los Angeles promoting the film, but the person there didn't seem to know very much about things. She didn't really say one way or the other, so I figured I'd go ahead; at least I had a name to drop if someone stopped me. But no one did. It was just, *"Let's walk in here and see what comes of it."*

I had no trouble taking all the pictures I wanted and observed a couple of hours of filming without any interference from anyone.

One thing I was to learn after we were married is that Priscilla is an assiduous rules-follower. If a sign says *"Keep Out,"* she keeps out. To use one of our dear old friend David Rhoten's favorite expressions, I'm a little more "loosey-goosey."

I mention this to explain why, while I was making my hike into the set of *"Sometimes a Great Notion,"* she remained behind in the '56 Chevy to read. When they shut down shooting for the day, I reversed myself and was making my way back down the logging road to the main highway and the car.

Before too long a dust-covered, *1953* Chevrolet four-door sedan borrowed from the set pulled up alongside me. It was painted that pretty saddle brown they had that year, a little banged-up, no hub caps—like a seven-year-old car owned by a logging family would have looked in 1960 when the story takes place. A man in the back seat hand-cranked the rear window down and asked me if I'd like a ride. This turned out to be Fonda.

He was still dressed in his costume, which this day was a tin hard-hat, a striped "hickory shirt" like the loggers wear, suspenders, and cut-off—or "stagged"—jeans. Loggers stag their pants off so the cuffs won't get caught in the underbrush. His arm was in a cast that stuck out away from his body in an "L" and he was sporting about a week's growth of gray-white stubble.

This should be the point at which I tell about the insightful interview I conducted with one of the greatest performers of our time, but alas an old character flaw reared its ugly head and I came away with very little I could use in my story.

What happened was that instead of talking about himself or the movie, Fonda began to interview me and I was only too happy to oblige him. He wanted to know what I knew about the Keseys. It wasn't very much.

I did tell him that Ken Kesey had a brother named Joe who liked to squirrel around Springfield in a big yellow Cadillac convertible with the top down and how Joe's wife, Nancy, was trying to market a new product out of their dairy business that most people had never heard of. (I just saw it in the dairy case at Fred Meyer's yesterday, 50 years later. It was—and still is—called Nancy's Yogurt.)

It became apparent to me that I should have gotten better prepared before setting out on this little escapade. I felt like I had let Fonda down. (At least I didn't ask for his autograph.)

Before I knew it, we were at the gate and the conversation was over. I had been hoping I'd have the chance to introduce the great man to my wife before he was driven away. But this was not to be. I'd been gone too long. Pris had decided she needed a nap and was soundly asleep in the back seat of our car when I climbed out of Fonda's and bid him adieu.

But the story came out fine and earned me a two-page by-lined spread in the *Springfield News* with photo credits. Sometimes it's better to be lucky than smart.

The Kicker

Now here's the kicker. I had gotten much better with the Nikon and ended up with a not-small stack of pictures—

some of them up-close and not too bad—of the major actors on the set doing their scenes. But I still had nothing from Kesey. I decided to try one more time.

I rang his number again; he picked up. I apologized for being a bother but told him I was looking at some nice photos of Henry Fonda as Hank Stamper. I wondered if we might print up a set for him. I further wondered if he might do us one little favor by providing us with a recent picture of himself.

Kesey seemed pleased and grateful to learn of the pictures I'd taken of Fonda and the others embodying his novel's characters. He told me that he would make a picture of himself available to me for the story.

He instructed me to go to a house at the corner of 10th and Jefferson streets in Eugene the next night to drop off my pictures and pick up the one of him. This turned out to be just a few blocks away from the area in downtown Eugene now known as Kesey Square.

Eugene was a hippie haven and Kesey was famous for his earlier LSD-fueled trip across the U.S. with a group called The Merry Pranksters in a 1939 International Harvester school bus painted in tie-dye. Therefore, I wasn't surprised when I knocked and a man who looked almost identical to Charles Manson came to the door.

I told him why I was there and handed him the envelope with my photographs. He disappeared into the house and returned with a 5 x 7-inch manila envelope. I thanked him and said goodnight, not bothering to open the envelope until I got back to the office. When I did, it was not at all what I was expecting.

There were two pictures. One was grainy, a little under-exposed, and slightly out of focus. It showed Kesey standing bare-headed wearing jeans and a T-shirt in front of a barn. This is the one we went with.

The other one, while technically a better photograph, showed the author sitting at a table facing the camera. He was smiling and appeared to be rubbing his hands in anticipation over something before him on the table. The "something" was a huge pile of what everyone we showed it to assumed to be cocaine.

I'm not sure what a newspaper today would do with such a picture under those circumstances, but probably more than we did. The subject of the photo didn't really fit with our story and we didn't know for sure what we were looking at. We decided not to use it.

That picture would probably fetch a fortune on eBay today. I think we tossed it in the wastepaper basket.

Talk about a prankster—I discovered for myself that Kesey was that.

CHAPTER 29

Pris and Don's Excellent Adventure

A s I said, it would be six years after Pris and I were married before we had kids. We tried to make the most of our unencumbered years.

We lived in a number of different places during this time, all rentals. One of the first was a farmhouse on Hazelgreene Road in the countryside just north of Salem owned by an orchardist named Diegnan. He couldn't believe we were old enough to be teachers. I told him, *"Well, everybody has to start sometime."*

We just about froze that winter, the house was so drafty. When the school year was up we relocated to another little white bungalow at 1850 Chemeketa Street near the state hospital in downtown Salem. Chemeketa was a pleasant enough neighborhood, although you had to be alert for some of the less-insane inmates from the state hospital who were allowed to roam around the area.

There was an 80-plus-year-old lady across the street named Mrs. Gemunder. She was so nearly blind that when Pris went to visit her she noticed that pictures of her daughter resting on the piano were upside-down. When Priscilla took her to lunch, she mistook an orchid for her salad and ate it.

The move to the 15 acres on Marcola Road outside Springfield in 1973 began our years of home ownership and became the first place our first two offspring—Kami and Michael—would know as a place we once lived.

But before all that, we had one last grand adventure in the period before the kids came along. A trip that lives long in our memories is one we took by car around the United States in the summer of 1973. Pris wasn't teaching because it was summer vacation for her; I had more than a month before I had to report to my new communications job with the Springfield School District.

Our life was so unencumbered at this point it seems like we came up with the idea to drive around the U.S. one day and took off the next. Pris says, though, that we took time to arrange for a cat sitter, so maybe it was a week. In any event, we did very little planning before hopping into our two-door 1970 Chevrolet Malibu on June 5, 1973, and hitting the road.

Pris had purchased two books to take along. One was a guide to campgrounds in America; the other was a book of places to see all over the country. Otherwise, we were just flying by the seat of our bell-bottomed pants.

We'd packed a pup tent, sleeping bags, a camp stove with cooking utensils and dinnerware, a gas lantern, and our swimming suits. Oh yes, and a two-gallon canvas water bag full to the stopper of clean Oregon water for crossing the Great Salt Lake Desert. (Cars were not nearly so reliable in those days as they are today.) That was about it. No reservations anywhere. No itinerary, really.

We had a few destinations in mind—some national parks and one stop in Visalia, Louisiana, that I'd promised one of my students we'd make. Otherwise, as the Southwest Airlines slogan says today, we were *"Free to roam about the country."*

And roam we did. When we arrived back home on June 29th we'd covered more than 9,000 miles and visited 33 states and the District of Columbia. I know this because Pris kept meticulous notes that included not only how far we went each day, but our average mpg—16.7.

The route we followed started in Oregon and took us down through California then east/southeast through Nevada and Utah where I maintained the family tradition of swimming in every body of water we come to by diving into the Great Salt Lake.

We'd been told that you float better in salt water. This turned out to be true. It's also true that you go blind, like, instantly if you open your eyes under water. Salt!

I staggered blindly from the lake to the car where I groped for the canvas water bag and finally managed to flush the salt out of my eyes. They should have a sign—maybe something like, "Hey, Dummies from Oregon—Don't Put Your Face in the Salt Water. Hurts Like Hell!"

In Salt Lake City we went to see the Mormon Church's Grand Tabernacle. We signed the guestbook. Two days after we got home, two young Mormon missionaries rode up on their bicycles and knocked on our door. We weren't interested in joining the church, but we <u>were</u> impressed with their follow-up.

(By the way, have you ever heard why they have to bury Mormon missionaries so deep in the ground? The first four feet are for the bicycle.)

After that it was on to Arizona and then across the bottom half of the U.S. all the way from New Mexico to Florida. This took us through Oklahoma and parts of Texas, Louisiana, Mississippi and Alabama. From Florida we made our way up the eastern seaboard through Georgia and the Carolinas, Virginia and into Washington, D.C. Once, we set foot in four different states on the same day—Maine, New Hampshire, Vermont and Massachusetts.

Coming back, we took in the upper half of the U.S., crossing from east to west through New York, Pennsylvania, Ohio, Indiana, Wisconsin, Minnesota, South Dakota, Wyoming, Idaho and then back to Oregon. Just as a cultural waterline, I'll mention that average people in the U.S. had only just begun to travel by car like this. I think my own dad never made it outside of the two or three Northwest states in his lifetime.

Here's some of what I remember about the adventure.

Sorry Officer, Now Clean this Place up

Any time you see one of our national parks it's a highlight. We saw several on this trip, starting with Mt. Lassen in California, then Zion in Utah and a couple of days at the Grand Canyon where I got a ticket from an Arizona State trooper for momentarily, and only slightly, crossing the center line.

I told him when he handed me the citation that somebody should do something about all the litter along their highways. Oregon's nation-leading bottle bill hadn't been passed yet but it was in the works. I made a point of telling him about that too. I don't know why, exactly, unless it was just to spit in his eye.

At a roadside stand on the Navajo Indian Reservation in Arizona, I stopped to snap some pictures of the little Indian kids manning the stand. The children's' father was plowing an adjacent field with a mule. I took a picture of him too. He stopped his work and came up to the fence, indicating I needed to pay to take pictures, which I did—50 cents.

I admit that I was a little miffed at the time but as I look at some of the images from that day I can see that I was being a little intrusive. It's fair to say that it was a moment of cultural insensitivity on my part.

Before we were done we'd taken in quite a bit of what our one guide book recommended we see, including Jefferson's Monticello and JFK's eternal flame at Arlington, most of the D.C. monuments and the Smithsonian.

At a pre-Civil War plantation house called Cedar Grove on the Mississippi River we saw a cannon ball fired from a federal gun boat still wedged in a parlor wall above a "fainting couch." Good place for it if you'd been there at the time.

Behind the Scenes at Jefferson's House

Thomas Jefferson's mountaintop estate, Monticello, embodied everything we were looking for in our little history tour of America. It was a dreary rainy morning and we were the only people taking the tour.

The guide said that typically only staff were allowed to walk up one of the four narrow and winding 24-inch staircases that Jefferson designed to reach the second and third floors of the mansion. There was barely room for two people to pass at the same time. It made me wonder if this had anything to do with how Jefferson and Sally Hemings "met."

She showed us the swivel chair Jefferson invented beside the desk where he wrote the *Declaration of Independence*. This way he could sit in one spot in his study and turn to follow the sunlight as he read.

I guess another thing that people don't usually get do was that she let each of us sit in Jefferson's chair while she spun it around. She said that was something that Jefferson and Sally Hemings used to like to do that a lot of people don't know about.

A weathervane on top of the portico was connected to a dial on the ceiling below so it could be read from inside the house. I don't know if it had anything to do with those two or not, but I wouldn't be surprised.

I've always loved a nice house and never miss a chance to see one. Hearst's Castle, Teddy Roosevelt's home on Sagamore Island, and Franklin D. Roosevelt's at Hyde Park; I was lucky to see them all. Thomas Edison's house in Orange, New Jersey, which we visited when I was working in New Jersey, is spectacular.

But nothing ever came close to Monticello. I totally got it when we saw that Jefferson had written, *"All my wishes end where I hope my days will end. At Monticello."*

I think he should have added "...with Sally Hemings."

CHAPTER 30

Finding Aunt Lizzie

T he most significant memories we have from our cross-country drive don't involve the famous landmarks as much as some of the people we met. At right about the midpoint, we had one of the most memorable and moving experiences of the entire adventure.

I'd had a wonderful boy in my journalism class. I'll call him "Alexander Owens" here to avoid violating anyone's privacy. Alexander's family had been fractured as a youngster when both his mother and father died within a few years of each other.

Theirs was an interesting story. His father was an African-American soldier stationed in Korea with the U.S. Army when he married Alexander's mother, a Korean. Her family promptly disowned her for marrying outside their race.

They planned to bring their family to America when Alexander's dad got out of the service, but he suddenly died of a heart attack. His wife and three children ended up coming to the U.S. by themselves. They weren't here very long before Alexander's mother also died, orphaning him, his brother and a sister.

By the time Alexander entered high school, homes had been found for all the kids through their church. But they knew virtually nothing about their father—only that he'd been born in Visalia, Louisiana, right across the Mississippi River from Natchez, Mississippi.

Alexander asked me if we might find time on our trip to go through Visalia, see if we could find anybody connected with his family still living there today. Specifically, he asked if we could try to retrieve his father's driver's license, as having that kind of ID had turned out to be important to him. We said we'd try.

So that's how I found myself shoving quarters into a telephone booth at a gas station/convenience store in Visalia one hot June afternoon calling the numbers listed for Owens in the telephone book chained to the little desk in the phone booth.

Actually it <u>had</u> a chain, but it wasn't attached to anything. I now remember taking it into the convenience story to ask for help. We'd been in the deep south long enough by then to see that there were distinctly different neighborhoods for blacks and whites. Since there were a number of Owenses listed in the directory, I asked the clerk at the store if he could tell me which of the listings were likely to be black neighborhoods based on the addresses shown.

The guy was friendly enough. He opened the telephone book on the counter and began putting a check mark by the ones he knew would be people of color. I heard him muttering, *"Niggra. Niggra. White. Niggra."* as he ticked them off.

Racial insensitivities aside, the man knew the area. Back at the phone booth I hit pay dirt on the second call. I'd no sooner begun to explain the situation to a woman who answered the phone when she interrupted and said, *"You're looking for Lizzie*

Shivers. That's their aunt. She lives in Natchez." She said she wished she could be more helpful but, *"We don't speak."*

I called the number for Lizzie Shivers and spoke to a creaky-voiced old African-American woman who confirmed that she was, in fact, the great aunt of the Owens' kids. She gave me general directions to her house and added, *"Just ask anyone on Waterline Street which one is Aunt Lizzie's."*

As I said, segregation was still very much the norm in the southeast at this time and the neighborhood we drove into was as segregated as it got. The streets were narrow and lined with small houses, some of them on stilts and every one in need of a paint job. Young black people lounged on the hoods of aged automobiles gawking at these honkies in a car with Oregon license plates.

When we thought we were close we stopped and asked a small group of teenagers if they knew which house belonged to Aunt Lizzie. They pointed it out immediately and Lizzie herself greeted us from her high front porch. There was a large neighbor man about 50 years of age sitting with her in a rocking chair when we drove up. He didn't say anything; before too long Lizzie told him, *"It's all right, Norman, you can run along."* You can deduce that she had asked him to come over *"Just in case."*

Typically, one might say that this was when we learned *"the rest of the story,"* but in this instance both sides helped to fill in the details.

We soon learned that Alexander's father and his siblings had also been orphaned when *their* mother died. Their father married a woman who wanted nothing to do with them. When she turned her back on the kids it was Lizzie who took them in. She said that education had been important to her so she had supplemented her income as a domestic by picking cotton in order to send all four kids through Catholic school. Lizzie basically sacrificed her life to raise those kids and never married.

Ironically, it turned out that the first woman I'd reached on the phone—the one who directed us to Lizzie—was the "wicked stepmother" in the story, which would explain why she said, *"We don't speak."*

Sadly, none of the four children Lizzie raised lived to be over 40 years of age. In fact, Alexander's father was the last of the four to go and he'd just reached that milestone when he died. Lizzie said she'd learned from the American Red Cross that he'd died, but knew nothing about his family after that.

Lizzie said that the last she'd heard from Alexander's father was that he'd had a daughter and named the baby after her. This we were able to confirm, as Alexander's sister was called *"Libby,"* short for Elizabeth; that was Lizzie's full name. She couldn't have been happier.

We took photographs from her walls of Alexander's unknown family and set them up against the front steps so I could take pictures of them with the Nikon. When we returned to Oregon we turned the pictures over to him. His family was delighted to discover they had a Great Aunt Lizzie and laid plans to go down to meet her.

If nothing else eventful had happened the rest of the trip we wouldn't have minded. Even 45 years later the experience of reuniting the Owens/Shivers family remains one of the best of our lifetime.

Think too what this unlikely summer-time encounter between a couple of young people from lily-white Oregon and these people in an all- black community in the deep south might have done to further relations between our races at a time when race relations in this country were not that good.

I do what I can do.

While U Wait

Pris's notebook says that we knew we were in the South when we stopped at a restaurant and one of the items on the menu was, *"Fry-Your-Own Catfish."* I thought we'd passed that point some time before when we passed a sign on a warehouse that said, *"Pecans Cracked While U Wait."*

In any event, we continued our sojourn deeper into the South. Late one hot and sultry night while we were looking for a campground someplace in Louisiana, I spotted a Pepsi machine outside a closed service station and turned around to go back. The machine was all lit up and appeared to be functional, but when I shoved a couple of quarters into the slot nothing happened.

I was banging on it a little bit when a local policeman wheeled up in a cruiser. He was a knockoff of what many people think of when they hear the words *"Southern Sheriff."* Short with a belly that hung over his belt, wearing reflecting sunglasses even though it was after dark. My first thought was *"Uh-Oh."*

He parked so that his lights illuminated the Chevy and took his time getting out of the patrol car before he approached me with a big aluminum flashlight. When he got within speaking distance he drawled, *"This thing givin' ya'll trouble? It does that."*

As soon as I confirmed that it was, he dove into his right pocket and extracted two more quarters which he shoved into the machine. This time it worked. I got the Pepsi and he wouldn't take my money.

This was the same guy who told us when we asked about places to camp that he didn't advise it. *"The water's been high this year. The snakes and 'gators are up in the campgrounds."* He recommended that we get a hotel. We had no trouble going along with that recommendation after receiving his wildlife report.

We did finally find a motel and took a room on the ground floor. Pris was so freaked out by now that she pulled up the legs of her bell bottoms and ran from the car to the room to avoid any chance of an encounter with a reptile. She managed to avoid that specific fate but ended up having a run-in with an amphibian just the same.

Once she was inside the room, she began trying to close the door but it wouldn't shut. She pulled it closed, but before the latch could catch it would spring back open. She tried several more times with the same result before we went in for a closer look and discovered to our horror that there was an enormous bullfrog caught in the bottom hinge of the door. She had been squishing it in the door jamb. There was a certain amount of blood involved and the thing was dead by the time we got it out. We couldn't wait to get to hell out of there in the morning.

Both the encounter with Aunt Lizzie and the one with the anti-Bull Connors turned out to be examples of Southern hospitality at its finest. Once we got up north, we had another one that can only be called a good example of *Northern* hospitality.

Bull's Island

In New Jersey we camped at a place called Bull's Island State Park where the ranger caught our Oregon plates and said he'd like to go out there some day. He told us you pay when you leave.

At night, Bull's Island became just ablaze in fireflies. Having never seen them before, we thoroughly enjoyed the show. We held them in our hands and marveled at their little electric generators.

But it was what happened in the morning that shocked us (Not really, I was just extending the metaphor there a little bit). We were surprised when we heard someone or some*thing* knocking on the tent flap. It turned out to be two little kids from a neighboring camp site, the one with a new Mercury station wagon and a travel trailer beside it.

The kids said they'd been sent over to ask if we wanted to come for pancakes. We did and they turned out to be pretty good pancakes served up by as nice a family as you'll ever meet. The man told us he worked at AT&T in Morristown, New Jersey. He'd won the Mercury in a jingle contest. I think I'd remember if he had sung it for us, so I guess he didn't. That's on me; I should have asked.

We enjoyed being at Bull's Island so much that we decided to camp a second night, despite what to Westerners struck us as a fairly steep campsite fee. That turned out to be of no concern. After we'd packed everything up on the second morning and driven to the exit gate to pay, the same ranger was there and now *he* wouldn't take our money.

He said, *"I'll come out to Oregon sometime and you can return the favor."*

Elsewhere in New England

Elsewhere in New England we found some folks not so welcoming. I see in the daily notes Pris took an entry that reads, *"Woonsocket, R.I. Clinton Street ARCO. Attendant named Norman Rivet snotty and refused to change oil."* Norman Rivet. You can't make this stuff up.

In New Hampshire we went shopping for one of those metal-cast eagles you see on everybody's houses back there and were refused the sale by a shopkeeper who said something to the effect of, *"Why don't you take your out-of-state plates and go back to wherever in the hell Oregon is. We don't need the business."* We finally got one somewhere else that I'm thinking might be a good item for the gift shop at the Camp Sherman dump one of these days.

In Vermont we caused a backup at the entryway to a state park because we had a failure to communicate with the ranger at the gate. He kept saying a sentence that ended in the word *"Purrmutt"* with no inflection on either of the two syllables. He said it several times before we realized he wanted to see our *permit.*

CHAPTER 31

The Heart of the Kickapoo Valley

To help you understand how little of what we saw and did on our inner-continental adventure was actually planned, we were more than half way around the country before we came up with the idea of going to Steuben, Wisconsin. That's where my Grandfather and Grandmother Wilt started out before moving to Oregon. We wanted to see if we could still find the schoolhouse where Alma taught all those years ago.

Steuben is a little town down in the southwest corner of Wisconsin near the border with Iowa on the Mississippi River. They call it *"The Heart of the Kickapoo Valley."* We knew it was small, but just how small was revealed to us within minutes of arriving there.

I knew that Alma had a brother named Neal for whom one of my dad's brothers was named, but I don't think I had any idea whether he was still alive. We only knew the name: Neal Wanamaker. We just pulled into town one day in the Chevy and things went from there.

We were able to locate the old school house and found it still standing. I picked up a square nail used in its construction. I can't for the life of me remember where I put that thing but I'm sure it's here somewhere.

There was a man working on a garden near the building so I approached him. I told him we were from Oregon and that my grandmother had taught at this very school. That's when we found out how small Steuben was. This man said to me, *"Alma Wanamaker? You must be one of Bill or Stan Wilt's boys,"* which I was: Bill's.

He told me that he'd heard a lot about Oregon after my grandfather went out there to homestead and seemed to have been kept thoroughly informed about events out that way. He held his fist out with the thumb sticking straight up, used his other hand to mark it about two inches from the tip, and said, *"They tell me you have blackberries out there the size of a man's thumb."*

My grandmother's mother was a Campbell, also from there in Steuben. The man I had approached at the school turned out to be Vern Campbell, her cousin. Turned out his wife's name was Fern, so they were Vern and Fern. We told him we were just passing through. He said, *"Well you're gonna go see Neal and Helen aren't you?"*

That's how we ended up sitting at Great Uncle Neal and Aunt Helen Wanamaker's kitchen table that afternoon.

One of Bill's Boys

When we drove up to their place I got out of the car and approached Neal who was working in his garden. I said, *"If I called you Uncle Neal, would you have any idea who I am?"*

He looked me over a little bit and repeated what Vern had said: *"You must be one of Bill or Stan's boys?"* Why neither one of them thought I might be one of my Uncle Neal's sons, or Joe's, I don't know. But I was instantly pleased to be identified with these two important members of my family tree.

It had been our intention to stop in Steuben for only a few hours. That all changed pretty quickly once the news of our arrival got around. Neal and Helen welcomed us with open arms and asked, *"How many months will you be staying?"*

Neal said that we were welcome to stay as long as we liked, but that we might have to help out around the place because Helen had recently had *"an accident with a dog."* (We subsequently learned that she'd tripped over one on a sidewalk and broken her wrist.)

We agreed to stay one night but felt like we were really letting them down, particularly after they got busy and started getting the word out that some Wilts from Oregon were in town. It really made Neal and Helen happy that we'd come. They were well into their 80s and talked with great fondness about the time my mother, my grandmother, my older brother and Uncle Neal had come by car in the early 1940s. They had stayed a month.

We ended up staying the night. It really wasn't long enough to see everyone they thought we should see but we had some awfully nice visits. One was with my grandfather's younger sister, Ethel Hippenbecker, who was in her 90s. We also met Neal and Helen's daughter, Noreen Joy, and her husband and kids. They came for dinner in our honor and couldn't have been a nicer bunch of people. They made us feel like the family that we were.

Vern Campbell turned out to be the town historian. He put us in touch with four of my grandmother's former students from the one-room-schoolhouse days. They thought the world of her and reinforced the image I'd always had of Alma as a smart, self-reliant, adventurous woman who had, as they say in the Midwest, *"Cut a pretty wide swath through life."*

Boscobel Has Everything

Neal had a 1963 Chevrolet Biscayne—that was the economy model. He'd bought it new 10 years before and it now had 3,200 miles on the odometer. It's simple math: his annual average mileage was about 300 miles.

How it could be so impossibly low became apparent when I was looking through their local newspaper and saw there was to be a reenactment of Marquette and Joliet's voyage down the Mississippi in 1672 at a town called Prairie Du Chien about 20 miles away. Neal called it "Purda-sheen."

The place sounded interesting but when I asked Neal what it was like, he said he wouldn't know because he never went there. He said, *"No need to. Boscobel over here's got everything a fella needs!"*

The next day we climbed into the Biscayne and Neal took us all over. We went to see the old Lee Wanamaker farm. Lee Wanamaker would be my great grandfather, so this is where my Grandma Alma had started her life.

The barn had a big "W" in the gable but it didn't stand for Wanamaker or Wilt either one. They said it stood for Western Farms, one of the big agribusinesses that were picking up a lot of the old places around there.

He also drove us to a place called Hoover Holler where my grandfather Albert was from, as well as the farms once owned by Albert's brothers, Charlie and Balzer. That's right, my dad had an Uncle Balzer.

For lunch Neal took us to his favorite café on the main street of Boscobel. He seemed to know everyone and introduced us to what seemed like the entire population. Even though it must have been apparent to them that Pris was female, he kept saying to everyone we met, *"I want you to meet my nephews from Oregon."*

There's an old joke about how many Midwesterners it takes to screw in a light bulb. It takes five—one to screw it in and four to talk about how good the old one was. I imagine it was many months—maybe years—before our relatives there stopped talking about the time Albert and Alma's "nephews" paid them a visit.

Who am I to talk? It's been 45 years and we're still talking about it too. We'd experienced Southern hospitality, then Northern hospitality, and now Midwestern hospitality. All things considered, it would be hard to top the Midwestern version.

CHAPTER 32

It Rained Backwards and We Saw Snakes

After the "delay" in Wisconsin, we decided we'd better start booking it for home, so we shot through the remaining states of Minnesota, South Dakota, Montana, Wyoming and Idaho. The most memorable event either one of us remembers from the stretch across the Midwest was when we woke up in our tent in the middle of the night with this hellacious rainstorm going on and us lying in about two inches of water.

We had no choice but to pack up and leave. We learned on the radio that we were in a big squall of some kind that was moving from west to east. We were headed west, so that meant we'd at least be driving out of the weather system, which I'll repeat was hellacious.

So we get up on Interstate 90. We drive and we drive and we drive. After about 45 miles, we're still in the downpour. Suddenly, Pris gets a good look at a highway marker and goes, *"Did that just say we are on I-90 East?"*

Oops. In the fog of leaving the campground I'd accidentally turned the wrong direction and we'd been driving right along <u>with</u> the storm for almost an hour. Have to thank my navigator for catching that one, but it still set us back a couple of hours. My nickname for Priscilla is "Margaret" because her Aunt Margaret was the navigator when she and her husband, Alan, traveled. He used to say, *"That's my Margaret, right on target!"*

"We are <u>not</u> Stopping There!" (Yeah, Right)

We'd crossed Oklahoma and the panhandle of Texas early in the trip and that was a long drive with not much to see. But it was nothing like traversing the state of South Dakota. I just checked; it's 423 miles from one side of the state to the other. I would have guessed twice that much anyway.

We drove it east to west on Interstate 90 and just about the only thing to see the entire way were alternating billboards for Wall Drug Store, the famous tourist attraction in Wall, South Dakota, and Reptile Gardens, the big snake farm in Rapid City.

South Dakota had some of the weakest billboard laws in the nation at the time. It appeared that Wall Drug and Reptile Gardens were free to put up as many as they liked. Wall Drug alone had something like 250 of them, most of them along I-90.

They'd literally put the business on the map. Reptile Gardens probably had about the same number; if you do the math, that comes out pretty close to one billboard for every mile you drive crossing the state.

Even after Congress passed the Federal Highway Beautification Act in 1965, South Dakota dragged its feet for 15 years before even beginning to comply. They lost out on a lot of federal highway dollars as a result, but apparently were content with the boost that the billboards gave to the tourist trade.

And that was no small matter. The year we took our trip, almost two million people visited Wall Drug in a state that didn't even have a million residents.

There used to be a place on Route 66 in the 1950s with a sandwich board out front that said, *"Stop. Eat. See Big Snake."* That's all the advertising they needed to really pull people in off the road.

But Pris and I were more resolute than that. We decided before very long that no matter how much advertising Wall Drug and Reptile Gardens threw at us, we were not going to stop at either one of these tourist traps. I think the exact words were, *"Ecch! No way are we stopping there."*

Free Ice Water in the Badlands

Wall Drug was still offering a free glass of ice water to anyone who came in. That was the gimmick that got the business rolling in the Great Depression. The owner's wife came up with the idea. Later they added free coffee and donuts for military people. The combination created a very appealing identity and made it a "don't miss" attraction out there on the edge of the Badlands, particularly in the days before automobile air conditioning came along.

So many people began to stop at the place it became an international sensation. Pretty soon visitors from all over the world began putting up their own signs indicating how far it was to Wall Drug from where they lived. You can see pictures of them on the Internet.

My favorite is the one of a U.S. soldier at Bagram Air Force Base during the war in Afghanistan standing in the blazing desert sun by a sign that says "6,964 Miles to Wall Drug. Free Ice Water."

We had planned to be among the only travelers going

that way that did <u>not</u> succumb to the allure of free ice water. But man, those signs can really grind you down. It wasn't subliminal advertising; it was full liminal. Long before you got there you already knew that Wall Drug had, besides free ice water and five-cent coffee, an ice cream parlor with an endless selection, a good-looking chicken fried steak and a wide selection of cowboy boots. You could also *"See a Jackalope!"*

We ended up pulling in. I still have a Wall Drug sign I bought there mounted in our garage.

When the druggist behind Wall Drug died in 1999, the governor of South Dakota eulogized him as *"A guy that figured out free ice water could turn you into a phenomenal success in the middle of semi-arid desert way out in the middle of somewhere."*

I noticed that as governor of the state he said *"middle of somewhere"* instead of *"middle of nowhere."*

Snakes on a Plain

As for Reptile Gardens, it was pretty much the same story; by the time we got there we almost felt like we *had* to stop.

Now, I myself come from a long line of snake bounty hunters. My mother was so afraid of them that she established a reward of one nickel for every snake we killed. She didn't need to *see* them; she'd take your word for it. With five kids all on snake patrol, the Wilt family was probably responsible for the eradication of an entire subspecies of garter snakes in the Mohawk Valley.

A friend told me once that although he is terrified of snakes he never misses a chance to see one. I think that's what got a lot of people into Reptile Gardens. That and the billboards.

Reptile Gardens got its start during the Depression when a guy named Earl Brockelsby had the idea to catch a few prairie rattlesnakes and make them a roadside attraction. By the time we were there it was in the Guinness Book of World Records as the world's largest reptile zoo and was well worth the price of admission.

We learned some fascinating things about snakes, like the fact that boa constrictors don't actually <u>crush</u> their prey—they <u>suffocate</u> it. Every time the animal exhales, the boa tightens its grip a little more. The King Cobra can inject enough venom to kill 13 adults. Some 15,000 to 20,000 people every year die from cobra bites because they're copious in a part of the world where people still go barefoot and hospitals are few in number. Stuff like that.

But one funny thing happened. The guy doing the show asked people, *"What should you do if you come across a rattlesnake in the wild?"* a little boy behind us guessed *"Stop, drop and roll?"*

As for the rest of the trip, if I told you we'd seen a dog die when his owners carelessly let him off-leash and he tumbled into one of the boiling sulfur ponds in Yellowstone National Park it would probably be the only thing you haven't already heard about Yellowstone, so I'll end this "travelogue" here.

By the way, we didn't actually see a dog get poached to death at Yellowstone; I'm just saying <u>if</u> we had.

CHAPTER 33

The Simpsons

O ver the next few pages I'm going to talk about my own family, which otherwise is being given short thrift in this account of my life and times. I'll say first, though, that what they say is true: the only people you cannot stop loving are your children. If you're lucky, you find someone to marry that you feel the same way about. I got that too.

I couldn't be more proud to see how our kids have excelled in their various pursuits. Each has distinguished himself or herself and our family in their own way. They give me complete confidence both in their generation and the one they're now raising.

In the end I have to agree with the first President Bush— (you remember, the one everyone liked?) He said the greatest achievement of his life was that his kids still come home.

In short, despite our collective shortcomings I have had—and continue to have—about as good a family as a man could hope for. Think, *The Simpsons*.

I wasn't in the corporate environment very long before I noticed how high the divorce rate was among the top people. Four of the six main bosses I had in my career were divorced and the job always had something to do with it. One of the guys' wives actually told him, *"You choose: me or that job."*

When I was home everything was okay with the world. You can't put a price on that. It helped me immensely in terms of how things went at work, I'm sure.

My boyhood friend, Edwin Head, and I both remember the summer when we were about 14. His cousins from Idaho came to stay a few days. Even to our barely-developed selves it was obvious that this family was something special. They actually seemed to like each other. Eddie and I agreed that when we had our own families this is the kind we wanted them to be. Here's a kid-by-kid look at mine:

Kami Teressa Wilt, b. November 8, 1975

Kami was the baby I didn't know I'd wanted all my life until she got here. But the picture of us together a week or so after she was born is all you have to see to know that that all changed very quickly. I'm sitting in an armchair under a floor lamp with a textbook from my graduate program propped up with my left hand and Kami cradled in my right arm. Utter contentment on both faces.

She was such a great little girl all-around that she brought out the best in both of us as parents—and the worst; once, when she was two, her grandfather and I were watching her play on the lawn at the farm on Marcola Road. Suddenly she inexplicably made a break for the road. It was a distance of about 15 yards and I didn't get to her until she was only 10 feet or so from the macadam.

When I did catch up to her I did something I'd never once even contemplated: I spanked her all the way back to the house. When you really love someone that much, you just can't stand the idea that they almost killed themselves.

It was, I'm told, a normal paternal response to a situation like that. And who wouldn't love someone who thought as much of me as Kami did. When she was 4, she learned at Montessori School that George Washington was the first U.S. President. Priscilla asked her, *"Do you know who's president now?"*

Kami: *"Daddy?"*

Like her dad, Kami's career thrust would begin at an early age with a great interest in the language arts. Once, when she was about 2 ½ and beginning to grasp the concept of reading, I took her to my office on a weekend. We walked by a driveway with a chain across it. The sign said *"Authorized District Personnel Only."*

Kami was already going to pre-school and learning her letters so I asked her if she could read what the sign said. She went over to it, touched each word with her little index finger, and pronounced: *"Everybody. Must. Stay. Out!"*

Kami's literary and dramatic talents began to emerge at an early age and sometimes made me, at least, think that she should have had a name more suited to her outsized persona. Perhaps Kamille; that way we could still call her Kami but her name on the playbill would be more substantial and befitting.

I'd probably still call her LuLu, like the Dell Comics cartoon character Little LuLu, whom she resembled at 7 coming up out of the pond, freckled and beaming.

She began reading on her own by 4, which of course didn't make her a prodigy; but once she started, you never saw her without a book. It was fun watching her natural talent with the language emerge and we'd often be amused by how the things she was learning were reflected in what came out of her mouth.

Once, I remember, we told the kids we had to turn the power off at the Sumner, Washington, house while we swapped out a light fixture. This would have been when Kami was about 7. She said to the boys, *"We might as well go upstairs and pretend it's the early 19th Century."*

And of course she had quite an advanced vocabulary for a little girl. I took her fly fishing with me on the Metolius one evening when she was 6. It began to grow dark and the bats started to emerge. I quickly drew in my line. Once in a while you hear about someone snagging one of these little creatures with their hook. That would be a big problem. I mean, how do you get a fish hook out of a bat without it biting you? Probably in the face.

Anyway, as we began walking back to the car I started explaining why I had stopped fishing when I did. I was choosing my words carefully so as to not alarm or confuse the poor little thing when Kami stopped dead in her tracks and exclaimed, *"Oh no! Not Hydrophobia!"*

Not surprisingly, given her way with words, Kami brought great honor to the family at an early age when she won the *Tacoma News-Tribune*—Pierce County spelling bee in 3rd grade. She correctly spelled *"Nectar"* to earn the right to take the last word, then spelled *"Pictorial"* to win. I was planning to write down every word she spelled on the way to the championship but I got so caught up in watching the competition that I later saw I'd only written down two words: *"Citizen"* and *"Myth."*

Meanwhile, sports were not too much her thing. One episode from family lore has her at age 8 counting daisies in the end zone of the soccer field instead of defending it against her team's rapidly-advancing opponent. Around 11, she did take an interest in basketball for a while and was telling me she'd "almost" beaten her friend Marcus in a game that ended 46-44.

I was impressed with the score until she explained how it happened. She said, *"I was ahead but then right at the end he hit a 20-pointer."*

Finally, I have to say in this little essay about my daughter that she distinguished herself as an older sister and took her responsibilities in that role seriously. Sometimes I thought it must be Priscilla's Aunt Margaret coming out in her.

Margaret was the famously formidable older sister on her father's side of the family. In about 1935 she watched her little brother, Paul, hop over the side door and into the backseat of the family's first automobile. Although neither one of them had ever been in an automobile before, Margaret knew immediately that this was not how you got into one. She sternly demanded that he exit the car and *"get back in the Christian way!"*

One of the times I'm thinking about with Kami was when her baby brother, Cooper, had begun to crawl, which would have made her about 6. I could hear him crawling around, entertaining himself under my feet as I worked at the dining room table one evening.

Pretty soon Kami came in from the main hallway and I heard her shriek, *"Cooper has a pen in his mouth! Cooper has a pen in his mouth!"* I took a quick glance and saw her little brother playing harmlessly with a ball-point pen from the office, making it click in and out. I said, *"Oh, I think it's all right."*

She glowered at me as she snatched him out from under the table and said, *"No it is not all right! It is nowhere near all right!"*

By the time she got to be 8 or 9, Kami was putting out a neighborhood newspaper called *The Wild Bugle* that covered the events in our woodsy and widely-scattered neighborhood. I think the news covered about 20 families with ours being the main source of content.

Fairly typical of the *Wild Bugle* was the story of a cat getting run over—but not killed—on our county road. It appeared under the headline *"Tragic Retelling of the Siamese Cat Who Looked Death in the Face and Lived"*

Because it has the strong family angle, I'm including here the full version of an article taken from the July, 1985, edition of the *Wild Bugle*. The story appeared under the headline, *"Resident of Our 'Neighborhood' Threatened Last Week by Menacing Fire."*

Last week, Don Wilt, a father of three, was driving along when a brightness caught his eye. At first, he turned his attention back to the road, but then, realizing what he'd seen, he quickly focused his eyes on the slowly growing fire in the car. As he was unable to stop, he frantically searched for a relief of some sort, a rest stop, a restaurant, a gas station. A gas station! There after five minutes of hysterical search, stood a gas station, which to Mr. Wilt must have seemed like the most beautiful thing in the world. Pulling up behind it so as not to ignite the gas tanks, he ran wildly into the station. He returned sweating but holding a fire extinguisher. Stepping bravely up to the flames, the fire licking at his feet, he turned his head and let the extinguishing gases fly. Relief filled him as a gust of steam blew in his face. He smiled, then collapsed, weary of the adventure behind him. A couple of minutes later, when the steam had cleared, Mr. Wilt's face was crinkled with disgust. The fire had melted the radio and flames had come out of the air conditioner. Mr. Wilt let out a gasp. "I hadn't realized how close I had come to a serious injury," he noted. Still, he continued faithfully on his way to work. That night, he returned to tell the story to his flabbergasted family. "All of us now realize how much he means to us," remarks Mrs. Wilt, lovingly. Luckily this car didn't belong to the Wilts, but was only on a test drive basis. The recent owner of the car has agreed to pay for the damage, leaving the Wilts happy and not in debt."

I made myself a little bit helpful to the *Wild Bugle* by Xeroxing at my office the 20 copies or so Kami distributed. I carried some regret for years that I might have done more. Now I'm more inclined to think it was right to just let her do her own thing; everybody loved it, and she got enough recognition and admiration from people to give her a sense of accomplishment that might not have been so genuine if I'd gotten more involved on the editorial side.

"Kam" turned out to be equally gifted in the performing arts and started early there too. I hope we still have the picture of her standing on a picnic table using a hotdog wiener for a microphone while belting out the theme song from *Little Orphan Annie* for her grandparents at a Shotgun Creek Park picnic one hot summer night.

When she was 12, Kami learned that the renowned Missoula Children's Touring Company was conducting auditions for a performance at the historic Pantages Theatre in Tacoma, 20 miles from where we lived. Being the overly protective father that I was, and knowing that hundreds of kids would try out, I tried to prepare her before the audition in the event she didn't get the part. But what does she do? Comes home with a lead role.

When she was a senior in high school, she won the part of Anne Frank in *The Diary of Anne Frank*, which the *Eugene Register-Guard* called *"a profoundly moving production at Lane Community College's intimate Blue Door Theatre."* It played a dozen sold-out performances. The paper said, *"Kami Wilt, a senior at South Eugene High School, is an endearing Anne. We clearly see her mature and grow."*

Following every production, the audience participated in a dialogue with the players who sometimes would answer <u>as</u> their character. At other times they would talk about the experience of <u>playing</u> that character. The way she handled these situations, the maturity and depth of emotion that she brought to the character, were very, very impressive, as was an extended interview she gave to one of the Eugene television stations.

But here's the funny thing: in the end, although Kami had her shots in the *Big Apple*, it wasn't acting or writing either one that intrigued her most. I guess she got the same gene Priscilla has because her real interest throughout all has been working with kids.

As a little girl Kami so longed to be a babysitter that when she finally did reach the age where people would trust her with their children—I'm going to say 13—she went straight to the top. Who wouldn't love a baby sitter who showed up with a lesson plan developed exclusively for her day with <u>their</u> children? Art projects were her specialty.

The law of supply and demand, together with her reputation, created quite a dynamic one New Year's Eve at the cabin. The area was full of people with young kids who seldom got a chance to go out and kick up their heels. She was so in-demand that she ended up babysitting multiple local family's kids for the evening so their entertainment-starved parents could go out to celebrate the New Year.

(I think she took in something like $12,000 that one night and nine months later two children born in the vicinity were named for her.)

Where I'm going with this is that today, Kami T. Wilt is the director of the Austin Tinkering School—which she founded and which has been named "Best of Austin" by the *Austin Chronicle*. The paper said, *"Kami Wilt has dedicated her career to giving children hands-on experiences in the interest of developing their creativity and confidence through art, glue guns, and power tools at the Austin Tinkering School, which is infecting kids today with a love of DIY and messy creativity."*

When the Obama administration invited representatives from every state to a conference at the White House on education through innovation, who do you think represented the largest state in the Lower 48? Yep—our daughter—Kami Teressa Wilt. Who wouldn't be happy with a girl like that?

Michael Jon Wilt, b. June 30, 1977

Michael is the one who quickly sized up the situation in our house. He decided he did not wish to compete with his older sister academically and went the opposite direction. When he was about 4, I was taking him for a ride on the back of my bike. When we came to a stop sign I pointed out to him what the word said and spelled it for him: S.T.O.P.

He waved his little hand dismissively, gazed off the other direction, and said, *"I don't need to know; I'm not going to learn to read."*

But thanks to his mother and an excellent first-grade teacher, he came around. And, like his sister, once he started reading it became second nature. I was tucking him into bed one night when he said, *"I like books better than television because the picture in your head is so much bigger."*

One of the gifts M.J. derived from learning to read was a good vocabulary early-on. When he was 5, I remember being struck as we drove past someone else's house and he observed that it had "similar features" as our own. I knew immediately he was going to have a facility with words, and he does.

Eventually the boy who wasn't going to learn to read made it all the way through college. He's a University of Oregon Duck like both his parents.

Mike was a great little kid and we went almost everywhere together, him mimicking my every move. If I rolled the window on my side of the pickup down, he'd roll his down too. If I rested my arm on the window, he'd do that as well. We had a lot of laughs because he was so damned lovable. His mother and I used to call him the "Baby Seal" because his face was speckled like one. I never got tired of palling around with him.

On Mike's 12th birthday, my friend Ray Nash took the two of us on M.J.'s first drift-fishing trip in Ray's McKenzie River boat on the McKenzie River. His little brother's middle name came from this river.

Ray was a meticulous note taker. He got out his tablet to begin entering the date and his passengers' names in his river log. He glanced up at Michael and asked, *"Do you go by 'Mike' or 'Michael?'"*

Michael mulled the question for a moment before telling him, *"Well, on a fishing trip I guess it would be 'Mike.'"*

He continued to be the source of a certain kind of amusement when he got into things like scouting and sports. When he was 10 and playing team soccer he liked to come home and tell us about the neat plays he'd executed. He told us that the other kids called him "The Darter" because he was so quick. I'm not sure <u>they</u> called him that. But that's how he saw himself.

For the longest time, another defining feature of Boy Number One was his incessant need for speed and the fearless way he approached any risky new endeavor. He could have been the poster boy for childhood injuries of the outdoors sort.

Mike's the one, when he was 12, who caused a Pflueger fishing lure with three hooks and feathers to become caught in his own ear so close to the lymph nodes that the local first-responders wouldn't touch it. On our last day of summer vacation we had to delay our departure to take him to St. Charles in Bend so it could be surgically removed.

Another time, a year or two later, he mistook my shouted caution from across the field. I hollered, *"Don't go near the electric fence!"* He heard, *"Go check out the electric fence!"* and would have continued to his own electrocution if I hadn't caught up to him.

We took him and his brother to the bunny hill at Hoo Doo ski resort when he was about 12. His little brother, Cooper, was taking it slow, trying out the modest slope and learning to go over bumps without falling—you know, *practicing.*

We turn around and there goes Michael on the chairlift headed for the top, completely confident that he could do this on his own with no further instruction. Turns out he usually could do something like that, but he got hurt a lot more often than his little brother did.

I read somewhere that a lot of famous athletes and daredevils exhibit a different brain pattern than the rest of us. Speeds that would terrify us don't affect them the same way. They see things more slowly and are able to deploy their physical abilities to deal with them as they come their way.

It's also said of test pilots and athletes like the great Boston Red Sox slugger Ted Williams. He famously said that even with a fastball coming at him at 90 miles an hour he could see the threads on the ball and which way they were turning.

Because they were former test pilots, a lot of the astronauts I met no doubt had this capacity, too, and it translated into how effectively they dealt with other people and situations. In Michael it shows up most when he's negotiating. You've never seen anything like it. He is relentless at driving the bargain where he needs it to be.

He's now an accomplished graphic artist. When he was getting his business up and going, we drove from Eugene to Coquille way down on the southern Oregon coast together to look at a piece of equipment he needed. The former owner of a long-time print shop had gone out of business. He had all these different items he was getting rid of.

I'd forgotten just how far it is to the southern Oregon coast, but it's a stretch. We were after a laser cutter. For some reason we weren't able to establish in advance that the guy might come off the price he'd listed it for, figuring that it would go without saying for someone going out of business. That was unfortunate because it put us in the position of possibly having to drive all the way back home—more than seven hours round-trip—for nothing.

Both of us figured this guy had to get rid of this machine—there couldn't be that many people out there looking for them, especially all the way down in little Coquille. Surely he would come down.

But when we finally got there, the guy says, *"Nope. I put $1500 on it when it's worth two grand; I can't let it go for any less."*

Mike says to him, *"Well, I see you have all these boxes of vinyl material laying around here; how about you throw those into the deal?"*

"No-can-do" says the guy. *"I'm going to donate those to charity."*

I had already sized this hard-ass up. He was obviously some sort of distressed Vietnam War veteran or something that was extremely hard-headed. Mike turned to me and said, *"What do you think, Dad?"* I said, *"It sounds like the man doesn't want to sell it. Let's go."*

Now that was a pretty smooth little bargaining tactic on my part, even it was unintended; I really figured this guy was not coming off his list price by a penny. It didn't seem to be about the money; he was just being belligerent. This is where I think Mike's brain waves slowed down, so to speak, and he began to fully focus his powers to deal with the situation.

The guy says, *"If you don't want it, I've had calls from two guys who are coming over today."*

Mike says, *"Yes, but you know when they get here they're going to offer you the same amount I'm offering, if not less. That's if they show up."*

"I paid $2,500 for that machine new and that was just a year ago."

"But it's not new now. It's used."

"We're done. Take it or leave it."

For the second time, I start back to the car. But wait. There's more.

Mike had sized the guy up, too, but instead of following me down the driveway he says, *"Wait, Dad,"* and takes a step closer to this cranky gray-beard. His voice drops a notch in volume and he says more intimately, *"Come on, man. You remember what it was like when you were starting out. When every dollar mattered and you needed a break on equipment like this just to stay in the game.*

"Think how much better you're going to feel when your head hits the pillow tonight knowing that you helped the next generation of people like us do what we do, instead of having a lousy few hundred more dollars in your pocket."

The guy caved. He ended up not just coming off his price but threw in a bunch of rolls of the vinyl worth a few hundred dollars themselves. I'll bet he did sleep better that night.

Getting going as a graphic artist on your own is not easy. But, like his dad, Michael sets a goal and he does not see the obstacles; he just sees the goal.

Yet he somehow manages to also accommodate another great strength. He is always for the underdog and willing to stand by him.

Mike has never deviated from this level of character and I'll give you some advice should you ever meet him: do not in any way—even as a joke—disparage someone else on the basis of their race. He won't tolerate it and once lost a job over insisting that another employee be spoken to for using an ugly racial slur at work.

He'd asked the guy what players he was following on his NFL fantasy team. The guy said, *"I don't know, just some N-----s."*

Mike knew from experience in this particular work place that things might not fall his way if he reported the guy, and they didn't. He took it to management because, he said, *"This is 2012; we can't be talking like this in the workplace."*

In the end, it was he who ended up leaving the organization instead of the wrongdoer. Once again I have to say that I never gave up a job on principle like my son did. He's a better person than I am, so don't give me the credit.

I admire the hell out of him.

Cooper McKenzie Wilt, b. April 11th, 1982

Coop's the one whose heart I broke when he was 10 by taking a job that required us to relocate to Southern California right when he felt he was about to be sponsored by the only skate board shop in Eugene, Oregon. I suppose he thought he'd never get that kind of opportunity again.

Later, of course, he discovered that Southern California was a hell of a lot better place to make a career of skateboarding that any place in Oregon. As a result, he skated right into the heart of the skateboard industry and became one of the best-known professional skateboarders in the world, with his picture on the cover of *Skate Board Magazine* and everything.

He ended up being sponsored by a place called *Boards 'N More* by the time he was about 14 years old. That was the first skateboard shop he started to frequent after we moved to San Pedro. Today he has a multitude of sponsors who gladly pay his way to places you cannot imagine all over the world as an ambassador for the sport.

At first we thought it was a pretty big deal when Coop went on the road to New York City or San Francisco. But then it was to countless destinations in Europe, South America and Africa.

Cooper's mother and I had one of the rare out-of-body experiences of our lives when we attended the premier of *Almost, Round Three*, one of several popular skate boarding films Coop has appeared or starred in. The premier was at a theatre at the corner of Hollywood and Vine in Hollywood, California, one summer evening.

The place was lit up with search lights. There had to be a thousand people there. It was packed with professional skateboarders and their admirers who were—somewhat to our surprise—a remarkably fun and well-behaved crowd if you overlooked some of the language. (For the record, my son does not participate, as a matter of course, in that part of the culture.)

Cooper's special place in the universe began to emerge fairly early on. Coming along five years after his older sister and brother, he was basically delivered into what he seemed to take as a household of servants, there to meet his every need.

He didn't start talking as early as the other two because he didn't need to; all he had to do was point at a water faucet and a glass of water would be made to appear. Sometimes two. And once, when I explained to the three of them over dinner that the parents would be going away for a few days to a development session the company had asked us to lead, the older two had questions like how long we'd be gone and how they'd get to school.

Coop, then 4, asked, *"What are we going to do with our kids?"*

One spring vacation we treated ourselves to a weekend at the Shiloh Inn at Seaside, Oregon. It was costing us a little more than we'd usually spend so everyone was really trying to make a good time of it. It wasn't a very nice day when we arrived, so after checking in we put on our swim suits and headed down to the indoor pool and sauna.

We splashed around in the pool for a while then huddled together in the hot tub, looking out through fogged windows at the Pacific Ocean in the mist.

I say something like, *"Boy howdy, isn't this place great?"* Mom says, *"I'll bet a lot of other people wish they could sit in a warm swimming pool and look out at the ocean."* Kami and Michael chirp in with their own enthusiastic endorsements as well.

Then Coop speaks. He says very soberly, *"The pool is too cold and the tub is too hot."*

We all <u>knew</u> this was true. Cooper was, and always has been, a truth teller. Gosh, I'd like to be like that.

And I will say this about Coop: he has always been an outstanding role model for others of all ages. I remember when he was 10 and his athletic abilities were beginning to manifest themselves in soccer. He was MVP of that team—if not officially, certainly in everyone's eyes—and as muscled as a Jack Russell terrier.

But modest. One day when I was working in California and the family was still living in Eugene, I called home to learn that Cooper had scored the winning goal in his team's soccer championship. They would be going to state.

His mother was excitedly retelling his achievement to me over the phone when I heard the screen door open, then slam. Pris says, *"Here he is now. Cooper, come tell your dad about your goal!"*

By now he was almost out of hearing distance but I could hear him say laconically, *"You can tell him."*

Self-effacing. That's another word I've never heard mentioned in the same sentence with my own name and one I admire a lot in him.

It was also about this time that Coop began to worry about the kinds of things he saw me eating and became concerned about my health. It wasn't like him to preach, but one day I suggested after his soccer practice that we go get milkshakes at the Dairy Queen. He patted his perfectly flat abdomen, looked at me dolefully, and said, *"I can't. I'm starting to get a gut."*

He has succeeded and is admired throughout the skateboard industry, which is a thing; last year about 10 million skateboarders accounted for sales of $5 billion in the U.S. alone. Coop's part in it today is as social media director for a well-known equipment and apparel supplier in L.A. Even in his 30s he skates almost every day because that's what professional athletes do.

Anyone who has met Coop can tell you that his remarkable athleticism is only half the story. It's his character that stands out to most people.

I could go on and on about how much people like our Coop; it always was that way. There's a picture that captures his magnetism. It's the one of him sitting in his first car—an olive green 1968 Volvo coupe he owned in San Pedro when he was about 17—parked on the street outside the Pacific Avenue apartment building where we first lived in L.A.

Posing with him is a group of happy kids from ages 6 to 12 holding skateboards. Every one of them looks like they would not trade places with anyone else in the world at that moment.

I've always loved to tell about the time Coop's friend Brandon was trying to get his skateboard shop going in the about-to-boom historic section of San Pedro. Coop spent a lot of time down there as shop pro, lending his support and engaging customers.

One of these customers—or at least a customer wannabe—was a 10-year old boy who admired Cooper a lot.

Now, Coop and I have birthdays just a few days apart. We usually would do something on one of those days so I asked him early in the week if he wanted to get together on his birthday.

He said, *"I would love to do that another day, but that 10-year-old who hangs out at the shop has a birthday the same day. He asked me if I'd spend the day boarding with him so that's what I'm going to be doing."*

To that little kid it must have been like having Jackie Robinson sign your baseball.

There's an old Hoyt Axton song about playing in honky-tonk joints called *"Getting Paid for Doing Something I'd be Doing Anyway."*

To me that defines success—to be paid for doing what you'd be doing anyway. For most of us those are two different things; we have things we <u>like</u> to do and then we have things we get <u>paid</u> to do. But they're usually not the same things.

I've only known a handful of people who could say they get paid for doing what they'd be doing anyway. One of them is most certainly Cooper McKenzie Wilt

What independence. What character. What a boy. He's much more like his grandfather, Bill Wilt, than he is like me, which is a good thing.

Oh, and the drollest sense of humor. He sent me a card on Father's Day once where he wrote, *"Happy Father's Day, Dad. You did a great job of raising most of your kids."*

Not far from where we live today is the ranch home of a famous professional athlete and sports broadcaster I don't need to mention by name. For a long time I would drive past his place and think what a perfect life he must live with his record of athletic accomplishment, his vast acreage, horses and cattle, barns and corrals and every kind of fun piece of heavy equipment. Real fame and fortune, too.

Then I picked up the paper a few years ago to read that his son, just a young man, had passed away. I knew with absolute certitude that despite all his success and riches, that man would have traded places with me without hesitation.

This is the way I would feel if anything ever happened to any of the four members of my wonderful family. A family like this has to be one of the great blessings of a person's life.

I don't mean to crap on them, but now I'm going to swing back to my main story line here—how I managed to claw my way to the middle. That story continues, beginning with a little roadblock I encountered when it came to first getting into graduate school in 1974.

Farm Life and Cabin Dishes

Our young family was very happy on "the farm" beginning in 1975 where we had several great outbuildings, including a barn and a turkey shed. Also, orchards of apples and plums and filberts and a garden that was well established before we got the place.

We bought it from Mac and Prue Landreth. Their youngest son, Lyle, who's still a good friend, said there was so much growing in the garden that sometimes in the summer, instead of cooking dinner, Mrs. Landreth would just give each of her kids a salt shaker and tell them to go out in the garden and find their own. Great raspberries too.

This is where we would live and work and begin to raise our family for the next four years, and also the place where the plan to build a cabin in Central Oregon was hatched and began to unfold.

In fact, it's where I took the first concrete step toward fulfilling that goal. In the district warehouse adjacent to where I worked there were stacks upon stacks of cast-off white ceramic dishes acquired from the U.S. Navy after WWII, since surplussed. They couldn't get anyone to take the stuff off their hands. Even the Boy Scouts didn't want it—too heavy. Everybody wanted the new Melamine.

I filled the trunk of the 1970 Chevy with twelve settings of everything. It cost me $2.00 because they had to charge something.

We carted those dishes around with us through two states and several different pieces of property before it ended up here at No. 8. We eat off them every day. They were built to last.

CHAPTER 34

Woodward and Bernstein Almost Ruined My Career

The whole Woodward and Bernstein Watergate story that brought down President Nixon had set off an explosion of interest in journalism as a career. Every high school kid in the country now wanted to go into journalism and the U of O had its pick of some of the brightest people out there.

Consequently, when I applied for admission to graduate school I wasn't deemed to be among this particular cohort and my application was denied.

What? How could this be happening to me, whom everybody loved? I called on the new dean who told me to my face that he wasn't feeling the need to accommodate any demonstrated academic slackers such as myself. My GPA as an undergraduate was no longer good enough to get a person in.

Had I not had the good fortune to bump into Alyce Sheetz, a more familiar and admiring professor, on my way out of the building that day, it would have been tah-tah to the master's degree and maybe to the rest of this story line altogether.

She intervened on my behalf and a week or so later the dean relented as long as I could score some pretty daunting number on the Graduate Record Exam. *"But,"* he told me, *"I don't like it!"* and put me on immediate double secret probation.

It was plain the dean did not think too much of me, which made what I did a few weeks later a little unusual, I guess.

Every candidate for a master's degree was required to have a faculty advisor who would approve his proposed curriculum and thesis project, meet with him periodically to assess progress, and oversee his final oral examination.

Our two choices that year, we were told, included just two faculty members. One of them was the dean. Guess which one I chose? Yep, Mr. "I Don't Like It!" himself.

My own father-in-law told me at the time, *"You need to start going around obstacles instead of straight at them."*

But it all worked out. Later, the same dean led the two-hour oral exam I was required to take at the end of my program— the last obstacle between me and a master's. There were three other professors at the table. After the exam they asked me to come back in an hour to hear the panel's results.

When I came back in and was informed that I'd passed, the dean, in giving me this news, said, *"I think I speak for the entire faculty when I say how rewarding it is to see someone come back to the school and excel the way you have after such a, well...crappy undergraduate exhibition."* He waved his hand in the air in a little circle before settling on the word "crappy."

Then he turned somber. He took off his glasses and said to me, *"Boy, you sure showed me! Thank you for proving me wrong. On behalf of the entire School of Journalism, I hope you'll accept my apology."*

Actually, that last part didn't really happen. But that would have been icing on the cake, wouldn't it?

I completed the degree in one year. It turned out to be more important in the long run than I could have imagined at the time. I know it looked good on a résumé. Someone told me once that the reason I got the best job I ever had was because I had an advanced degree and the other front-runner didn't.

Many years later the company I was working for expected to be sold. They offered free career counseling to anyone who wanted it.

Well, I love to talk about myself so I jumped right on that. I lined up six sessions with a licensed career therapist in Torrance, California, a small Japanese man who exuded confidence and wisdom. (Think, Mr. Miagi in *"The Karate Kid."*)

He asked me what my greatest concern was about the situation. I told him it was probably the same as everyone else's—that I might end up without a job and be unable to support my family or meet my mortgage.

He said, *"Then you must get ready to fight the tiger!"*

Later, during that initial session, I told "Mr. Miagi" about the time I chose the recalcitrant and unadmiring dean to be my advisor and final adjudicator. He looked at me over his half-glasses, gave me a slight, deferential bow and said, *"Oh, so you are the kind who says, 'Tiger, I am here!'"*

I try to cling to that image.

School Bus in the River

Just about the most interesting aspect of the Springfield School District job is how I came to have it in the first place.

The job came open after a school bus carrying 75 kids home from outdoor school ran off the highway and into the wild and scenic McKenzie River in 1973. For several minutes the bus bobbed in the water, completely susceptible to being swept away in the swift and deep current—with a good chance of rolling over too, most probably.

Fortunately there were a lot of log trucks and loggers coming and going on the McKenzie Highway in those days. Some of them went to work with their cable-rigging know-how to get lines on the bus. They offloaded the passengers and saved all of them.

Jay Rickford, later a member of my book club, was a faculty member on the bus. He said no one even got hurt much; one counselor had a broken arm and someone else a bump on the head.

The incident got a lot of media attention and the accident investigation showed that the wreck happened because the steering mechanism on the bus seized up. It was an older bus because the district had a philosophy of getting its money's worth out of equipment.

This resulted in a lot of criticism directed at the school district; the superintendent himself took quite a beating and it made for an altogether miserable experience for him.

The superintendent was the aforementioned Bill Llewellyn, a legend among Oregon school superintendents. He'd put in his time in several smaller Eastern Oregon school districts over a long career.

Bill applied his small-ball philosophy of school administration to the running of this larger district. That meant keeping a lid on expenditures. He used to brag that although the much larger Eugene district had a more modern administration building, ours was better because it was paid for.

Llewellyn had apparently liked the article I'd done on him while I was with the *Springfield News*. He looked me up in Salem and asked me to come to work for him.

The two school district jobs paid about double what I'd been making as a teacher so that was the principal motivation for leaving that profession and moving into the fairly new field of organizational communications. As I mentioned, the move to Springfield had the additional advantage of putting me back in close proximity to the University of Oregon where I could start work on my master's.

The deal to go to Springfield was made all the sweeter when, after I was hired, Priscilla became one of the first in her field of Gifted Education to work for the same school district.

We moved to a farmhouse on 15 acres in the Mohawk Valley where I grew up. This was shortly after our first baby, Kami, was born. It's also where we lived when her first brother, Michael, came along a couple of years later.

The Springfield School District had a program that allowed you to take time from work to attend classes. I'm grateful that they did as it made getting my graduate degree much easier than it otherwise might have been.

There was a bike path that ran from Mill Street in Springfield, where my office was located, through Alton Baker Park and all the way to the university, a distance of about four miles. I'd just jump on my 10-gear Nishiki and zip over there for a class or two. Not having to find a parking spot saved a lot of time and I became very efficient about getting to class and back.

It was easy to make up for lost time by working late, writing and laying out publications or working in the darkroom. In a lot of ways, it was like owning your own newspaper.

Work First—Play Later

I also worked a lot on weekends and rode the bike from the place we were renting from Pris's folks in South Eugene over to the Springfield office. Early one Saturday afternoon I was riding home from work with plans to turn my attention to some important homework.

As I pedaled uphill from the university I heard an enormous roar go up from Autzen Stadium on the other side of the river. A football game was in progress and Oregon had obviously just scored. For just a moment I hesitated and considered turning my bike back down the hill toward the stadium. Ditch the homework; go watch the Ducks play football.

But then a voice in my head said, *"Don't. Wait. If you continue working like this—go home and do the homework now—it won't be long before you'll be in a position to go to as many ballgames as you want for the rest of your life. Work first—Play later."*

I followed my own advice and things worked out just about the way the little voice said they would. I've watched Oregon play in two different Rose Bowls, and once in the national championship with both of my sons.

Nothing to Write Home About

Career-wise, the years between the time I left teaching at McNary High School and the time I left the job with the Springfield School District were nothing to write home about, and not just because I was already back home.

This isn't to say that we weren't doing good work, even progressive for the day. As I leafed through some memorabilia from that era I found myself pleasantly surprised to be reminded of all the accolades that came our way, particularly for publications.

There's an item from the *Oregon Statesman* newspaper here that says the *Salem School Report*—that's the one that went out to the community—had been named the top publication of its kind in the United States.

From the Springfield era I see a nice write-up in the *Register-Guard* that reads, *"Three of this year's top 25 school publications are in Eugene or Springfield according to the results of a national competition in which some 1,300 school publications were rated. Receiving the Award of Excellence— the highest presented by the National School Public Relations Association—was the Springfield School District's community newsletter, 'Springfield Schools Report'."*

Partly because of our publications and some other well-received communication products, we were generally seen as a progressive district and I was often asked to go to other school systems to talk with them about their communication programs. That gave our program even more visibility at both the state and national levels.

Sometimes I made presentations on my own, separate from whatever organization I was working for. One of the highlights of this period was an address I made to the Oregon School Boards Association annual conference in Portland that went over well.

I remember holding on to the check they gave me for a long time before cashing it. Unlike any previous compensation I'd received professionally, this was not from the organization that employed me; it was for a skill I'd perfected on my own and managed to "monetize."

I enjoyed seeing and touching the tangible rewards of this small accomplishment because it said I had worth outside of the organization; that's something a person should always try to maintain. Too many people tie their fortunes completely to the company they work for; when they lose that job, they lose their identity.

Still in the Dark but Starting to See the Light

The only problem was that I really didn't know what I was talking about. Yes, we'd demonstrated a certain amount of competence in creating, writing and producing communication products across a wide range of print and visual media.

We'd also introduced some innovative public relations techniques. One was the practice of sending a personal response letter from the superintendent to anyone who wrote a letter to the editor of either of the local papers concerning the district; either that, or arrange a personal meeting between the individual and the superintendent.

The Super was an affable guy to whom people responded well so this fit perfectly with his own communications style. Things like this we got right.

But someone who really understood what organizational communications is all about wouldn't have been impressed. They would have said, *"Show me your plan!"* or, *"What does that have to do with achieving the district's top operating objectives?"*

We gave <u>some</u> thought—but not all that much—to such matters because we still saw ourselves as internal journalists responsible for putting out the paper, so to speak. The people who signed our pay checks didn't expect too much more. I remember no conversations about aligning communication goals with district goals or even strategy sessions with the administration on more immediate concerns like teacher morale, school security or generating public support for changes in the schools.

We did this pretty well when we were campaigning for the annual budget renewal, but day-in, day-out our messages weren't purposely aligned with what the district needed to accomplish.

It's important to point out here, though, that I was starting to get it, the best evidence being that when I enrolled in the master's degree program in the UO School of Journalism I identified "Organizational Communications" as the subject of my main course of study. Whatever that was.

Until then there had been no course of study called Organizational Communications. But more and more, graduates of the school were beginning to get into jobs like mine. It was seen as an emerging profession and a field where communication professionals could begin to add real value to organizations—not just school districts, but large companies, government organizations, hospitals and more.

The J-School agreed and we laid out a course of study that gave me academic credit for the work I was already doing at the school district. My terminal project was to be a blueprint for planning and launching a comprehensive communication program for the school district. It would identify all the critical audiences, our plan for establishing effective communications with each, and with what objective in mind.

Moreover, it spelled out the role of everyone in the organization for carrying out an effective public relations program. This included the school board right down through the principals and other administrators to the teachers, and then to "classified" personnel such as bus drivers, cafeteria workers and custodians.

This at least showed that I understood communications applied to, and could affect, everyone in the organization.

Second-Round All-Star

Thanks to the unique arrangement between the J-School and my employer, nobody ever had an easier graduate school experience. I only needed 45 credit hours to graduate and I see from my transcript that they gave me seven for what I was doing at work and three more for a "reading" class. The latter required only that I spend one hour a week with the head of the J-School's P.R. segment leader talking about the whole idea of organizational communications and how I was applying it at work.

This would have been Jack Ewing. He taught the public relations courses I'd taken as an undergrad. We enjoyed a congenial relationship. He was also a notorious tightwad. I didn't know this until I told him after graduating that I wanted to take him to lunch to show my appreciation. We went to the *Black Angus* across Franklin Boulevard from the university and had a steak sandwich. He kept looking around the room, saying, *"How much can this be costing?"*

They gave me 10 more hours for a class called *Advance Photography* where I drove around in the Eastern Oregon desert with a bunch of hippies for three weeks taking pictures of ghost towns. One of them took a group photo of almost everyone in the class naked in front of an abandoned hotel; that might have been a lot of fun but I was too square to participate in anything like that.

Taken together the hours accumulated in these few classes alone put me practically half-way to finishing my advanced degree. Unlike my undergraduate years, I excelled as a graduate student. I pretty much got perfect scores in the courses I took at this level with the exception of a statistics class called *Communication Research Methods* that went right over my head and ruined my chance to ever see *magna cum laude* after my name in a commencement program later.

If I had to point to what the vainer side of myself would call the "best" moments in my life, this one would have to be right up there: Priscilla and I were walking through the Valley River Shopping Center in Eugene at Christmas when we ran into one of the most celebrated members of the J-School faculty, Roy Paul Nelson. He taught political cartooning and the magazine segment. Plus, the entire back page of *Ad Week Magazine* was reserved for his column on design every week. A lot of people knew who he was.

We talked for a little bit about how things were going with my graduate program before he turned to Pris and said, *"It's always great to see one of our former students come back and be such a star."* You had to love that.

The fact that he uttered the words in the presence of the one person on earth I most cared to make a good impression upon is what made it memorable for me. (I wonder if Pris remembers that happening. Probably not.)

Educational advancement aside, I'd have to sum things up in this period work-wise as being pretty much status quo; I didn't grow that much in the job. The focus was on doing what I'd been doing, primarily publications. We improved somewhat as time went along, but I wasn't advancing the organization or myself the way I might have. It was a case of not knowing what you don't know.

What these jobs *did* do, though, was two things: one was to serve as a long incubation period for the first significant ideas I'd come to formulate about organizational communications; the other was to give me a boost to the big leagues where I began to meet the people and receive the opportunities I needed to not just grasp the bigger communications picture but to become part of it.

The Book Club

Before I leave this period I want to mention a development that occurred when I was in this job that's turned out to be an important part of my life to this day: the book club, Le Groupe.

My Grandmother, Alma Wilt, belonged to a book club clear up into her 80s, so she was no doubt the inspiration for me on this one. In 1974, another friend from the office, Frank Walch, and I got the thing started by inviting, I think, three people each.

We had just one rule, borrowed from Ruben Moore's father-in-law's club in England: you couldn't leave unless you died. So far everyone has fulfilled that oath; they are either still members in good standing or are no longer standing. You don't even have to attend meetings, I guess, because I lived out of state for about 35 years and it didn't seem to affect my affiliation.

The club started out nameless and went through several early phases (We'd been calling it the Group, but Ray Nash thought that didn't sound literary enough and "upgraded" it). The first phase was a serious attempt to really get into a big fat book every month and have a roaring discussion about it. That was a short phase—two meetings, I think. And we hadn't been up and running more than a year before we began taking annual recreational outings to Central Oregon and the coast where sometimes that month's book selection barely came up.

For a while some of us also pooled our financial resources and added "investment club" to our portfolio. Ray refused to participate and labeled it the "Le Groupe Sinking Fund" in his monthly report. That phase didn't last long.

Today Le Groupe is a "grown-up" book club with selections made annually, discussion leaders assigned for every title, etc. But first, it morphed into a combined book and dessert club when one of the guys' wives made up a particularly delicious post-meeting confection—a blackberry cobbler as I recall. The next month, the next host's wife made an equally spectacular apple crisp and the race was on.

None of us can probably tell you who recommended the best book Le Groupe ever read, but all of us remember who we think set out the best sweet course.

Ray generously took responsibility for the club's minutes, keeping me informed of the monthly selections and the club's activities wherever I might be working in the world. He signed his letter each month "Ray Nash, le Directoire de Le Groupe Archives."

Ray wrote wonderful minutes and no one got into the theme of Le Groupe as a combination book and dessert club more than he did. Here's one of his entries from back there in the 1970s:

> Besides this month's book, there was the extraordinary matter of Judy Moore's warm strawberry sauce. Frank and I left the meeting in solemn reflection upon our latest gourmanding experience.
>
> With a catch in his voice, Frank said, "I'm 59 years old and this is the first time in my life I've tasted warm strawberry sauce."

In my mind, I heard the strains of 'Some Enchanted Evening' as I realized we had experienced the sudden, magical, pulse-pounding "Love-at-First-Taste."

Oh warm strawberry sauce, where have you been all our lives?

Ray may now be Ex-Ray (That's what I used to tell him I'd call him when he was gone), but the club lives on. We just held our monthly meeting in the governor's conference room at the state capitol arranged by Jim Sellers, one of the original members. Jim and I went to journalism school together. He went on to become a speech writer for the highly respected Oregon Governor, Victor Atiyeh.

The meeting in Salem was where everyone brought their suggestions for next year's reading list; we settled on some good titles, with the one that most jumped out at me being Conrad Roemer's suggestion that we read a book called *I Hear You Paint Houses*.

This turns out to be a term from the mob world meaning "I hear you kill people." There's another phrase in the book: "I also fix furniture." Conrad said he wouldn't ruin it for us by revealing what that might mean.

Anyway, it looks like it's going to be another year of good reads, made all the more enjoyable by the social network it creates for those of us still standing, still reading.

I sometimes think about how, as we move through life, we pick up fellow travelers who end up becoming important and enjoyable parts of our journey. That, for me, has been the book club.

The obituary for Ray Nash, when he passed away recently, mentioned that he belonged to Le Groupe for 40 years. I'll try to see that it's mentioned in mine, too.

CHAPTER 35

I Turn Corporate

I n 1979, when I was 31, I was lucky to make the leap from the public sector to an interesting career in corporate communications, an emerging field at the time. Most of the name companies already maintained corporate communications departments, but their resources were not generally applied as fully to the business as they would be later.

I've been looking forward to writing about these working years because—for better or worse—that's where I expended the largest proportion of the physical, mental and emotional energy I had to expend.

Of course when push came to shove, the family came first. But day-in, day-out it was the job. I'm sure I spent far more time thinking—often worrying—about what was going on at work than anything else in my universe. It drove everything to the point that a good day at work made for a good day at home; a bad day at work was just a bad day, period.

I was rewarded for my efforts in the customary ways, but also in terms of the adventure and recognition that came with the job, which can only be described as ample even by the craven attention-hound that I could be.

Among the many extraordinary people I met on the job were eight American astronauts— and some of the greatest of them at that—including Sally Ride, the first American woman in space; Jim Lovell, commander of Apollo 13; and Neil Armstrong.

I probably had more fun days at work than most people ever get to have and the lifestyle was easy to get used to. In fact, for a good period of time the company was not only providing me a paycheck but meeting 100 percent of my main living expenses as well, including lodging, meals, ground and air transportation and membership in the nationwide system of University Clubs.

When people ask me what I miss most about work I tell them *"The nice hotels."*

All in all, when it came to jobs my whole generation had it pretty good. Because I wound up in the advanced and fascinating aerospace industry, I probably had it a little better than that.

My Overseers

Real quickly—so you'll have some reference for what comes later—three companies figure prominently in this narrative. They are:

> **The Weyerhaeuser Timber Company** headquartered at Federal Way, Washington, 20 miles south of Seattle. This was the largest vertically-integrated forest products company in the world when I worked there. It's where I learned most of what I came to know about internal communications management and a lot about working in a corporate environment.

Just as reference to how times have changed, there were more than 3,000 employees at the HQ building when I was there. They've since relocated and employ only about 250.

Nissan Car Company in U.S.A. This was the arm of the big Japanese car maker that distributed and marketed Nissan automobiles in the United States. I was based in Los Angeles and was the company's first director of internal communications, but not for very long.

And finally, **AlliedSignal Aerospace,** which became **Honeywell** a few years after I joined the company. It was also headquartered in the Los Angeles area, just down 190th Avenue from the Nissan building I'd worked in earlier. Later the headquarters were relocated to Phoenix because the new president liked it better *"in the desert" and* it's where we had a good portion of our engineering and manufacturing facilities. I kept a company apartment there.

Honeywell made engines and complicated control systems for every kind of aircraft from helicopters to the space shuttle and everything in-between. It was said that every single aircraft flying at the time had Honeywell components on it, so you can see it was a sizable business.

A Job Made for Me

From the Weyerhaeuser years on, the kinds of things we were doing in communications began to attract more and more attention from organizations outside the ones I was working for—enough that one of my employers created an entirely new communications consulting organization and made me its chief consultant, backed by the considerable resources of our department.

It was pretty much a dream job that required me to give a lot of talks to big organizations all over the country and then turn my speaking fees back to the company.

Years later I'd receive another "gift" position when I was made director of public affairs for the first time. It was a job made for me.

No, really. They made the job for <u>me</u>. Here's how it happened.

CHAPTER 36

I Didn't Go to War and I Still Got PTSD

A s rewarding as my career was overall, I thought I'd
mention early-on that there was also something a little
nerve-wracking about going to work in this profession
a lot of times.

People used to say you're only as good as your last project, so that was one thing. The other was that this kind of
work was largely subjective so it was hard to please everyone. I once saw a carefully-researched, multimillion dollar
advertising campaign scuttled at the last minute because
the final decision-maker's aged secretary happened to come
into the room during the final review.

He asked her what she thought. She looked over the
artwork for a few seconds then said something about never
having liked that shade of green. That was all it took—back
to the drawing boards!

I worked with a guy who did an outstanding job for
us—we'll call him Paul. The company hired him at about
age 30 and only a couple of years later endorsed him for a

leadership position in one of our larger businesses. Before too long that business showed him the door.

The "problem" was one that Paul had been telling me about: instead of reporting to the president as planned, he ended up reporting to the head of H.R. who, as so often happens, considered himself to be an expert in the field of communications.

He kept telling Paul, *"You're a 'Big-Bang Guy.' We don't need a Big-Bang Guy; we need a Bang-Bang guy."* Or maybe it was the other way around. Either way, neither one of us knew what in the hell he was talking about.

Go-Time

Here's an experience I wouldn't want to relive: I was in charge of organizing the global senior management meeting held annually for the company's top leaders from all over the world. The meeting was about to begin. I could see the ballroom of the hotel was almost full.

As event organizer, it would be my job to step to the speaker's lectern and begin the conference. The expectation was that I would lay out how the next few days would unfold, make advance introduction of the keynote speakers and introduce the chairman and CEO.

But for some reason, I was completely unprepared. I'd written out some notes but couldn't find them. Neither had I gotten around to formulating an agenda. Worse, the kickoff speaker's office had called to say he was running 30 minutes late. In other words, I had nothin'.

About five minutes before start-time, the chairman comes over to me and says we better get this thing rollin'. I'm glad I don't have to tell you what happened next because it couldn't have been pretty.

But I don't, because it never happened. It's just a recurring nightmare I began having long before my working years ended and continued for several years afterwards. It pops up every once in a while even to this day.

I told someone this once and they said, *"You must not have been very good at your job."* I hope that wasn't true, but I'll admit that sometimes I didn't <u>feel</u> I was very good at my job and there's a lot of anxiety in that.

My wife pointed out recently that it's probably the people who could be counted upon to do a good job who have these kinds of nightmares, not the other way around. That's a comforting thought and there's probably something to it. My friend Bill Marvin is the same age I am. He has a stellar reputation as a finish carpenter but he still wakes up with nightmares that he's severely underbid a job and is going to lose his ass.

"It's all your fault!

What was it like working in the communications department of these massive organizations? On just about every measure, the jobs I held were as good or better than I had any right to expect: good pay, lots of recognition and rewards, travel, and the opportunity to be part of something bigger than yourself.

But there's a reason that I sometimes told people, *"I have the best job in the company and I don't intend to do it one day longer than I have to."*

While I never experienced a meltdown on the scale of the one that haunts my dreams, the slightest miscue—a guest speaker fails to arrive on time, say, or a satellite temporarily loses connection in the middle of a broadcast—would be seen as a catastrophic failure from which the event organizer might never recover.

I worked with a young woman who said that where she went to college, whenever an athlete made a mistake like dropping the winning touchdown in the end zone or missing a basket at the buzzer, the crowd would begin to chant, *"It's all your fault! It's all your fault!"*

I don't remember it ever being that bad, but I'll just say that whatever the organization and its issues, if things weren't going well, someone would always try to lay it off as poor communications. As in, *"People aren't signing up for the new health care plan cutting their benefits in half. Must not have communicated it right."*

Among our responsibilities were the production of publications and videos seen by tens of thousands of employees, customers and people in the community. Oh the slips I've seen happen between the lip and the cup: the next-to-final version of a video gets distributed to God-knows-how-many locations; a press release goes out in the wrong language in a foreign country; the *Power-Point* presentation supporting a top executive's remarks to customers at the Paris Air Show won't work off the electrical system in France. You always had to be on your toes to avoid things like this.

Once, the Teleprompter with the CEO's remarks went hinky just before he was supposed to arrive for the companywide broadcast. In this instance, it was because the operator had fallen asleep in the men's room sitting on the remote control. He'd driven all night from Los Angeles where he was working the *Super Bowl* and was exhausted. Somebody had to go drag him out of a stall to get the thing working again.

Another time, pretty early in my corporate career, I was partnered with a woman new to our department to produce what was called a management forum. This was a series of presentations by the company's top leaders on events of importance at the time. They ranged from discussions on company strategies like advertising to topical events like reorganizations and mergers. About 500 headquarters employees at a time would attend.

The woman I was working with was new to Communications, being cross-trained from her job in another department. We'd put together a multi-media, rear-projection slide show to accompany the speaker's presentation.

This was the height of technology at the time and involved not one, but two projectors, each operating independently of, but in sync with the other.

The slide carousels were mounted on two tall tripods positioned equidistant from the center of the screen. This turned out to not be the best setup. While an A-V guy was standing on a ladder checking the slides to be sure he didn't have any of them upside down or something, the tripod on stage left suddenly collapsed. Slides scattered half the length of the stage and of course the projector was in no shape to go on. It looked like an impossible situation.

We still had 15 minutes before show time. The auditorium was already nearly full. My new partner and I looked at each other. We both chose the same human gesture for the situation—that one where you slap your palms to both sides of your face, open your eyes wide and screw your mouth into the shape of an "O."

I didn't know what we were going to do, but I knew we had to do something—quick! She on the other hand calmly placed her hands on my shoulders and said, *"You're just going to have to go out there and tell them there's not going to be a program today."*

Even under the circumstances this made me laugh out loud because it was so entirely out of the question; the show *always* goes on.

With failure not an option, someone was sent for a backup projector and everyone dropped to their knees to begin recreating the slides in order. Showtime came and we didn't miss a beat.

Later, the kind of things we would be handling—think, delicate labor negotiations or multi-billion-dollar business transactions with names in them like *General Electric* and *Air France*—held much greater potential for seriously negative consequences if anything went wrong.

Because we played on a world stage, even relations between the U.S. and other nations could sometimes be affected. I think the nearest we came to setting off a nuclear disaster—or whatever would have happened—was mixing up the Republic of China's flag with that of the People's Republic of China at a big function for important customers from the PRC.

You probably know they hate each other's guts. Our flub would have been like waving a red flag at a bull. A Communist red flag.

As in the case of the unsteady slide projector, things worked out okay in the end; but you can see why I sometimes still have nightmares with situations like these as the theme— probably a mild form of Post-Traumatic Stress Syndrome.

Finally, on the subject of Communism, I'll leave you with a thought I recently came across. It said, *"We should have known Communism was not dead; there were red flags everywhere."*

CHAPTER 37

What Daddy did for a Living

I t might be the rare reader who would want know what a career in corporate communications was all about and why all the big companies had people like me on the payroll in the first place. But for that reader I'm going to go into some detail about those things. It covers a period of about 35 years, so if you want to get a snack or something now would be a good time.

I like to begin an explanation of what I did for a living by inflating the importance of it. I had numerous opportunities to do just that on the public speaking circuit where I'd often begin by recounting a television interview I'd once seen on the 20th anniversary of the of the U.S.- led invasion at Normandy, France, on June 6, 1944—*"D-Day."*

The interview was conducted by the great CBS newsman Walter Cronkite with the five-star American general who led the invasion and later became president of the United States, Dwight D. "Ike" Eisenhower.

D-Day was the largest coalescence of men and equipment in the history of the world. It involved more than 500,000 allied soldiers, sailors and airmen, more than 11,500 aircraft, 56,000 cars and trucks, and nearly 7,000 ships.

It had been a massive and complex undertaking at one of the most pivotal moments in the history of the world, literally a showdown between good and evil. Keeping all those people and parts working in concert must have presented communication challenges beyond anything anyone had seen until then. But that wasn't where I was going in my presentation.

Cronkite and Eisenhower did the interview from a small boat as they drifted just off the coast of Normandy, looking back at the 100-foot-high white rock cliffs the allies had scaled that day to successfully begin the battle to push Hitler's army out of France and the rest of Western Europe.

One of the first questions Cronkite asked Eisenhower was, *"General, what was your first objective here that day?"*

I would then confide to the audience that <u>my</u> mind had jumped right away to what critical hard target or objective Ike would mention first. The cliffs were heavily fortified with tank-top turrets and barbed wire guarded by four German Panzer tank divisions with cannons, so I figured he would say they needed to take out the biggest guns first or come in with air power—something along those lines.

But no. I would then point out, *"What Eisenhower <u>actually said was, 'The first objective, Walter, was to take out the enemy's <u>communication systems</u>, because then he would be disorganized'."*

You could almost see all these business and organizational leaders before me lean forward in their seats at this point because they quickly understood what Eisenhower was saying: without communications you don't <u>have</u> an organization; you have <u>dis</u>organization.

After that, whatever I had to offer about achieving better communications was something most people in leadership positions wanted to hear. One of the great benefits I experienced in my career was working with some of the most progressive leadership teams of that time; they were always big supporters—and participants in—the communications effort.

So what Daddy did for a living <u>was</u> important. Not "D-Day" important, but important enough to explain why organizations had people like me on the payroll to keep their communications systems up and going under every possible set of circumstances, some of them pretty challenging.

In the following pages I'll try to describe what it was like to have a communications career in these big organizations at the time, how we went about doing what we did, and how it all turned out.

For better or for worse, I can tell you one thing my career was <u>not</u>, and that was a career like everyone else's.

That's because I was one of the first people to ever hold the position of manager or director of internal communications for a major U.S. company. Up until then, there just hadn't been that many big companies around and they're the only ones that employ people like me.

The employee populations of America's big corporations, like General Motors and IBM, didn't really explode until the post-WWII years. For example, IBM had only 30,000 employees in 1950 but by 1960 was up to more than 100,000.

Up until that time there had been only a small number of what you could call "mega-organizations." The biggest two were the Catholic Church and the military. It should be no surprise that it was from them that most of the big organizations that followed adopted their methods of organizing and managing themselves, including how they communicated.

As the size and number of big companies grew, so did the profession of internal communications management.

This was the wave I caught and rode to the end of my career.

CHAPTER 38

Journalism with a Purpose

W hen I came into the internal communications profession it was one thing; when I left, it was still that
thing and a whole lot more.

Let's start with why the company would have a communications department in the first place. The answer to
that was simple: it was good for business.

I became friends with Alvie Smith, the head of employee
communications for General Motors. He went so far as to say
in his own autobiography that, *"Handled well, communications
becomes the single most powerful tool available to the leader."*

Our job was to see that it <u>was</u> handled well—first by
formulating policies that committed the company to good
communication with its workforce, then managing the
programs and systems that made it possible.

Journalism with a Purpose

The big change that occurred on my watch was the con-
version of the communications function from "internal
journalism"—just getting information out—to something
that's been called "journalism with a purpose."

That's when we became responsible for actually making something happen through what we did—like galvanizing people around certain goals and priorities, accelerating acceptance of change and things like that.

There's a neat analogy I came across somewhere in the process of learning about organizational communications. It points up the distinction between the way most companies had historically gone about managing communications with employees and the way they came to do it later.

The person who wrote it said that most organizations communicate with their employees as if they are passengers on a ship. A communications survey in these companies might ask employees how satisfied they are with the food in the cafeteria, or how they like the new inventory system.

But of course they're not passengers; they're the crew. The communication needs of the two are entirely different. What you should really want people to know is whether they understand where the ship is going; the hazards to be avoided; their own role in getting the ship to its destination safely and on time; and the information they need to perform their jobs well. And you want them to feel motivated.

When companies like ours did get around to asking employees what they thought about their companies' communications efforts, almost universally they said, *"You do a good job of providing information to me but a poor job of getting information from me."*

That's not good. In order for the organization to function at its best it has to communicate effectively in three directions—downward, upward and across.

The Need to be Heard

Here's a quick lesson on what each kind of communications does for an organization:

Downward communications. This is what management relies on to organize, direct and control the activities of the company. Make no mistake, this is the one it cares most about.

Horizontal communications. This is the kind that goes on between employees at the same level in different work groups. It's what gives you coordination between departments and functions.

Upward Communications. This is information from people in the organization to the leadership. It was greatly overlooked before my time. Nobody used to care very much about what the working man or woman thought.

More enlightened management came to see that listening to the people who do the work is the only way to get a sense of how the organization is running and how people are responding to current leadership efforts. You have to know where things aren't working. Often it's because of poor management, inadequate resources or equipment, or dozens of other common and fixable deficiencies.

Finally, upward communication fulfills the need for people to be heard on things that affect them, which at the time was becoming stronger than it had ever been.

This wasn't an entirely foreign concept at the time but it did differ as a management style from the one that many managers had come up under. It wasn't uncommon to hear one of them say, *"Nobody told me anything when I was on the floor and I got along all right."* Changing this attitude required a cultural shift as much as a change in this one behavior. It also became part of the new internal communications mission.

A Convict Mentality

There's a wonderful quote from a book called *"The Fatal Shore"* about the founding of Australia as a British penal colony in the 1700s. It said, *"No convict ever invented a new tool or a better use for an existing one."* It meant that the first European inhabitants of Australia—all incarcerated—did little to advance the country. It wasn't until they became free men that Australian civilization began to advance.

It wasn't uncommon for employees in some of the big companies of my time to have this "convict mentality." Their work was heavily regimented and closely supervised with little or no opportunity to influence how it actually got done. A lot of people questioned why they should bother to think of better ways to do things if no one was going to listen to them and they saw nothing in it for themselves.

It would be overstating it to say that people in America's work places were treated like convicts, but it's fair to say that many of them felt deprived in some important ways that were getting in the way of doing their jobs better.

I heard a college football coach say one time that the difference between a good team and a great one is the amount of "discretionary" performance its players give you, i.e., that little extra effort that resides within each of us and requires good leadership to bring out.

Creating mechanisms and developing supervisor abilities and behaviors that made it possible to elicit this discretionary level of performance became the heart of what our communications function was there to do.

We wanted people to feel that they weren't there only for their physical expenditure of energy but for their mental and emotional qualities too. In other words, a good employee is a well-informed and involved one.

Change Is Good for the Communicators

I need to mention one more area that emerged as the province of Internal Communications. It was helping companies manage through <u>change</u>.

People hate change. They resist it. They yearn to maintain the status quo. But organizations <u>have</u> to change, and never more-so than in my time. All the big companies were going through some of the severest upheavals in their history—a veritable avalanche of mergers, plant closings, leadership changes, strategic shifts, and downsizings.

Change like this can cripple an organization because people spend all their time speculating about what might happen next instead of doing their jobs. It's one of the most powerful laws of human nature; the bigger the change, the more people resist it. The only remedy—the only way to keep people focused on the work and moving in the new direction—is to communicate.

You can't achieve successful change without communications. You have to operate on the principle that a void of <u>information</u> will quickly be filled with <u>mis</u>information. In other words, if you don't tell people what's going on, someone else will do it for you. That can lead to all kinds of organizational dysfunction, from declining morale to your best people abandoning ship.

As understanding grew of how important communication is in time of change, the more vital the internal communications function became. Whenever the company foresaw an important change coming—a layoff, a change in leadership, a change in policy, or any other major issue or development—our phone was the first to ring.

Actually, I have change to thank for the fact that I landed a badly needed job in the aerospace industry at the very time that 250,000 other aerospace employees were being terminated in southern California—the largest layoffs in history.

A cataclysmic change like that might be bad news for a lot of other kinds of employees, but not the professional communicator. Change requires lots of communication and someone has to manage it. Change is good for us; it's when we're needed most.

Putting It All Together

The full potential of internal communications to influence the performance of an organization—and how to apply that knowledge—was just beginning to be universally understood when I started out. I take some satisfaction in knowing that I had a hand in shaping the profession that eventually developed to manage it.

There were good things being done all over, but we were among the first to pull it all together and apply it to the running of a company. That in turn made us the first to reap the personal rewards of doing so as well.

CHAPTER 39

What People Like Me Did at Work

've been asked any number of times what people in corporate communications jobs did. It's not the easiest thing to explain; the responsibilities could be all over the place. What might be a relatively low-stress, secure position almost entirely separate from the business side of a company and requiring little more than a firm handshake and a nice smile in one place, could be a pressure-cooker job right in the wheelhouse of the organization in another.

It all depended upon whether company management was progressive enough to have brought its communications function into the leadership circle where it belongs or instead hobbled it over in the Human Resources department or some other outpost.

Some communication jobs in business weren't very challenging or complex at all, even though they paid just as well or better than the kind of work I was invariably engaged in. I knew someone who worked for the big telephone giant Pacific Northwest Bell before it was broken up.

His most important assignment one year was choosing the photograph for the cover of the new telephone directory.

Mine leaned more toward the boiler room variety. Every time I landed someplace where it looked like I might get to put my feet up a little bit, the shit would hit the fan.

Using that expression reminds me of something we always called *"The law of unequal distribution."* That's the one that says when the shit hits the fan it won't be distributed equally.

We would know.

What I Was Looking for and What I Found

I had to laugh a while back when I heard someone talking about the re-training he was getting through the State of Oregon so he could work in a career other than logging. He'd recently had his ankle crushed by a rolling log after 30 years in the woods. He told me he was learning to operate machine lathes using computers.

I said, *"Oh. That sounds interesting."*

He replied, *"Not to me it don't. But it sounds easy."*

Truth be known, I felt the same when my career path led to the field of corporate communications. I somehow envisioned that once comfortably ensconced in the corporate cocoon, I'd make more money and wouldn't have to work so hard.

The situation as I envisioned it was very attractive, but it put me in for some surprises. Namely, there is no such thing as a corporate cocoon, at least in my field. If anything, my personal accountability soared.

Someone told me about a friend's 8-year-old son who, when asked what his dad did for a living, said, *"He sends paper to other people and other people send paper to him."*

That would be one way to describe a lot of the positions occupying a corporate headquarters building and I did my share of it. But unlike a lot of the luckier bureaucrats, our papers required a lot out of us.

We were in the idea-generation and proposal business as much as anything so everything we produced had to come out of our own imaginations. Sometimes it was like being the producer, the writer, the creative director and the best boy on a film all at once. And this was every day, like at the post office.

One thing anyone working in internal communications had to do was write. It was something most organizational leaders either couldn't, or wouldn't, do for themselves. If I learned anything over 35 years of doing it, it's this: if you can write, you will almost always be able to find work in this field.

We wrote features for the company paper, advertising copy, press releases (for taking our message to the media), media response statements (for when we preferred to sit back and wait for them to call us), newsletters, messages from leadership, magazines, annual reports, video scripts, web sites, issue papers, bulletins, broadcasts and speeches, to name some. Social media was just becoming a thing about the time I left, but if it had been around I'm sure we would have been Tweeting our guts out.

Every time you hit the "send" button on one of these company-wide messages you were putting your judgment, ability and reputation on the line. And the closer you got to the top of the organization the more everything had to go right.

The communications we produced often touched every individual in the company, which could be as many as 120,000 people at a time. Being able to get this all right involved skills that companies valued highly. As a result you ended up working with some extremely capable people; that's always good for a person's own development.

By way of example, I'll mention the second V.P. I served under. He'd been director of communications for the U.S. Secretary of Defense and was still at only the mid-point of his career. I really had to step up my game to hang with individuals like him.

The Dark Side

The typical arc of a career in my time was that you started out in newspapers or television then went over to what my friends in journalism called "The Dark Side"—public relations or corporate communications.

I've never forgotten an exchange I had with the capable and highly admired editor and writer Don Bishoff at the *Register-Guard* the day after a story appeared in the paper saying I'd taken my first P.R. job. He would have been aware that I was a product of the U of O journalism school from seeing me around the paper during my college years.

I was no longer working at the *R-G* but stepped over to his desk to say hello. Instead of returning my greeting, he gazed up at me with this doleful expression and half-snorted, *"A perfectly good education!"*

I Learn a New Formula—for Disaster

Once in the new field, you pretty much had to master a whole other kind of writing and develop a lot of other knowledge besides, like communications troubleshooting, communications planning and the vocabulary of business.

The writing demands intimidated the hell out of me at first. To be honest, it was a number of years before I had enough experience with the genre of business communications to do it with any alacrity. I remember once being mortified to see the first vice president I worked for take a red pen to a three- paragraph letter he'd had me draft. Turns out I wrote "long." It was the first thing I had to correct. I know I really never got over that tendency either (as if anyone reading this has to be told).

Without a doubt, the number one thing I learned about writing for a living is that you have to know what you're talking about before you can write about it, and sometimes the people you worked for made that harder than it needed to be.

I remember once early in my career getting a call from a senior executive's secretary informing me that "Dale" wanted me to draft a speech for him to give to some industry group. No topic.

Naturally, I inquired as to when I might get some time with him to talk about what he was looking for. She informed me, first, that "Dale" did not have time for that and, second, that he wanted a draft on his desk when he returned from an overseas trip the next week.

It wasn't long before I learned that this was a guaranteed formula for disaster. I did my best to get some guidance from one of the man's lieutenants and to fill in some gaps, but the draft that was on "Dale's" desk when he got back from China was a flop, as was the one after that.

This went on until there had been enough give-and-take about what he wanted that it was actually a pretty good talk, but not before I felt like I'd been hammered down to nothing in the process.

This was my first exposure to a corporate management style of any kind; it was a poor one to start out with as it really made me question my ability and self-worth.

I came to refer to people like this as the ones who confused "writing" with "typing." Their reasoning seemed to be, *"If a speech is 20 pages long and it takes, what, two minutes to type a page? Then the speech should be ready in 40-45 minutes, am I right?"*

My "Speciality"

I'm lucky to be able to contrast this early experience with other much better ones working with a number of top executives who really valued communication and took the time to get personally involved. You can spend enough time with these kinds of leaders that you understand their priorities and what they're trying to make happen. It's then easy to help them communicate it. When you can master the "voice" of the leader it's even better.

In the corporate world, the guy who can do this for the CEO is often the only one on the whole staff who enjoys complete job security. Often this person will stay with the same top executive the entire length of the CEO's career, as if they aren't allowed to retire and leave him without his "voice."

I knew a guy in this role once. He told about the time he was camping with his family on a river island when a company helicopter came flying low over the island. Someone with a loud speaker was calling out his name over and over: *"Dan Alexander...Dan Alexander...Go to the nearest clearing."*

He did and was immediately whisked away to perform some kind of writing assignment for the big guy before they brought him back to the island, his family, and his vacation.

When he told this story at a department Christmas party one year, someone asked, *"Did it turn out to be something really important?"*

Dan contemplated the question for a moment, took a sip of his Bourbon and water, and said, *"It could have waited."*

I took a lot of pride in crafting communications that went beyond the *pro forma* requirements of keeping people in the organization informed to something that would really connect with people. I wanted them to find it not just informative, but also interesting and worth their while to read. I was always seeking to make a connection between the leadership of the organization and the "followership."

If I had a specialty it was preparing the letter people would get from the CEO in the face of big events or developments affecting the company, the country or even the world.

One of these was the message that went out to all 120,000 employees in Honeywell International from the chairman, Larry Bossidy, after the events of September 11, 2001—the World Trade Center disaster. The response from people in the organization was positive and immediate.

One note to the chairman came from a plant manager in a foreign country. It said, *"Your message on the New York City catastrophe was well stated. I suspect you wrote it personally. It reflected an emotional sensitivity and sense of priorities that were good to hear. Thanks."*

Just doing my job.

CHAPTER 40

Where I Was in the Organization

I wasn't the first person from the sticks to end up working at the big Weyerhaeuser Company corporate headquarters. There were guys there who'd put themselves through college working on the green chain in Aberdeen, Washington, or setting chokers at Kamloops, B.C. Now they might have jobs as raw materials director or research manager.

To hear people back home tell it, every one of them was practically running the place. *"He's way up there,"* they'd say.

I'd later see that the ones I'd heard of from my neck of the woods were actually in the middle-management range; they had plenty of responsibility within a specific business or functional area, but rarely of the magnitude that people back home imagined. My job would have fit in this range.

Generally speaking, everyone who works at a corporate headquarters is aligned with one of the top handful of senior executives who run the company. There's one "Senior Manager" for each of the major business groups and staff functions that make up the enterprise.

At Weyerhaeuser, for example, you'd have a senior V.P. for paper products, a senior V.P. for lumber products, one for human resources, and so on. The "SVP" after someone's name at the top of a memo always meant it was top priority. Our department reported up to the SVP for Law and Corporate Affairs—William D. Ruckelshaus.

Together this group made up a level of the company called the "Senior Management Committee"—or "SMC."

Some jobs, like ours, cut across all the businesses and functions; an important part of our responsibility was to help these top leaders achieve the goals of their own organizations as well as those of the entire company.

Anyway, sitting atop these various management towers resides the Chief Executive Officer—the CEO. He or she might also be called CEO and President, or Chairman and CEO, depending on how much power the company has vested in them.

A little further down the chain of command were your "regular" V.P.s. There were quite a few more of these than SVPs. It was a title that extended out into the operations and applied to people who ran large manufacturing organizations or oversaw important companywide functions like Economic Forecasting or Communications.

Then we came to "my" level made up of people reporting to those V.P.s. Reporting to us, in turn, were the several thousand managers and first-line supervisors necessary to carry out the prairie dog-like operations of a vast enterprise like that. And then of course you had the prairie dogs.

This was the hierarchy everywhere I worked in corporate communications. Our department had director-level leaders for Advertising, Marketing, Executive Communications, Internal Communications, Community Relations and Media Relations. I held the director of internal communications job for the bulk of my career and then director of community relations for the best part of it. This was the highest position for these functions in the Fortune 500 companies I worked for, but a good deal more hands-on than a lot of others working at that level. You could call us blue collar executives.

Here's a story that puts this level of job in perspective:

Our boss, the V.P. of Communications, was holding a meeting of his six directors, which included me. He informed us that he was now being required to carry an electronic pager so each of us was to get one as well. *"Get with I.T. and start wearing them,"* he ordered. This was long before anyone carried a cell phone, and even pagers were just starting to be worn by people outside the medical profession.

(Mobile phones were so rare that, at first, the Southwest Airlines attendants used to modify their pre-flight safety spiel to say, *"If you have a cell phone we're all impressed, but we'd ask that you turn it off at this time."*)

Anyway, as soon as the boss left the room one of the other directors spoke up. He said, *"I don't know about you guys, but I am* not *wearing a pager."* He added, *"Let's face it guys: we're middle managers, doing things of medium importance. We do not need to be paged."*

Of course you know who won that battle. Within days every one of us was electronically tethered for the first time in our lives and has no doubt remained that way ever since. It wasn't too long after this that we were each issued another new electronic device called a *BlackBerry.* Even the president of the U.S., Barack Obama, had one. Once again, we were instructed to, *"Get with I.T."* and start carrying one.

I did serve as the *Acting* Vice President of Communications for Honeywell's aircraft engines division for about six months once. I knew everyone on that staff and they knew me, so at our staff meeting on my first day as A.V.P. I told them, *"You might find that I'm not a very good <u>vice president</u> but I think you'll see that I am a very good <u>actor</u>."*

It didn't bother me to turn the job back to someone else later but I have to admit that the air up there was pretty intoxicating.

I don't know how many people still remember the comedian Paul Novello's character, *Father Guido Sarducci.* He was a regular on the early days of *Saturday Night Live.* His character was a hip, chain-smoking Italian Roman Catholic priest with tinted glasses.

Part of his charade was to be entirely self-centered and self-serving. One night he announced that he'd gotten a letter from the Vatican informing him that he'd been promoted. He said the next time we saw him he would have a red stripe down the length of each arm of his garment. In the thick Italian accent he was famous for, he said he was *"rilly rilly excited"* because, *"they say nothing brings out the good veal in an Italian Restaurant like that-uh red stripe!"*

I can tell you from personal experience that the "V.P" on your office door didn't hurt, either. I couldn't help noticing how much more helpful people were.

So you might say that my career topped out in the high middle. I can tell you from personal experience that there are a lot worse places to land up. You have the satisfaction of being somebody in the organization, but without the crushing and unrelenting demands of a top executive reporting, say, directly to the president.

In my instance, circumstances led to me being further developed not as your typical manager, progressing from managing a few people to many, but instead being an "I.C."— "Individual Contributor." This is someone responsible for personally carrying out most of the responsibilities of a particular position. Speech writing would be a good example. A highly valued I.C. is practically a protected species.

This was the way to go as far as I was concerned, because managing large numbers of other people was not for me. Better to be in a position, I thought, of either personally delivering results or working through other people (loaned resources, hired contractors, etc.) to get things done cooperatively as opposed to supervising people, if you can appreciate the difference.

I could only admire those who had the ability to track the activities of two scores of people and know right where everybody should be on a project at any given time. I'd more likely find myself listening to someone reporting on their big hot project at a staff meeting and wondering, *Who's this one again, and what's he talking about?*

CHAPTER 41

The Times

There were a lot of significant social changes occurring about the time I started in corporate communications, some of them driven by the great military escapade of my generation, the Vietnam War.

When it came to being employees, the previous generation had many attributes; they were, after all, the *"Greatest Generation."* That doesn't mean they didn't have their issues.

A lot of the GI's who came home from WWII definitely had a chip on their shoulder based on their experiences. Many were cock-sure of themselves and, as a generation, they had a right to be. After all, it was <u>they</u> who put their lives on the line to save the world and they didn't come home to take any you-know-what from anybody afterwards.

They were always skeptical of what the company was trying to feed them in the way of information. But, as a rule, they had no trouble taking direction from above and held no great expectations when it came to being kept informed.

The Vietnam vets who came home from "our" war brought issues to the workplace based on the experience <u>they'd</u> had. Many of them had been put through hell in a military campaign that the famed Vietnam veteran and writer Philp Caputo said had *"...all the organization of a crowd at a train station."*

There hadn't been much satisfaction in participating in the conflict and it had made doubters of many vets when it came to trusting in the organization and its leaders. Beyond their own military unit—and sometimes even in it—life-long sentiments developed which said the brass didn't always know what in the hell it was doing.

A lot of them had heard of, or experienced situations where things had gone bad because of poor planning or decision-making by people up the chain of command unfamiliar with the actual situation on the ground. They'd almost been conditioned to question orders from above.

They <u>were</u> like the generation before them in one way: they both had a strong dislike for authority. But the Vietnam generation—not just the ones who served in the military, but their entire generation by then—had also developed a certain attitude as well. Sometimes it seemed like they didn't believe <u>anything</u> they got from the company.

I liked to eat in the employee cafeteria and sit with different groups of employees to gauge how the latest communications were going over with the workforce.

There was this one table I called the "Grumpy Old Men." They would put a negative spin on anything we put out. Just for fun I told them once that I was working on an announcement that would give every employee a thousand dollars for Christmas. It wasn't true; I just wanted to see how they would react.

Before I came out with the truth, they'd already concluded that the company was somehow trying to trick them in some way that would later cost them a hell of a lot more than the thousand dollars. This was my audience. It was not easy to convince them of anything.

It certainly didn't make the job of supervisor any easier either. The men who spoke up to question policies and directives in Vietnam came home and went to work for companies like ours. Their attitudes and predispositions began to infuse the workforce about the time that I joined it.

Their attitude was that the leader was not the only one with answers. Their expectation was that they would be informed and involved in decisions that affected them. This was the new work force. Companies had to adapt to the changes in people's communication needs if they expected to secure their full contribution to the enterprise.

In what I've always thought was quite a revealing moment, I happened to say in a staff meeting one day, *"We're finding that the old chain-of-command kind of communication doesn't work anymore."*

We had a former WWII Army guy in our department who had served in Europe. He said, *"I'll let you in on a little secret: it never did."*

I think he was right. The good leaders have always known how to elicit the best results from the people in their command—and it usually wasn't just to be more commanding. Our new mission was to help managers at all levels see the light and begin operating that way themselves.

CHAPTER 42

I Dive Into the Corporate Pool and Don't Come Up Where I Went In

There seems to be a lot of contempt for big corporations these days for reasons I "get," but which I think are mostly misguided. All that aside, there was just no better opportunity for an individual with my background to advance than by hiring on with one of the name corporations of the time. They all had good products and reputations, paid well and were expanding. I went to work for Weyerhaeuser—the "Tree Growing Company."

Lots of people wanted jobs like mine. They found them in the same kind of companies I did—Fortune 500 enterprises like G.E., Kodak, General Motors and Boeing. The pay was better than just about any other segment of the job market and people liked being part of something prominent and successful. I know I did.

Consider, for example, the reputation that Weyerhaeuser enjoyed at the time: surveys of the forest products industry showed that overall recognition of the company was two-to-one over our nearest competitor. When people in the industry were asked what forest products company most impressed them, that too came out two-to-one in Weyerhaeuser's favor.

Better yet, surveys showed that when the company had something to say, eight of 10 people said they would believe it. The same number said they believed that when it came to replanting trees, Weyerhaeuser really did plant more than it cut down. These predispositions were enormously helpful when it came to communicating with the public about our forestry operations and their inevitable environmental impact.

And finally, among readers of the *Wall Street Journal,* Weyerhaeuser ranked first against our 20 largest competitors on reputation and good investment. In short, I was joining an ethical company universally recognized as a good place to work, a good place to do business and a good investment.

What It Took

I discovered over time that it really only took a few—albeit significant—successes in any given year to extend your value in the eyes of the company, and that this could help shield you from the occasional downsizing.

I also came to see that in a company of global proportions, every assignment that comes your way is an opportunity to not just distinguish yourself by doing the job, but to advance your personal objectives in terms of fortune, adventure and fun as well.

Although I wasn't so much aware of all this at the beginning, I feel extremely lucky to have landed a job in the internal communications department at Weyerhaeuser. It was the culmination of something I'd been angling to make happen for at least three years, maybe longer; even as a youngster I knew most people thought of Weyerhaeuser as a good company, one that anyone could be proud to be associated with.

The fact that it was bigger and better-known than any other place I'd ever worked created that old siren song in me to keep moving upward and into the biggest arena I thought I could get to.

It would be overstating it to say that I loved everything about my first corporate job, but looking back I don't see how things could have gone much better. Indeed, my 11 years in that job served as prelude to every good thing that would happen to me in my work life after that. Yet I did not foresee that the job would transform my career the way it did.

Through the company-provided relocation service, we came to reside at 17319 51st St. Ct E. in Sumner, Washington, which I thought represented a particularly unimaginative and dreary mentality in street-naming. A better and more descriptive name would have been "Windy Ridge Road."

However the house was just right. It was a brand new cedar-sided split-level built in the Northwest style with plenty of sky lights about 12 miles east of the office near Lake Tapps. That one acre of Northwest jungle turned out to be a perfect place to raise our three monkeys.

There was an advantage to my commute worth mentioning. My friend Fred Westerlund had a college professor who told his students to always buy a house that is east of where they work. That way the sun is never in your eyes during drive time. That was pretty good advice and possibly one more thing that will have no application in the future; they say the pandemic is going to lead to most people working from home from now on.

The Cheerleader in the Grey Flannel Suit

You could say I was a company man. I read and believed everything about the founding of the company, how from the beginning it believed in being a responsible steward of the land; how the founder of the company, Frederick Weyerhaeuser, had emigrated from Germany before the turn of the century, started out in farming and then worked his way up in the lumber business to become founder of the largest forest products company in the world; and how everything he did was just honest and good and wonderful. Like George Washington, or Jesus.

One thing that really did make the story inspiring is that when Frederick acquired the 900,000 acres of timberland in the Pacific Northwest in 1890 that became the foundation of the company, he set himself apart from the cut-and-runners who dominated the timber industry at the time by committing the new company to "environmental stewardship." His famous quote was, *"This is not for us. Nor for our children. But for our grandchildren."*

I also bought into and did my part to advance the company's reputation as an innovative enterprise bringing many good things to the modern world. These would include the fact that our six million acres of timberland in the U.S. were kept open for use by the public at no charge. You have to admit that made for a pretty sizable public park.

Also, we'd been the first big company to seize on the idea of "sustained yield" forestry, which meant that we were perpetually both harvesting <u>and</u> planting trees. For every tree it cut down the company committed to planting six more in its place.

Just like being named "Most School Spirit Boy" in high school, I was a real cheerleader for my company. I'd sit next to someone on an airplane sometimes and couldn't resist telling them about all the imaginative and important things the company was into.

I think people were genuinely interested because it was true, and some of it was amazing. They liked hearing about how we were making forest products stronger than steel and setting aside eagle nesting habitat on our lands as "No Log" zones. Sometimes they asked me a lot of questions and I enjoyed satisfying their curiosity because I did know quite a lot about the forest products industry and, of course, the biggest player—Weyco!

The question people asked me more than any other was, *"Do you have any jobs?"*

The Palace

The headquarters building we worked in 20 miles south of Seattle was the nicest office I would work in during my long career. It was an architectural masterpiece that had won more awards for its architects than any building in the history of the American Institute of Architecture and had lots of the most modern features.

The most prominent of these was its "Open Landscape" architecture, which eliminated a lot of the walls separating people in a conventional office building. This helped to improve communications between work groups, very advanced thinking at the time.

People worked in cubes, but they were spacious with high walls and some sort of modernistic *"white sound"* system that masked the noise levels to create a sense of privacy on the cube farm. By the standards of today's Google-inspired workplaces, ours was nothing to write home about. But it seemed like it at the time.

The exterior walls on every floor were composed of seamless 3/8-inch-thick glass manufactured in Germany. As a result, just about every employee's work space had a view of either the lake on the north side of the building or a grassy meadow on the south. I believe they were the largest plate glass windows in the world.

Research showed that people who could look up from their desk and see some distance—particularly with a view of water or trees—were happier in their work, more creative and effective. By contrast, my own wife visited the office I had at an earlier job one time and asked me, *"How do they expect you to be creative in a space like this?"*

The physical work environment at Weyco was exceptional and carried off with an uncommon degree of quality. This included a carpeted employee cafeteria looking out over the lake and a free exercise club with miles of jogging trails that wound through the Douglas fir forest surrounding the building.

There was no restriction on when a person might leave his desk to go exercise, which everybody was doing at the time. You saw employees of every rank on the trails and pickle ball courts at all hours of the day.

As you moved up in rank you got closer to the windows and were awarded more space—and more things you could put in that space. It reminded me a little bit of that *New Yorker* cartoon where someone is showing a group of people around the new office. He's telling them, *"Each cubicle can have one plant or one picture, but not both."* Ours was quite a bit more relaxed.

I started out one row of desks in from the windows on the meadow side with a handsome L-shaped desk made of solid red oak and a nice layout that afforded everyone plenty of space. I had no complaints with it whatsoever, but I'd be lying if I said I didn't eye those nice offices along the windows and think that when I grew up I wanted to be one of those guys.

And I did. I don't mean I grew up; that would be a lie. But I was fortunate enough to become one of "those guys." I wasn't thinking so much about the expansive views from their window offices or their more handsome salaries. I was struck more by how much easier their jobs seemed. Again, this was very attractive to me (and just as misguided as some of my other earlier misconceptions about corporate work). I came to see in time, of course, that more pay almost always comes with more responsibility, not less.

I was particularly taken in by a fantasy involving one window-sitter who, it was said, *eats lunch for a living.* He did appear to always be coming back from some long lunch he'd had with somebody in the community around 3 o'clock in the afternoon every day. I wasn't even aware they had jobs like that.

I had little idea as to what the guy actually did, but knew immediately he had the job I wanted. Turned out he was in charge of community relations.

In any event, I'll just say my own job grew pretty quickly to the point that it was apparently deemed window-worthy. A nice location on the southeast corner of the third floor is where my desk ended up along with a couple of nice bamboo plants and a sofa. I wasn't eating lunch for a living, but when I ate at my desk I had a better view.

Because the building was what they called a "reclining sky scraper," it constituted just five floors but occupied the floor space of a 32-story sky scraper. The top—or 5th—floor was the executive suite where the CEO and about half a dozen senior vice presidents had their offices, arrayed in the open landscape format but quite a bit farther apart.

Those of us who had reason to be on that floor from time to time thought it was pretty cool that we could pass by the legendary George H. Weyerhaeuser's office—known as "GHW" inside the company—to see (and smell) him at his desk puffing on a cigar. He was the grandson of the founder.

A Kinder Culture

Like all companies, Weyerhaeuser had a distinct culture that had developed over its nearly 100-year history. I think I was the beneficiary of that because it wasn't terribly fast-moving or demanding like offices I'd work in later, especially some on the East Coast.

Don't get me wrong. I was challenged to the extreme, but that was more because of my own limitations than because anyone was pushing me too hard. People rarely got fired, and when they did there was usually something worked out that allowed them to make a soft landing somewhere else.

I remember once that one of the guys in our department got the axe. When he told me what had happened, the description of his new assignment made it sound like he'd been promoted. He was going off to a much better situation someone had arranged for him—the human equivalent, you could say, of a kid's dog being taken to "the farm." All I remember thinking was, *"Geez, I hope they don't give me his work too!"*

I was lucky to have this relatively genteel environment to start out in, particularly since the work began to require more and more risk-taking on my part. Sometimes risks don't work out the way you'd hoped, you know? But you could make a mistake or two without it imperiling your prospects for continued employment too terribly much.

I would need that cushion, because I hadn't been in corporate communications more than a few months when I received the assignment that would throw me into some deep and uncharted waters. It looked like I might have been sold the old switcheroo.

End Vol. I

Author Don Wilt alongside the Metolius River—
Fall, 2020 (Mike Wilt photo)